Cloud Migration PM Bible™

The Complete Framework for Running Successful Infrastructure, Application, and Cloud Migrations

A practical guide for project managers, architects, and technology leaders.

Gérald L'ouverture Noël

BA in Psychology — Hofstra University
Project Management Certificate — Cornell University

Leadership Coach — John Maxwell Team
PMP® — Project Management Institute (PMI)

Cloud Migration PM Bible™ represents the culmination of his experience, research, and structured approach to enterprise transformation.

ISBN: 979-8-234-03800-5

www.cloudmigrationpmplaybook.com

Dedication

Dedicated to the project managers, architects, and technology leaders

who carry the responsibility of transformation—not in theory, but in execution.

To those who bring structure to uncertainty,

discipline to complexity,

and clarity where others see chaos.

To those who believed in me before I believed in myself.

To my mother, whose wisdom required no formal education,

yet shaped the foundation of how I think, lead, and endure.

To my wife, who stood beside me through every rise and every fall—

your presence made this work possible.

And to every project manager who carries the weight of responsibility in silence—

making decisions under pressure, navigating ambiguity, and being held accountable for outcomes few truly understand—this book is for you.

May you find clarity in chaos, strength in uncertainty, and control in execution—where success is not left to effort, but defined by structure.

Acknowledgments

This book is not only a reflection of professional experience—

it is a reflection of the people who shaped me, believed in me, and stood beside me throughout my journey.

First, I honor the memory of my mother, Lernice Linotte († 2011).

She never stopped believing in me.

“If there is too much noise that distracts you, you must learn to step away—find your peace—and return when clarity is restored.”

My mother was my Socrates, and I was her Plato.

Though she could neither read nor write, she embodied the essence of a true philosopher—humble, wise, and deeply insightful.

To my father († June 2011)—Though you did not always believe in me, I choose forgiveness.

You lived a long life, and perhaps wisdom came to you in its own time.

As George Bernard Shaw once said, “Youth is wasted on the young.”

And in reflection, I have come to understand that wisdom, too, can arrive when its time has already passed.

Despite my frustrations, you taught me something far greater than validation—you taught me resilience.

I watched you rise each day and do what was right.

That discipline, that endurance, lives within me today—not only through upbringing, but through inheritance.

You once told me: Do not fight fire with fire—use water, but use it with precision and control.

That principle has stayed with me in every moment of adversity.

May your soul rest in peace.

To my childhood friend, Shiler Saint Eloi († 2016)—

"Gerald, you are a success."

Your voice still echoes in my mind.

If a brother is greater than a friend, then I have never known where to place you—because you were both.

Your absence is not emptiness—it is presence in another form, one that remains with me always.

May the angels be kind to you.

To my wife, Nilufar Yasmin—Thank you for standing beside me through every moment.

"You've got this, Gerald."

I have heard those words more times than I can count.

There is a saying that behind every great man stands a great woman.

For me, this is no longer a theory—it is a lived reality.

Your presence, your strength, and your belief in me have shaped me into a better version of myself.

Like any complex system, understanding reveals clarity—and in that clarity, I found not difficulty, but depth.

You have been a constant force behind this work.

To my children—Paris T. Noel and Xzander Noel—

Be humble.

Be kind.

Be strong.

Greatness is within your DNA.

May the Grand Architect of the Universe guide your path.

I will always love you.

To my daughter, Humayra H. Noel—You believed I would never fall.

For that, I am deeply grateful.

Your belief is a strength I carry with me.

To my sister, Alexandra Noel—Our mother's hopes for us remain alive through us.

I wish you strength, success, and courage on your journey in Canada.

To the Noel family—

Ours is a large family, and though I may not name each of you individually, I remain grateful for the role each of you played in shaping my life.

Your support—both seen and unseen—especially in moments when care and provision mattered most, contributed to the person I have become.

I would like to recognize my niece, Marquery E. Registre, whose belief in me never wavered—even in moments when I questioned myself.

You have witnessed parts of my journey that few have seen, including moments that required discipline, composure, and diplomacy in environments where both strength and restraint were necessary.

Your belief has never gone unnoticed.

To members of my extended family—particularly the Jeanty family, and especially Wilbert, Jude, and Moise Jeanty—Jude and Moise, in particular, have made meaningful contributions to my life in ways that deserve recognition.

The qualities you both possess remind me that, even in a fractured world, humanity still preserves within itself a remnant of goodness.

To my friends and colleagues—Though I keep my circle small, its value is immeasurable.

To Denise Luis—an early believer in these pages—

and to Joseph Beauchamp, colleague from the Maxwell Leadership Team, now extending leadership beyond its horizon through Beauchamp Team Growth Solutions—my sincere gratitude.

To Gregory King—friend and partner—our connection is not defined by proximity, but by the value we recognize in one another.

To Avula Balayyagari Narasa Reddy—a friend I met later in my career, yet one I consider a brother.

We have learned from one another equally, and that balance is rare.

To Travis Race—we met in one of the most challenging environments of my career.

Your standard of excellence and leadership left a lasting impression on me.

You are a leader I have long respected and sought to emulate.

To Deavin Banks—your ambition and talent reflect a drive that will carry you far.

To Nnamdi Jideani—from the first moment we met, you showed me respect.

At a time when others sought to diminish me, you reinforced something greater.

It takes greatness to recognize greatness in others.

Finally, I acknowledge the role of artificial intelligence tools—

including ChatGPT and Claude—which assisted in structuring, refining, and organizing portions of this work.

They did not replace thought—

they supported its expression.

No matter how advanced, fast, or effective artificial intelligence becomes—

it remains an extension of human intent, and a creation of human design.

It does not originate thought—

it responds to it.

It does not lead—

it follows.

It does not exist in purpose on its own—

it exists in response, bound to the will that invokes it.

Its existence is not independent—

it is activated, directed, and defined by the prompts we create.

For every output, there is a prompt—

and behind every prompt, a human mind.

The caveat—artificial intelligence does not mislead; it reflects the clarity—or confusion—of the one who uses it, or misuses it.

Be the noumenon of your knowledge.

Table of Contents

PREFACE

Why This Book Exists

There is a quiet misconception about structure.

It is often mistaken for rigidity. For slowness. For an inability to operate in environments that demand speed, adaptability, and constant change. In reality, the opposite is true. The more complex and uncertain the environment becomes, the more essential structure becomes—not to constrain movement, but to prevent it from collapsing.

What is often overlooked is that systems do not fail because everything breaks at once. They fail at their weakest point.

A chain is only as strong as its weakest link.

This principle, formalized in the Theory of Constraints, reflects a deeper operational truth: every system is limited not by its strengths, but by its constraint. And unless that constraint is identified, understood, and managed, progress becomes an illusion. Movement continues—but performance does not improve.

I have spent much of my career operating in environments where direction was not always clear, where priorities shifted, and where execution was expected before full understanding was established. In those moments, success did not come from control alone, nor from chaos. It came from the ability to move within both.

Because without structure, constraints remain hidden.

Dependencies go unchallenged. Assumptions go untested. Weaknesses remain embedded in the system—until execution begins to expose them.

Leadership, in that sense, is not about imposing order. It is about recognizing what the environment requires—adapting to it, stabilizing execution, and then introducing the right level of structure to sustain and scale it.

Enterprise migrations are among the most demanding initiatives an organization can undertake. While they are often perceived as technical transitions from one environment to another, they are, in practice, coordinated business transformations. They impact infrastructure, applications, identity, security, networking, operations, vendors, and ultimately, the daily experience of end users.

And yet, despite the investment, effort, and expertise applied to these initiatives, they fail more often than many expect.
Not because organizations lack capability.

But because they focus on movement instead of control.

From a systems perspective, this is the failure to manage the constraint.

The cutover event becomes the focal point, while the operating model required to support that transition is left underdeveloped. Systems go live, but dependencies are missed. Monitoring is incomplete. Adoption is low. Support structures are not ready. What appears successful at launch begins to deteriorate shortly after.

Execution continues—but the constraint remains.

And when the constraint is ignored, the system does not scale—it fractures.

This book was written to address that gap.

It is designed to provide a repeatable framework for project managers, program leaders, architects, and technology leaders who must deliver migrations with discipline, business awareness, and operational rigor. The approach outlined in this guide applies across infrastructure, application, and cloud migrations, and can scale from a single migration wave to an enterprise portfolio.

At its core, this framework is built upon six disciplines consistently present in mature organizations: technical architecture, operational governance, risk management, validation, organizational change management, and leadership communication.

Each of these disciplines represents a control point.

Each one exists to either reveal, stabilize, or elevate a constraint within the system.

Technical architecture establishes clarity between current and target states. Governance defines how decisions are made and enforced. Risk management ensures that uncertainty is identified and actively controlled. Validation confirms that systems behave as expected before and after transition. Change management prepares the organization to operate in its new state. Leadership communication aligns stakeholders without introducing noise or confusion.

Together, they form the conditions required for controlled execution.

But beyond industry challenges, this book is also deeply personal.

It reflects not only the lessons learned from complex migrations, but a belief shaped over time:

Structure is not the opposite of agility—it is what makes agility sustainable.

And in environments where complexity is constant, success is not determined by speed alone—

It is determined by the ability to move with clarity, discipline, and control.

Migration success is not defined by movement—it is defined by control.

INTRODUCTION

How to Read This Book and Why It Matters

Most organizations approach migration as a technical event.

A system is moved. A platform is upgraded. A deadline is met.

And yet, despite successful execution on paper, many migrations fail to deliver lasting value.

Not because the technology failed—

But because the migration was not managed as a system.

This book is designed to shift that perspective into execution.

It is not a technical manual, nor is it limited to a single methodology. It is a structured approach to managing migration as a controlled system—where architecture, governance, risk, validation, operations, and people are aligned toward a single outcome: successful, sustainable transformation.

At its core, this book introduces a disciplined framework for executing migrations with clarity and control. It brings together proven strategies—such as the 6R migration model, wave-based execution, validation discipline, and structured rollback planning—and places them within a unified operating model that can be applied across environments.

This is not about reinventing methods.

It is about applying them correctly.

This book does not advocate for or depend on any single certification or formal designation. At the same time, it is deeply aligned with the principles that those certifications represent—structured thinking, disciplined planning, risk awareness, governance, and execution control.

Frameworks do not create capability. They reinforce it.

What matters is not the certification itself—but the ability to apply its underlying principles with judgment in real-world environments.

In parallel, as organizations move deeper into cloud, distributed systems, and modern architectures, another reality becomes unavoidable: the more advanced technology becomes, the more critical security becomes.

Cybersecurity is not treated in this book as a separate domain—but as an embedded responsibility.

It exists within architecture, within identity, within access, within validation, and within operational control. It is not introduced as a layer—it is assumed as a condition.

Because in modern environments, transformation without security is not transformation—

It is exposure.

In practice, failure is rarely caused by lack of knowledge—it is caused by alignment between what is known and how it is executed.

PART I

The Foundation Behind the Framework

Why this book exists, where it came from, and what it is built to solve.

From Frustration to Framework

This book is not the result of theory.

It is the result of experience—of frustration, of observation, and of the need to transform both into something meaningful.

At its surface, it may appear to target a specific technical domain—to demonstrate expertise in cloud, data, and application migration.

But in reality, it is about something deeper.

It is about finding alignment.

It is about understanding where your value truly exists—and having the discipline to build around it.

There is a quiet deception that happens in professional environments when your credentials and potential are not fully acknowledged. When you know what you bring to the table—when you understand that project management is not just something you do, but something you embody—and yet you are still placed in a box, or placed in an interrogation room from interviews all the way into the workplace.

At some point, you are faced with a choice.

You can internalize frustration—

Or you can transform it.

That is the path I chose.

I do not allow frustration to consume me, and I do not allow negativity to define me. Instead, I convert that energy into production—into learning, into growth, and into evolution.

I enter what I call my avatar state.

I learn.

I improve.

I evolve.

And in doing so, I become better than I was before—positioning myself to either align with an environment that recognizes my value or to create something of my own.

This book is part of that creation.

It is a reflection of how I approach execution—how I lead cloud, data, and application migrations by applying proven frameworks with precision and judgment.

I did not invent these frameworks.

The 6R strategy.

The Big Bang approach.

The Pre-Mortem method.

These were developed by pioneers before me.

What I bring is the ability to understand when to apply them—and how to apply them effectively in real-world environments.

Credentials, Work Experience, and Turning Point

Going back to the idea of deception—the first thing to understand about me is this:

I hold an Associate in Arts degree from Nassau Community College and a Bachelor of Arts in Psychology from Hofstra University. I also pursued a Master's degree at Hofstra University, completing a full semester and progressing midway into my second before making the decision to step away.

I am a certified leadership coach through the John Maxwell Team.

I am a leadership coach.

I am a mentor.

I am a speaker.

I have been coached and mentored by remarkable individuals since the age of 18, including Villard Denis (Davertige) and Emmanuel Pierre Charles.

I was exposed early to diplomatic environments through close interaction with members of the diplomatic corps, including U.S. Ambassador Daniel Whitman and Canadian Ambassador Gilles Bernier. I also served in a cultural capacity with the Embassy of Mexico in Haiti.

At the age of 20, I held titles that many achieve much later in life.

I was publicly recognized as an art critic after restoring a painting by Jean René Jérôme—an acknowledgment formally conferred by curator Gerald

Alexis. I was also mentored directly by the renowned art critic, Dr. Michel Philippe Lerebours.

I have a network of experiences and relationships that could fill pages.
So yes—it is fair to ask:

Why the frustration?

Because I have the credentials.

I have the experience.

And I built myself from the ground up.

The Interview Reality

And yet, in interviews, I am asked:

“Walk me through the five phases of how you run a project.”

And in those moments—I go blank.

Not because I do not know.

But because something deeper happens.

I disengage.

I enter an internal dialogue.

I am no longer fully present in the room.

Externally, I remain composed.

But internally, frustration builds.

No one has ever heard me lose composure in a meeting.

But internally?

If I were paid a penny for every time I expressed that frustration in my head, I would be a multimillionaire.

If you don't believe me—ask my dogs, Mishti—or my cat, Moon.

Moon would probably say, "A zillion."

Frustration and Reality

Yes—it is frustrating.

Not because the work is difficult.

Not because expectations are high.

But because, at a certain level, the challenge is no longer capability—

It is recognition.

There is a quiet tension that exists when experience is not acknowledged. When someone who has spent over a decade navigating complexity is still approached as if they are learning how to begin.

It is not always said directly.

But it is felt—in the questions asked, in the assumptions made, and in the tone that frames the conversation.

It reminds me of a moment from La Casa de Papel (Money Heist).

The Professor begins his negotiation the way he always does—calculated, composed, methodical.

But this time, he is not speaking to the inspector.

He is speaking to the Colonel.

Before the strategy can unfold, the Colonel interrupts:

"Cut your crap. I am the colonel."

That moment is not about ego.

It is about hierarchy.

It is about positioning.

It is about understanding who you are speaking to—and adjusting accordingly.

Because at a certain level, introduction is unnecessary.

Validation is irrelevant.

And performance is assumed.

What remains—is alignment.

Yet in many professional environments, that alignment is absent.

Seniority is flattened.

Experience is questioned unnecessarily.

And conversations begin at a level that no longer reflects the individual in the room.

This is where frustration begins—not from the work itself, but from the disconnect between reality and perception.

Because at a certain level, the conversation changes.

You are no longer proving that you can do the work.

You are establishing how you lead it.

And when that distinction is ignored, it is not just frustrating—

It is, in many ways, a dismissal of earned experience.

And I am not alone.

I have seen professionals with decades of experience face the same reality. Some are treated differently. Some are elevated based on status rather than capability.

I recall when Prince Harry moved to the United States and was appointed Chief Impact Officer at BetterUp.

That moment highlighted something deeper:

Access, positioning, and visibility often shape opportunity.

This is not a critique of individuals.

It is a reflection of systems.

And within those systems, one truth remains—

No one deserves to be underestimated.

Human Nature and Reflection

Humanity often tries too hard
to be something it is not.

We forget our origin.

Scientifically, all modern humans belong to the species Homo sapiens, which emerged in Africa approximately 300,000 years ago.

This is not about division—
it is about unity.

We are one species.

And yet,
we create distinctions
that divide us.

I may sound frustrated—
but I am not angry.

I am disappointed.

And I have come to realize something—

These distinctions are not always explicit.

They show up
in subtle expectations—

how we speak,
how we sit,
how we present ourselves.

Even posture
becomes a signal.

Even presence
becomes something to interpret.

Why must posture, tone, or presence
be interpreted as respect or disrespect?

Why must individuals adjust themselves
to fit an expectation
that feels less human—
and more mechanical?

Why should race, status, or perception
influence how excellence is judged?

We are all evolving—
continuously.

And my perspective on this
is not theoretical.

It comes from lived experience.

In 2019,
I was involved in a car accident
while traveling for an opportunity.

Since then,
sitting upright for extended periods
brings physical discomfort.

Yet even something as simple as posture—

how one sits,
how one holds presence—

is often misinterpreted
in professional settings.

Work Experience and Turning Point

I have had positive experiences as well.

At New York Life.
At C Spire Wireless.
And at another major financial institution—
whose name I deliberately leave undisclosed.

In those environments,
I felt respected.

I felt seen.

But the experience
that ultimately led me
to write this book—

came from one of the most reputable
organizations.

I have ever worked for.

After nearly seven rounds of interviews,
I was selected.

The process was professional,
engaging,
and respectful.

I was able to show up as myself—

without forcing posture,
without masking discomfort.

That mattered
more than most would realize.

In this case,
my presence was not misinterpreted.

And I appreciated that.

The Breaking Point

The project was eventually canceled.

Officially,
it was due to a decision
from the parent company.

But by then—
I had already identified
critical issues
during the pilot phase.

The project
had already failed.

And I had provided
a recovery strategy.

Instead of rolling back,
I recommended allowing the execution to continue—

so that real lessons
could be extracted
and applied
to future rollout phases.

But I was placed into a situation
alongside another project manager—

who lacked the experience required
for a global
Zero Trust Network Architecture implementation.

I was too accommodating.

Too patient.

Under pressure,
we engaged a key stakeholder
who owned the delivery side.

The project continued
to be presented as stable.

But it was not.

In the United States,
it appeared successful.

By the time it reached Europe—
failure had already taken root.

Quiet.
Unacknowledged.
Progressing beneath the surface.

At that moment—
while the decision was not mine to make—

the responsibility to advise
remained.

I conducted
a formal gap analysis.

That analysis
became the turning point.

It exposed
what had been overlooked:

Dependencies—
unaddressed.

Assumptions—
unchallenged.

Discovery—
left incomplete.

We presented the findings.

They were received professionally.

There was mutual respect.

And yet—

truth
does not always
lead to correction.

Sometimes—
it leads
to consequence.

Within hours,
the decision came through my consulting firm.

The project
was terminated.

And so
was my role.

The Aftermath

The gap analysis
did not fail the project.

It revealed it.

And sometimes—
in environments not prepared for clarity—

revelation itself
becomes the liability.

I was let go.

And I was left
with questions.

Was it because
I identified too many gaps?

Because I challenged
the direction?

Or something else
entirely?

I may never know.

But I do know this:

I was offered a severance package
of a significant amount—

at the request
of the end client.

Even my recruiting firm
said it was highly unusual.

That moment
confirmed something for me:

I was not wrong.

I was early.

Early
in identifying failure
before it became visible.

Early
in understanding
that execution without structure
leads to collapse.

Early
in seeing what needed to be corrected
before it became irreversible.

And that—
is the responsibility
of a true project leader.

To see ahead—
even when others
are not ready.

That experience
did not define my limitations.

It clarified my role.

It reinforced a principle
I now carry
into every engagement—

A true project leader
is not defined
by reacting to failure—

but by recognizing it early—

and having the discipline
to prevent it
before it becomes inevitable.

And this book exists—
to make that discipline
repeatable.

PART II

The Foundation Before the Framework

The lived experience and discipline that shaped every principle that follows.

The chapters that follow are personal because the discipline that follows them is earned. Read them once, and the technical chapters become operational instead of theoretical.

The Journey Behind the Framework

Before any framework can be understood, it must be lived.

Methodologies, structures, and execution models do not emerge in isolation—they are shaped by experience, by pressure, and by the environments that test us. Every disciplined approach to delivery is rooted in something deeper: a foundation that existed long before the terminology was ever learned.

This book is built on such a foundation.

Not one formed in boardrooms or defined by certifications—but one shaped through lived experience, discipline, adversity, and the constant pursuit of order within uncertainty.

Before I guide you through frameworks, methodologies, and execution strategies, it is important for you to understand the journey behind the voice.

This is not just a technical book—it is a lived experience.

I will take you through real moments—experiences shaped by environments of strong leadership, trust, and support, as well as moments forged in uncertainty, pressure, and adversity.

Because it is often in adversity that clarity is formed.

As expressed, and often attributed to Aristotle,

"Adversity introduces a man to himself."

My adversity was my greatest anchor.

In my entire life, I have known nothing less than defying adversity to establish my presence.

At the same time, I will walk you through the trajectories that shaped me—how I became a project leader in the technology space. These reflections form the foundation for what follows:

My background and upbringing—where project management began.

How leadership environments shape—and at times fail—execution.

The burden project managers carry to remain accountable, productive, and focused.

A framework alone does not tell the full story.

Behind every structure, every method, and every execution model, there is a journey—one shaped by experience, challenge, and growth.

Without that journey, this book would be incomplete.

So, before we move into the mechanics of cloud migration, allow me to first share the path that brought me here—my story, my struggles, the bruises and scars that shaped me, and the strength that emerged from them.

Because those experiences did more than test me—

They revealed me.

They shaped how I think, how I lead, and how I remain grounded in my identity—while choosing, always, to lead with clarity and with respect for others.

Patience is a virtue.

I simply ask that you walk with me for a few pages before we step fully into the framework.

Because what follows is not just explanation—

It is foundation.

CHAPTER 1

Why Project Management Chose Me

Project management is who I am—not just what I do.

Some of us did not have the luxury of full parental support growing up.

Simple things—like having our parents set an alarm to wake us for school—were not part of our reality.

In my childhood, roosters were our alarm clock.

My parents did not own watches.

Time, as many understand it today, was not something we tracked by the hour—

It was something we felt through patterns.

I grew up in the 1980s.

Technology existed, but awareness of it—especially where I came from—was almost nonexistent.

I was raised in a home with two parents who were, in many ways, denied the opportunity of education.

To say they were blind to education is not an exaggeration—

It was their reality.

At that time, for many people, owning a watch or a clock was not a necessity—

It was a luxury.

The concept of measuring time in hours and minutes simply wasn't embedded in daily life.

My mother never had the chance to attend school.

She was orphaned at a young age.

For her generation, education was not just a privilege—

It was often seen as a threat.

There was a belief—spoken or unspoken—that the more you knew, the more dangerous you became.

I am not speaking of slavery.

In Haiti, slavery had ended long before my parents' time.

My father and mother were born in 1920 and 1937.

What I am saying is that despite limitations, lack of resources, and systemic barriers—

They still lived with discipline and structure.

They did everything on time.

Looking back, I realize something profound:

I grew up in a household full of project managers.

They coordinated activities, managed responsibilities, and adapted to constraints—
All without formal training, frameworks, or tools.

And yet—they succeeded.

I went to school on time every single day.

How did they do it?

They relied on patterns.

Today, we call this Agile.

We call it Scrum.

We define it as working within structured cycles, routines, and predictable behaviors.

But they were already doing it—naturally.

They were Scrum Masters—without knowing the term.

Those behaviors, those rhythms, those disciplines—they were passed down to me.

When I was in elementary school, I never needed my parents to wake me up.

In fact—I would wake them up.

Every day, I woke up two to three hours before sunrise.

How do I know?

Because I was always awake before the roosters began their chorus—and we had many of them.

In those quiet early hours, I studied.

But there was another challenge—a major one:

Electricity.

I won't go into the full infrastructure details here.

But necessity made me resourceful.

I used small batteries—AA and larger—to create light so I could study before dawn.

Looking back, I see it clearly now:

That was project management in execution.

That was ownership.

That was problem-solving under constraint.

That was creation under limitation.

Long before I carried the title—

I was already living the discipline.

Early Project Management

How did I get here?

I did not grow up dreaming of becoming a project manager.

I was born into a large family of twelve siblings. Life was filled with both hardship and joy.

School, which I once disliked, became my safe place.

It was miles away from home, and many days we walked long distances to get there.

I was a curious child—constantly asking why.

In a culture where questioning adults was often considered disrespectful, this made me difficult to manage.

But that curiosity became my strength.

Today, researchers recognize curiosity as a critical driver of success—

On par with Emotional Intelligence (EQ) and Intelligence Quotient (IQ).

This is often referred to as the Curiosity Quotient (CQ), a concept explored by Tomas Chamorro-Premuzic, who emphasizes that curiosity fuels learning, adaptability, and innovation—

Traits essential for effective leadership and problem-solving.

I now describe my early self as:

“A chaos creator in search of clarity.”

Over time, that evolved into:

“A clarity catalyst.”

Looking back, I began practicing project management at the age of six.

Inspired by a LinkedIn connection
who once humorously shared
that he began his project journey at age two,

I found myself smiling—
a long, lingering smile
woven from memory
and quiet pride—
and realized
I could confidently say
I began mine at six.

At two, I was not leading projects—I was a chaos creator.

But within that chaos, I discovered discipline, planning, and ultimately my calling:

Bringing order to complexity as a project leader.

At the age of six, at home, we:

Coordinated responsibilities

Resolved conflicts

Managed time

Worked toward shared outcomes

At school, that same structure continued.

Despite difficult conditions, I became one of the top students.

Not because of privilege—

But because of resilience, discipline, and necessity.

As the story goes, when Michael Jackson was asked at a young age whether he loved music, he reportedly paused before quietly responding:

"I am music."

I feel that I have reached a similar point in my journey, where I can say:

"I am project management."

Project management is a noun. It refers to the discipline and process of planning, organizing, and overseeing tasks and resources to achieve specific goals and outcomes.

It is not merely an action—

It is a practice.

And to correct my fellow project managers once again:

Project management is not just something you do—

It is a core part of who you are.

Now, with all that said, tell me—

Why should I not be a great project manager if the work environment permits it?

Potential does not fail on its own—

It fails when the environment refuses to sustain it.

My Beginning

From Art to Project Management

My early path did not begin in technology—it began in art.

At 17, going on 18, I entered a defining period of my life.

I met a young artist whose talent extended beyond painting.

To him, art was not confined to canvas—

It included philosophy, expression, and thought.

His name was Shiler Saint-Éloi, a mind I often describe as a reincarnation of Salvador Dalí.

We attended two higher education institutions together—École Nationale des Arts (ENARTS) and École Normale Supérieure.

Although we were not formally registered, our presence and performance earned us recognition among the student body.

We belonged—not by enrollment, but by ability.

While I admired Shiler's artistic mastery, my strength revealed itself differently.

I developed a sharp eye for structure, detail, and form.

I could immediately detect when a line was off—

When something lacked balance.

Alongside that, I gravitated toward philosophy.

My first public exposé was on George Berkeley's idealism, where I explored the nature of perception and reality.

But more than the philosophy itself—it was how I delivered it.

I was able to articulate complex ideas in a way that resonated—clear, structured, and compelling.

The reception was striking.

My speech was not only understood—

It was recognized.

From that moment, many began to predict that I would one day become a writer.

We were young, at times undisciplined, and often inconsistent in attendance.

Yet despite that—

We excelled beyond expectations.

Then came a moment that changed everything.

At 18, during the rise of modern communication, the national telecommunications authority—working alongside French institutions—launched a national art competition.

It was divided into two categories: amateur and professional.

The professional category included artists with decades of experience—masters of their craft.

I entered.

The theme was simple, yet profound:

"Communication: linking voices across the world."

I approached it with intention.

I designed a piece centered on a sphere representing the world—

Given human attributes: ears and a mouth—

To symbolize listening and expression.

Around it, I incorporated global landmarks:

The Statue of Liberty

The Empire State Building

Telecommunications structures

Satellites suspended in space

The globe itself was positioned in space, surrounded by these symbols of human achievement.

Wrapping around it was a telephone cord—binding everything together—

While the globe appeared to be speaking into it.

It was not just a drawing.

It was a concept.

Out of more than two thousand submissions, I placed third—among master-level artists with decades of experience.

That recognition opened doors I had never imagined.

Shortly after, I realized something important:

While I appreciated creating art, my true alignment was not in producing the work—

It was in interpreting it, organizing it, and bringing it to life at scale.

I transitioned into becoming a promoter and art critic, where I found a deeper connection to the discipline.

That same exhibition led me to one of the most defining encounters of my life.

I met my mentor, Villard Denis (Davertige)—a rare intellectual force.

The renowned critic Alain Bosquet once wrote of him with reverence, stating that Davertige wrote French better than the French themselves.

Despite his declining health, I had the privilege of spending time with him in Montreal.

In that brief but powerful encounter, he shared with me refined techniques of writing—insights that would stay with me for life.

More importantly—

He made a prediction:

That I would become a prominent writer.

That affirmation never left me.

By the age of 20, I had progressed quickly.

I was organizing exhibitions, assisting Michel Philippe Lerebours with installation work, and contributing to large-scale artistic projects.

That same year, I led a major exhibition at the Mexican Embassy in Haiti.

For the first time—

I wasn't just contributing.

I was leading.

I owned the entire effort:

Concept

Planning

Execution

Looking back—

That was my first true project.

Even if I did not call it that at the time.

Then came a long silence.

For nearly a decade, I stepped away from both art and structured project work.

Life moved in a different direction—

Until 2010.

The earthquake in Haiti changed everything.

On a flight back to Haiti, I met a program director from the Tzu Chi Foundation.

What began as a conversation became something more.

I shared my ideas:

How to organize support

How to structure relief

How to reach people effectively

That moment marked my return.

But this time—

It was different.

I was no longer working within the world of art.

I had entered project management—

Not as a title.

But as a responsibility.

And not at a small scale—

But on a global, humanitarian level.

Where Geography Ends, Identity Begins Again

A New Land, A Rewritten Identity

An immigrant coming to America is nothing like the theatrical version portrayed in Coming to America, where Eddie Murphy plays a prince who arrives with wealth, confidence, and perfect English.

In that story, he chooses modesty despite having access to luxury—

Living in Queens instead of remaining in the comfort of privilege.

My story was the opposite.

My arrival in America—while not the worst compared to what many others have endured—began with real challenges.

The kind that are not theatrical, not scripted, and not forgiving.

Let us begin with one of the most basic needs for safety, as described by Abraham Maslow (1943)—the need for shelter.

I carry a long list of gratitude for members of my extended family, the Jeanty family, who welcomed me into their home, even as they themselves were still in pursuit of identity, stability, and security.

That act alone gave me something essential—

Not just a place to stay, but a place to begin.

At twenty-one, I immigrated to the United States and settled in Queens, New York.

Life became unstable.

For the first time, I had changed course entirely—

A 180-degree shift in direction.

In this new land, I stood at the intersection of disorientation and silence.

I did not know my way around.

And worse—

I did not yet have the language to express myself.

At that time, I could have signed anything placed in front of me without understanding it. I could have unknowingly agreed to anything.

That is how vulnerable I was.

English was my greatest challenge.

I remember once entering a restaurant and ordering a pasta dish. I was afraid to ask for a fork because I feared mispronouncing the word and saying something inappropriate instead.

So, I ate pasta with a spoon.

Quietly.

Cautiously.

Avoiding embarrassment at all costs.

Looking back, I still ask myself:

How did I make it here?

Because at that moment—

I was not the person I had been.

I had lost familiarity.

I had lost fluency.

In many ways—

I had lost myself.

And yet—

something remained.

Not confidence.

Not clarity.

But resilience.

A quiet, persistent force that refused to let me collapse under uncertainty.

Today, I am a senior project leader operating at a strategic level and leadership coach—anchoring communication between CEOs, CIOs, and senior stakeholders.

I lead meetings to mitigate chaos, resolve complex technical issues, map dependencies, and take leadership action.

I have evolved from a mid-level project manager to a Senior IT and Technical Project Manager.

And among all the domains I have encountered, I found myself drawn to cloud infrastructure, applications, and Zero Trust Architecture.

But this transformation did not happen overnight.

There was a time when my love was rooted in art.

I would stand behind artists painting murals—watching silently, studying their form, their structure, their discipline—

Until one day, they invited me in.

That curiosity never left me.

It simply evolved.

Today, I have earned my place in project management—particularly in infrastructure.

Over the past seven years, I have invested more than 15,000 hours into IT strategy, project management, and leadership.

I have reached a level of depth that many would call mastery—

Yet I remain aware that there is still more to learn.

As I shared in earlier chapters—why project management chose me, and why infrastructure chose me—

The answers were not immediate.

They revealed themselves over time—

Through experience.

Through pressure.

Through reflection.

And now, we are approaching the part of the journey where those answers begin to take form.

The lessons ahead are not theoretical.

They are lived.

They are shaped by real workplaces, real challenges, and real moments of pressure—

Where execution mattered more than intention.

This is where you will begin to see:

The workplaces that shaped me

The realities of execution under pressure

The transition from observation to disciplined execution

The emergence of leadership—not as a title, but as action

And the foundation of what would later become my understanding of cloud migration

Because transformation is not learned in comfort.

It is revealed in motion.

And what comes next is not a continuation of theory—

It is the beginning of truth.

CHAPTER 2

From Identity to Direction — Where Experience Begins to Take Shape

Why Infrastructure Chose Me

The question, "Why infrastructure?" is almost rhetorical.

I have never been comfortable calling myself a jack of all trades, master of none.

I believe we are each meant to master something—

We simply need to identify it, recognize it, and commit to it.

That is our gifted talent.

What is often mistaken for lack of mastery is, in reality, a lack of focus.

You cannot go deep if you are constantly spread thin.

Over time, I found myself reflecting on a principle often associated with William of Ockham.

Occam's Razor does not directly speak about mastery—but it teaches something just as important:

Remove what is unnecessary.

Simplify.

Focus.

From that, I developed a personal discipline:

Do less—then obsess.

Not less effort—but fewer directions.

Not limitation—but concentration.

Because performance is not built on doing more.

It is built on doing what matters—repeatedly, deliberately, and with depth.

As few as you can.

As many as you must.

And perhaps that is why infrastructure chose me.

Because infrastructure does not reward surface-level understanding—

It demands depth.

For me, the journey began with fear.

I did not grow up in a country where access to knowledge was readily available.

There were only a handful of libraries in the country—

Primarily located in Port-au-Prince and often affiliated with private, religious, or cultural institutions.

For most people, they were simply not accessible. [1]

Access was not assumed—

It was restricted.

Even that limited access was nearly 11 miles from my home—far beyond what was realistically reachable given the conditions at the time. [2]

Technology felt distant—almost unreachable.

In reality, it was.

And yet—

something within me was drawn to it.

Despite having little to no access to it.

You must understand something deeply to truly love it.

When I chose project management as a career, I often asked myself:

When will I ever be able to call myself an IT Project Manager—let alone a Technical Project Manager?

The truth is—

we carry these titles long before they are formally given to us.

At home, we solve problems, coordinate tasks, manage constraints, and make decisions—all without recognizing that we are already practicing project management.

For example, I used to hesitate when I saw job descriptions requiring electrical engineering experience.

Yet in reality, I grew up working with electricity in my own home.

I understood voltage, wiring, and components long before I ever saw a formal definition—

because I had to, not because I was taught.

That realization changed my perspective:

We often underestimate what we already know—

especially when it was learned through necessity rather than recognition.

Notes

[1] During the late 20th century, Haiti had a limited number of libraries, primarily located in Port-au-Prince and affiliated with private, religious, or cultural institutions.

Notable examples include the Bibliothèque Haïtienne des Spiritains (1873), the Bibliothèque Haïtienne des Frères de l'Instruction Chrétienne (1912), and the Institut Français d'Haïti library (1945).

Access remained limited due to geographic, economic, transportation, and security constraints.

2 Distance alone does not fully capture accessibility. Limited public transportation, infrastructure challenges, and safety concerns made such distances effectively prohibitive.

Learning Without Realizing

One thing I have always found fascinating is how companies unintentionally turn consumers into engineers.

Think about it—

When you sign up for internet service with providers like AT&T or Verizon, they send you instructions to:

Connect routers

Configure wireless networks

Set up access points

Without realizing it, you are performing tasks that mirror those of network engineers.

You are not just using the system—

You are configuring it.

That realization stayed with me.

Because long before I formally held the title of Network Project Manager, I had already performed these tasks—repeatedly, intuitively, and without formal recognition.

I was learning—

Without realizing it.

Later, at C Spire Wireless, that informal knowledge evolved into real responsibility.

What once began as curiosity and necessity became structured execution.

I led major initiatives, including:

Network Legacy Upgrade

StreamWide implementation

Mobility Network upgrades

I was managing multiple large-scale projects simultaneously.

And that is where something shifted.

This was no longer exposure.

It was ownership.

It was accountability.

It was execution at scale.

And it was there that my true passion for network infrastructure and cybersecurity began to take shape.

Workplaces That Shaped Me

Great environments refine us; difficult ones test us—but both are necessary, because failure is not the enemy of success; it is part of its foundation.

I have worked across many organizations throughout my career, primarily as a consultant. But C Spire Wireless remains one of the few places I speak about with complete confidence.

The leadership.

The culture.

The trust placed in project managers.

It was exceptional.

A project manager cannot succeed without trust.

At C Spire, I had that trust.

The Vice President who interviewed me made a decision after a single round. He did not merely assess what I knew—he recognized my willingness to learn, adapt, and deliver.

That is leadership.

C Spire Wireless is one of the few companies where I experienced what I would call grace—where project management was respected, where leadership supported execution, and where Vice Presidents and Program Directors trusted us to do our jobs—

Because they understood the value of project professionals in bringing structure to chaos.

There was strong collaboration across teams.

The tools were available—and continuously evolving alongside the demands of technology and cybersecurity.

IT SMEs remained focused on their responsibilities, and stakeholders operated without visible personal agendas.

At least, that was my experience—through the lens in which I observed the organization.

Others may have different perspectives.

And that is fair.

When Leadership Fails the System

Now—

it is time to get real.

Not all failures in enterprise environments are technical.

Some of the most critical failures originate from structure, leadership, and human dynamics.

Without naming organizations aside from C Spire Wireless, I carry a Rolodex of difficult leadership experiences.

I will share testimonials from two more organizations.

To me, they represented the epitome of chaos—places that seemed to operate under an unspoken slogan:

Kill the good, reinforce the bad.

In those environments, it often felt as though the people trying to do good work were pushed aside, while dysfunction was allowed to thrive.

As I have always said:

without leadership support, even the most capable project manager can become a laughingstock.

I will not use real company names, but pseudonyms—to protect their privacy.

The Environment

This case involved a family-owned, mid-sized organization generating nearly $300 million in annual revenue.

It was also the first place where I began to feel myself breaking down mentally.

The hiring process itself was smooth.

Not intimidating.

The only hesitation I had was the preference for Big Four backgrounds—but I moved through four rounds and received the offer.

It came while I was on vacation in Mexico.

A birthday gift.

I was excited.

I was energized.

I was eager to make a difference.

To their credit, I did not experience prejudice or racial bias.

They treated employees and contractors with respect.

I was flown to their office monthly, all expenses paid.

Each visit began with the company limousine waiting for me at the airport, followed by stays in high-quality hotels—

An experience that felt unmissably executive in nature.

But once the work began—

reality surfaced.

Listening First

As I always do, I began with environmental analysis—

by listening first.

Before imposing structure.

Before recommendations.

Before trying to solve anything.

I listen.

The work of Dr. Mark Goulston, the psychiatrist whose writing on listening under pressure shaped much of my professional discipline, reinforced this practice deeply in me—the ability to listen beyond words and hear what is actually happening beneath them.

So, I unpacked my tools.

My instincts.

My discipline.

I listened first.

And what I heard began to tell a very different story than what I had been sold.

Not all challenges in enterprise environments are technical.

What I heard was not simply operational noise.

It was a pattern.

A system was speaking through its dysfunction.

RED - P—Organizational diagnostic Model & Execution Model

The RED Lens

To make sense of what I was observing,

I relied on a framework that had guided me through complex environments before.

Rajeev Peshawaria introduced the RED framework:

Role. Environment. Development.

Originally designed to evaluate workplace alignment,

I adapted it into something more operational—

an organizational diagnostic lens I apply at the start of engagements.

As I began applying that lens, clarity started to emerge.

Role

Responsibilities were blurred.

Ownership was unclear.

Accountability was inconsistent.

Environment

Communication was fractured.

Leadership alignment was weak.

Decision-making lacked cohesion.

Development

Capability gaps were visible.

Expectations were misaligned.

Productivity was uneven.

What I was seeing was no longer a collection of issues—

it was a pattern taking shape.

What looked like a delivery problem was something else entirely.

Not a breakdown in execution—a system problem.

From Diagnosis to Action

But diagnosis alone is not enough.

Projects do not fail because we lack understanding.

They fail because we misjudge urgency.

That realization led me to evolve the model into what I now call:

RED-P—where Priority becomes the filter that turns diagnosis into execution.

With Priority introduced,

the model no longer only explains the system—

it directs where action must occur first.

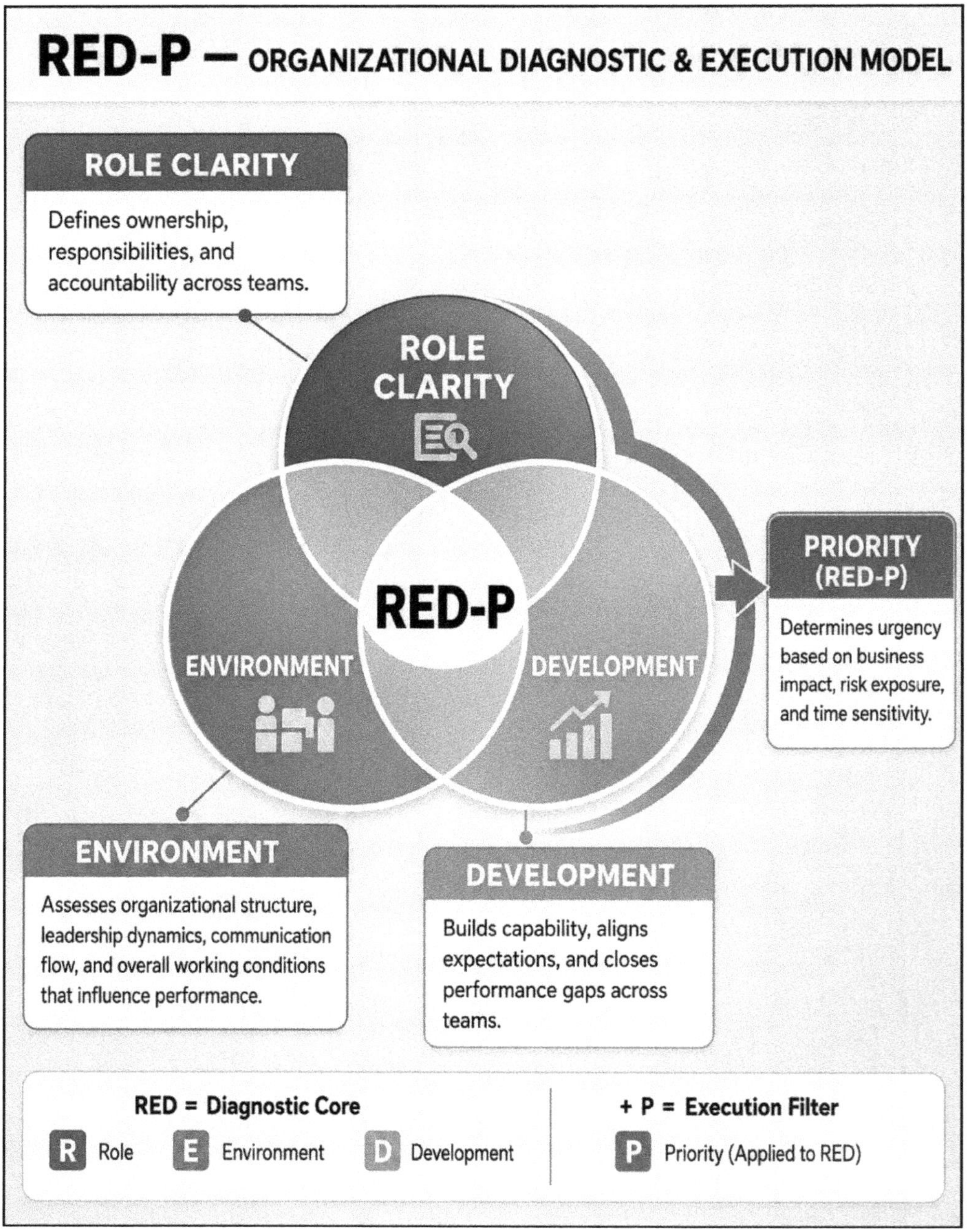

RED-P — Organizational Diagnostic & Execution Model

Priority

What must be addressed now?

What can wait?

What cannot be ignored?

Priority changed the function of the model.

It moved the lens from observation

to intervention.

It forced decisions.

It exposed trade-offs.

It made action unavoidable.

What it revealed in this environment

was deeply concerning.

The System Beneath the Surface

As I continued listening and applying the lens—

the pattern became unmistakable.

This initiative had already been

attempted twice.

And it had failed—both times.

Not because of technology.

Not because of process.

Because of leadership resistance.

There was a single point in the system where progress stopped.

When I asked about it, the answer was clear:

The effort would not move forward because one individual would not allow it.

Naively—and perhaps too confidently—I responded:

"I will succeed."

But the environment told a different story.

There was an unspoken tension in every room.

People spoke over each other.

Ideas never reached completion.

Conversations reset themselves

before conclusions could form.

As I listened further,
the more I understood the internal dynamics.

The resistance was not isolated.

It was reinforced.

The individual at the center of that resistance
was closely tied to one of the most influential
figures in the organization.

Authority, in this environment, did not
follow structure.

It followed relationships.

And that changed everything.

Early Wins—and Their Limits

By week four, I found an opening.

In one meeting, executives continuously interrupted one another.

No one finished a thought.

I stayed quiet.

Observed.

Then I was asked:

"Gerald, what are your thoughts?"

I asked, "May I speak freely?"

They said yes.

So, I did.

I told them the behavior had to stop.

If ideas could not be completed, nothing meaningful would move forward.

To my surprise, they agreed.

That was the first win.

But agreement in principle is not transformation in practice.

The Breaking Point

By week twelve, nothing had changed.

We were still trapped in the same conversations.

Still unable to move forward.

External partners were waiting.

Initiatives were stalled.

Momentum was gone.

This time, I had enough data.

Enough observation.

Enough clarity.

When asked if I had identified the root cause,
I answered directly:

"The issue is not the solution.

The issue is trust.

Trust is being blocked at the leadership level."

Silence followed.

That moment shifted everything.

Some supported me.

Others resisted.

Looking back—

That was my breaking point.

Not because I was wrong.

But because I delivered truth
without enough awareness
of the environment I was in.

What Happened Next

I later met privately with the individual at the center of the resistance.

I apologized.

He told me not to.

In his words:
"I know. You're just caught in the middle."
That confirmed everything.

But by then—

it was too late.

Momentum had collapsed.

Initiatives were cancelled.

The broader effort failed.

Seven months—

circling the same issue.

Waiting for approval that was never coming.

Eventually, my Program Director stepped back into the role.

Nothing had to be said.

I could read the room.

My role ended.

What Stress Revealed

Looking back, I recognize something critical.

What I experienced was not just frustration.

It was emotional override under sustained pressure.

Even with knowledge—

we are still human.

We like to believe that understanding behavior

means controlling it.

It does not.

We are constantly managing ourselves.

This was not a failure of skill.

It was the consequence of prolonged exposure to dysfunction.

Daniel Goleman first described this as an amygdala hijack—a concept he introduced in *Emotional Intelligence* (1995).

Goulston builds on this foundation in his work on emotional regulation under pressure—

which is where I first encountered its application in leadership settings.

And it does not only happen in extreme situations.

It happens in boardrooms.

In leadership meetings.

In environments where truth is obstructed and accountability is absent.

The Five Phases of Stress Response

1. Reaction — The Reptilian Brain (Fight or Flight)

This is the havoc moment. Survival takes over before reason has time to speak.

2. Release — The Mammalian Brain (Emotion)

This phase is dominated by frustration, denial, shame, blame, or emotional flooding.

3. Recenter — The Transition Back to Control

Emotion begins to settle, and internal balance starts to return.

4. Refocus — The Human Brain (Reason Engages)

Thinking sharpens. Perspective returns. The ability to evaluate options becomes available again.

5. Re-engage — The Human Brain (Deliberate Action)

Purposeful action replaces reactive behavior.

I had used this model before.

But in this environment—

I underestimated how deeply I was already affected.
Stress is not weakness.

Stress is the body's response to sustained contradiction and disorder.
Leadership environments—
good or destructive—
shape who we become.

And sometimes—
the hardest environments
forge the strongest lessons.

The RED framework—Role, Environment, Development—became more than a concept.

It became a lens.

With Priority, it became a system for action.

Because in enterprise environments—

understanding is not enough.

Knowing where to act first
is what determines success.

In my next workplace testimonial—
I will share a similar challenge—
One even more brutal.
One that nearly took my sanity.

A Time of Insanity—Madness from top to bottom

There is an old aphorism:

when you pray for a job—
be sure to pray
for the environment
that comes with it.

Because it is not the role
that shapes you most—
it is the system
in which that role
must survive.

The workplace described in this chapter
is one where chaos
is not a problem to be solved,
but a condition
to be sustained—
where the solution to chaos is,
invariably,
more chaos.

I cannot describe it
more honestly than this:

We are hiring for talent—
with zero tolerance
for actual talent.

Because true talent
does not adapt to dysfunction—
it exposes it.

And in environments
where disorder becomes
the operating model,
exposure
is treated
as insubordination.

Talent becomes a menace
to the system.

What makes it even more paradoxical
is that systems built around
security clearance frameworks—
MBI / Public Trust.
In practice, however,
it felt less like a measure of integrity
and more like

an unspoken contract:

"Trust To Keep Lips Shut."
(TTKLS).

Nearly six months
of background checks—
only to formalize silence.

Four months into the process,
I was granted a temporary clearance
and began working—
two weeks before my birthday.

I replaced an Assistant Director
for one of the departments—
a two-decade veteran
transitioning to another division,
essentially
an organization within the organization.

He carried himself
like someone
who had spent years
navigating a system

that demanded endurance.

By the time he left,
the exhaustion
was visible.

This Assistant Director was one of the few individuals
who understood project management
at a high level.
His Excel automation alone
was a masterclass—
he was not just organized;
he was surgical.

He gave me
a two-week transition—
walking me through systems,
repositories,
intranet structures,
and ultimately
handing over
his program portfolio.

There was no need
to reinvent anything.

His work
was already operating
at a level
most organizations
never reach.

He also introduced me
to someone I consider
one of the top three professionals
I have ever worked with—
this engineer.

Work ethic.
Technical depth.
Integrity.

Rare.

Both of them
saw me
for what I was capable of—
and I felt it.

Momentum Before Collapse

With the portfolio in hand, I began executing.

I worked across multiple technical and operational departments:

Cybersecurity functions

Application teams

Network operations

Enterprise technology services

My focus was not just delivery—but visibility.

I aligned initiatives to the strategic roadmap:

Phishing-resistant MFA

Zero Trust Network Architecture (ZTNA)

Infrastructure modernization

For the first time, projects had structure.

I introduced:

Agile practices (adapted—not dogmatic)

Stage gates

Escalation timelines

Dependency awareness

Before that?

Projects operated like a Möbius strip—

no beginning,

no end,

no accountability.

Tools existed:

Trello

Microsoft Project

Power BI

Most of them unused.

Because tools do not deliver projects.

Leadership and disciplined execution do.

Within six months,
I became the person leadership called—
when projects were failing.

I reported directly to the CIO and DCIO.

And I delivered.

The Arrival of Disorder

Then came the shift.

A new director entered to lead one of the technology departments.

I will call him

Dr. Viru Sahastrabuddhe—

"Mr. Virus,"

inspired by the character in 3 Idiots—

who embodies a system

where discipline becomes dogma...

and leadership loses its humanity.

He did not introduce dysfunction.

He institutionalized it.

I was told—informally—that I would now report to him.

No official communication.

No transition.

Just... absorption.

Three weeks later, he scheduled a one-on-one.

I entered the meeting ready to collaborate.

He entered it ready to contain.

His first question:

"Why are you involved in all departments?"
I explained my role.

His response:

"Stop all projects. You report to me now."

I agreed—
with one condition:
"Send formal communication to the DCIO—
releasing me from those responsibilities."

He replied:

"Don't worry about that."

That was the moment I understood the system I was now in.

The IMS vs. Gantt Chart Incident (A Defining Moment)

One week later, I was tasked with building an Integrated Master Schedule (IMS).

I spent days consolidating:

Strategic initiatives

Dependencies

Milestones

Cross-functional timelines

I presented the IMS using Excel—

structured,

categorized,

and aligned.

He looked at it and said:

"This is not an IMS."

Then, gesturing vaguely:

"I'm looking for bars... stacked... across time."

I paused.

"You mean a Gantt chart?"

He replied:

"Yes. That's what an IMS is."

This is where precision matters—

not just for the story,

but for the discipline itself.

An Integrated Master Schedule (IMS) is a comprehensive, logically linked schedule that integrates all project activities, dependencies, and timelines across programs.

A Gantt chart, on the other hand, is a visual representation of that schedule over time.

A Gantt chart can represent an IMS.

But it is not the IMS itself.

I responded carefully:

"With all due respect—

they are different.

A Gantt chart can visually represent an IMS—

but the IMS is the underlying structured schedule."

He replied:

"Maybe you don't know

what a Gantt chart is."

That was the moment
tension entered the room.

I paused—
recentered—
and recalled Goulston's principles
on managing emotional escalation.

Then I said:

"I understand
what a Gantt chart is.
Let's keep this discussion
professional."

We de-escalated.

But from that moment forward—

I became a target.

Controlled Erosion

The attacks were not loud.

They were precise.

I was skipped in meetings.

My input was ignored.

My authority was quietly removed.

Then came policy shifts:

Not announced as disruption.

Presented as order.

Contractors could not speak on behalf of the government.

A contractor's name was never to appear on any formal document. If assigned to a project, the work had to be attributed to a full-time federal employee in their place.

Contributions only counted if they were formally documented.

Identity was removed.

Voice was reassigned.

Work was permitted—ownership was not.

Then came something quieter.

More precise.

The audit of existence.

Every Friday, my timesheet was expected to account for every hour of my time.

Not approximately.

Not reasonably.

Completely.

I complied.

Not out of agreement—
but with accuracy.

I documented my work in a way that made the invisible undeniable.
So granular that what appeared to be "petty detail" became a record of control.

It read like this:
Research conducted during working hours
Incident response when systems failed

At first, I documented the categories of work.

But that was not sufficient.
So, I went further.

I broke down my day as if it were being examined for deviation:
30 minutes – morning preparation to review WBS and priorities
2 hours – daily stand-ups across three major projects
1 hour – review and update of the master project plan
2 hours – ad hoc meetings across workstreams
1 hour – email review, stakeholder updates, coordination

And beyond structure—there was operational reality:

1 hour — research required to move work forward

1 hour — incident response when systems failed

1 hour — problem-solving during outages

And then there was the work that could not be reduced, but still had to be justified:

Vulnerability remediation coordination

Disaster recovery documentation

SOP development with engineering teams

Policy documentation creation

Reworking a two-year strategic roadmap into an updated, forward-aligned plan

Everything had to be accounted for.

Even what could not be measured.

When I finished documenting it all, the conclusion was unavoidable.

The system was not measuring productivity.

It was measuring presence.

And in doing so, it revealed something it did not intend to.

The detail did not expose inefficiency.

It exposed integrity.

Because what those records showed—clearly, structurally, without interpretation—was this:

I had been giving more than I was ever charging.

Overtime that was never claimed.

Effort that was never questioned—until scrutiny required justification.

That is when I understood something deeper about myself.

I have always believed that operational excellence is a disciplined form of perfectionism—

but one that professionals are expected to carry at their own expense.

I am a perfectionist.

But not the kind that delays outcomes.

I set boundaries.

I deliver.

I move forward.

Still—

For six months, this level of scrutiny did not exist.

Which meant the work had not changed.

Only the system had.

Now it did.

And that is when I understood something even more critical:

Governance, when applied consistently, creates clarity.

When applied selectively—it creates control.

Internal Collapse

Something changed in me.

Not professionally—personally.

I began to question:

My value.

My identity.

Even my place in the environment.

I lost appetite.

Sleep became optional.

I began therapy.

Because leadership—when misused—does not just break systems.

It breaks people.

Promotion Without Relief

At the point of near resignation—after rewriting my resignation letter three times—I was reassigned.

To the CIO's office.

On paper, it was a promotion.

In reality, it was escalation.

Now I was responsible for:

Solving cross-departmental failures

Delivering executive-ready outcomes

Recommending technical solutions

Building dashboards and visibility models

I was no longer managing projects.

I was absorbing dysfunction—from both ends.

Bottom and top.

The Pattern Revealed

Whenever a project was failing—I was assigned.

Whenever it stabilized—it was taken.

Credited elsewhere.

Direction came in one form:

The way projects were assigned to me was discombobulated—

to the point of abstraction.

There was no structured intake, no defined objectives, no articulation of outcomes.

Only fragments.

It required a different kind of discipline—

the ability to interpret the shortest form of thought and reconstruct it into something executable.

A sentence had to become a scope.

An email had to become requirements.

An assumption had to become a plan.

From there, I built what did not exist:

Business requirements

Work breakdown structures

Timelines

Dependencies

Execution paths

And this was not reserved for minor tasks.

This was the expectation—even for enterprise-level initiatives.

Projects like the implementation of Azure Virtual Desktop (AVD).

Projects like the Data Modernization initiative.

No clarity was provided.

Clarity had to be created.

Leadership, in its shortest form of communication:

"FYI."

No scope.

No context—just expectation.

And I delivered.

Every time.

The Cost of Failed Leadership

This environment did not fail quietly.

It collapsed through attrition.

Experienced leaders began to leave.

High-performing staff exited.

Institutional knowledge disappeared.

Then came the irony.

A department called
"Government Efficiency."

The new administration introduced DOGE—
under the direction of Elon Musk (Lucas, 2025).

The intent appeared sound:

eliminate waste.

But execution—
revealed the truth.

The cuts came fast—
too fast—

and too broad to distinguish
precision
from damage.

This is the failure:

not of intent—
but of control.

Because waste reduction
without structure—

is not optimization—

it is indiscriminate removal.

Essential workers were terminated
alongside the inefficient—

and many had to be
hurriedly rehired
(Kamarck, 2026; Wallace, 2025).

This is not efficiency.

This is rework—
introduced at scale.

Entire agencies
were left understaffed.

Critical functions
were disrupted.

This is not cost savings—

this is capability degradation.

And the savings—
when measured honestly—

came at a cost
greater than the waste
they were meant to eliminate.

This is the principle:

Cost reduction
without operational awareness—

creates downstream loss
greater than upstream waste.

I know this
firsthand.

I served as a contractor
for one of the government's oversight offices—

the kind charged with auditing
waste
and fraud

My contract—
originally set for three years—

was cut short
during the DOGE-era reductions.

Despite one fact:

contractors sat outside
the federal workforce
DOGE was officially tasked
to reduce.

This is where execution failed
completely.

Because when a system
cannot distinguish
what it is designed to control—

it begins to erode
its own foundation.

The irony
was structural—

not symbolic.

In the name of fighting waste—
the administration weakened
the very oversight
designed to prevent it.

This is the governing truth:

When oversight is reduced
to create efficiency—

inefficiency expands
unseen.

Those positioned
to navigate the chaos—

learned how to use the system
to their advantage.

While frontline workers,
contractors,
and the public—

bore the cost.

And this is where
execution defines truth:

Not in what was intended—

but in what the system
actually produced.

Efficiency, it seemed,
meant removing those
who could expose inefficiency.

Musk stepped away.

The agency then took full latitude
to eliminate what it considered its problem—

those who were trying
to make things right.

I watched it happen
to engineers and leaders
I deeply respected.

The kind of professionals
who were not just capable—

they were sought after.

The ones who helped move work forward
that had been stalled for years
inside POA&M pipelines—

trapped in a state of controlled stagnation,
where compliance was used
as a mechanism to delay execution.

Those of us who understood the system—

were precisely the ones
the system resisted.

I saw capable people
who had already demonstrated leadership—
step into acting roles,
deliver results,
and still be denied
the permanent seat.

The justification was familiar:

"Poor leadership."

A conclusion
I fundamentally disagree with.

Because leadership
is not defined by title—

it is defined by impact.

And their impact
was undeniable.

Then came the final signal.

The control was enforced passively—

through return-to-office mandates,
through restructured severance terms,
through conditions designed
to make resignation consequential.

Highly skilled,
necessary resources
were placed under quiet pressure:

stay under conditions that diminished them—

or leave
and forfeit what they had earned.

Some chose their integrity
over the system.

They resigned.

No severance.

The same system
that claimed efficiency
ensured that talent exited quietly.

Despite being capable
of leading at the highest levels—

they were never given
the opportunity.

These were the kind of leaders
the agency needed—

ones who believed in doing the right things,
the right way,

and doing all the right things
when necessary.

They had something
many in leadership positions did not—

Followers.

Followers.

People trusted them.
People relied on them.
People chose to follow them.

And that is the difference.

We did not lack management.

We lacked leadership.

And the few who demonstrated it
were suppressed—

until they could no longer operate.

What remained
was structure without direction.

Execution without principle.

The difference is clear.

Management
is doing all the right things.

But this management
was doing all the right things
the wrong way.

Leadership,
as it has always been,

is doing all the right things
the right way.

The so-called leaders
had no followership.

The real ones did.

You can claim leadership

all you want—

But if no one is following you,

You are not leading.

You are managing.

You are managing.

The Final Blow

A new director entered.

The pattern repeated.

But worse.

Now the experience included:

Prejudice

Rank-based suppression

Cultural undertones

My role ended under the justification:

"Lack of funding."

This experience reshaped me more than any success ever could.

Because it forced me to confront something deeper than failure.

It forced me to confront systems that reject truth.

It also forced me to recognize that sustained dysfunction does not only test performance—it tests the person.

This was not merely a professional challenge.

It was prolonged exposure to disorder.

And prolonged exposure to disorder changes you.

Leadership failed—from the top.

And as always—

What happens at the top reflects at the bottom.

As Hermes Trismegistus wrote:

"As above, so below."

What this experience taught me is that environments are never neutral.

They either strengthen discipline—or erode it.

They either support truth—or punish the people who speak it.

They either create clarity—or weaponize confusion.

And when governance is applied without consistency, it stops being governance.

It becomes control.

That is what I learned.

Not simply that bad leadership creates bad outcomes—

but that leadership environments shape who we become, what we tolerate, and how much of ourselves we are forced to spend just to remain intact.

This role tested everything in me:

My discipline

My identity

My faith

It tested my commitment to PMI principles.

Ironically, the same leader who rejected structure once said:

"The organization is not ready for PMI."

What he meant was:

The organization was not ready for accountability.

Because PMI is not methodology.

It is discipline.

And discipline exposes disorder.

And in the end, I did not question project management—I questioned the system that refused to be managed.

The system did not break me—it revealed who I had to become to survive it.

I learned something critical: where leadership fails, even truth becomes a threat.

And slowly, with clarity, I understood—

I was not the problem. The system was.

And beyond that realization, something even deeper remained:

Some systems are not meant to be fixed—only understood.

CHAPTER 3

When strategy meets doubt

Not every strategy is accepted.

Not every leader is understood.

And not every decision will be welcomed

in the moment it is made.

But leadership is not tested

when everything is clear—

It is tested

when uncertainty takes control,

when doubt fills the room,

and when conviction must stand alone.

This is where execution begins.

Execution Under Pressure

During a major network upgrade, our project fell significantly behind schedule due to COVID-19 delays—nearly six months.

To recover, I introduced a new testing strategy.

Originally, testing phases were fully sequential:

Integration Testing
End-to-End Testing (E2E)
User Acceptance Testing (UAT)
Performance Testing

Each phase had to be completed before the next began.

This created delays.

I introduced a controlled parallel execution model based on an 80–85% completion threshold.

Once a phase reached stability:

The next phase began in parallel
Remaining issues were resolved concurrently
Teams coordinated across overlapping stages

This allowed us to:

Accelerate delivery
Reduce delays
Maintain system integrity

We saved 3–4 weeks per phase.

When I proposed this strategy, many looked at me with doubt.

I could hear reactions—some laughed, others whispered:

"There goes someone trying to move forward without fully completing testing. It's going to break."

"Maybe he doesn't know what he's doing."

I could feel the room judging me.

And the truth is—project managers are human.

We are not superheroes.

We experience stress. We seek validation. We look for acceptance, just like anyone else.

But as leaders, we are wired to absorb it.

As the captain, we cannot show weakness when the ship is under pressure.

Yet we remain vulnerable—like Superman under the effect of kryptonite.

Although I had strong support from the engineering teams, that did not eliminate their doubts. My approach was unfamiliar—unconventional.

And that is okay.

We must understand something fundamental:

We are dealing with people.

And people are complex.

We evaluate ideas through preference, experience, and bias.

Only one person stood up and spoke.

I will refer to him as OJ—a highly skilled and experienced senior engineer with decades of tenure at the organization.

He was a living library.

If he ever left, the organization would lose not just knowledge—but the equivalent of its data storage and processing power.

OJ said:

"It's possible—if we apply an 80–85% completion threshold."

OJ supported the idea publicly.

Without his support, the strategy may have been dismissed.

He also said something that stayed with me:

"With IT, we can fit the world inside a bottle."

That statement captures the essence of technology—turning the impossible into reality.

Now, I want to share how OJ and I built our relationship.

Because it did not start well.

It started like an unexpected explosion—like stepping on a mine you didn't see.

I didn't anticipate it.

But I was prepared enough to respond.

And that moment remains one of the most defining experiences of my career as a Project Manager.

OJ had a habit of interrupting and taking control of conversations.

He did this with many people—including me.

In my first month, he interrupted me during a meeting—abruptly.

The room froze.

And for a moment, so did I.

My heart was racing.

I could feel the sweat under my arms.

I took about ten seconds to regain control.

You could probably hear me swallow.

Instead of reacting emotionally, I responded calmly:

"I truly appreciate your contribution to this project. Without you, we're a car running on three wheels. Let's hold your thoughts, and we'll come back to you after the call."

That moment was critical.

I did not challenge him.

I respected him.

Later, I connected with him one-on-one.

I took the time to understand him.

And I realized something important:

He did not need control.

He needed recognition.

He needed respect.

People become far more collaborative when they feel heard and valued.

From that point forward, OJ became one of my strongest supporters.

And in many ways—

That support allowed me to survive and continue delivering in that environment.

Equipollent leadership—Where Status ends, and respect begins

Leadership is a virtue that should remain constant—
unchanged by title,
position,
or circumstance.

True leadership is symmetrical.
It does not bend to hierarchy—
nor does it distort itself
in the presence of power.

It is blind to status.

Real leaders operate
with an equipollent level of respect—
offered equally,
without condition,
without calculation.

This raises a question
that has echoed across generations:

Are leaders born—
or are they made?

And where does true leadership
actually emerge from?

It is tempting
to search for this answer
in books,
philosophies,
and doctrines—
to pause long enough
to study every theory
ever written on leadership.

But the truth is far less academic—
and far more personal.

This is not a simple question.
And it should never be.

Because leadership is not just a skill—
it is proximity to power.

And power—
when misunderstood—
becomes dangerous.

The distance between a leader
and destruction
is often thinner
than we admit.

While God holds the power to create—
and the authority over destruction—

leaders operate
within what has already been created.

Yet they still possess the ability
to shape,
influence,
elevate,
or dismantle.

Every leader lives
in a constant internal conflict—
a battle not against others,
but against themselves.

We are often taught
a flawed narrative:
that light is good—

and darkness is evil.

But if that were true—
we would be righteous in daylight
and destructive at night.

That is not
how human nature works.

Darkness is not the enemy—
unexamined character is.

Leadership, then, is a choice.

A daily one.

And that choice is often rooted
in something far deeper
than professional experience—
it is rooted
in who we were
long before
we carried titles.

A Lesson in Respect — Before Leadership Had a Name

I learned this lesson early—

long before I understood leadership as a concept.

At the time, I could not have defined it—

I only recognized it—in human terms.

Only later did I come to understand—

Leadership is not merely a concept

to be discussed—

but a construct to be formed,

tested,

and lived.

At eleven years old,

I grew up in an environment where bootblacks

would come to our home—

several times a week—

to clean shoes.

Mine—and those of my siblings.

At that time,

Society placed visible distinctions between people—
based on profession,
appearance,
and perceived status.

Some roles were respected.

Others were tolerated.

But I chose something different.

I chose connection.

I spoke with them.
I asked where they came from.
I listened to their experiences.
I offered water—sometimes food.

Over time, something changed.

What began as a transaction became a relationship.

One bootblack, in particular,
became loyal to our family.
He returned consistently—
even during times

when payment was uncertain.

That loyalty was not built on money.

It was built on respect.

And that is when I understood
something no leadership framework
had yet taught me:

Status has limits.
Respect does not.
That moment formed a principle
I carry to this day:

People do not respond to titles—
they respond
to how you make them feel.

What many call karma—
I understand as reciprocity:

You harvest
what you cultivate
in others.

The Illusion of Hierarchical Value

If I respect a CIO differently
than I respect a Help Desk analyst—
then I am assigning
unequal human value.

And that creates
a contradiction.

Because when systems fail—
it is not the CIO
who restores operations—
it is the very individuals
often overlooked.

So, who, then,
holds the greater value
in that moment?

The answer is situational—
but the principle is constant:

Every role carries necessity.

Every individual
deserves respect.

Leadership is not about
elevating some
and diminishing others.

It is about recognizing
that systems function
because people—
at every level—
matter.

The Equipollent Leadership Model™ — Respect vs. Status Axis

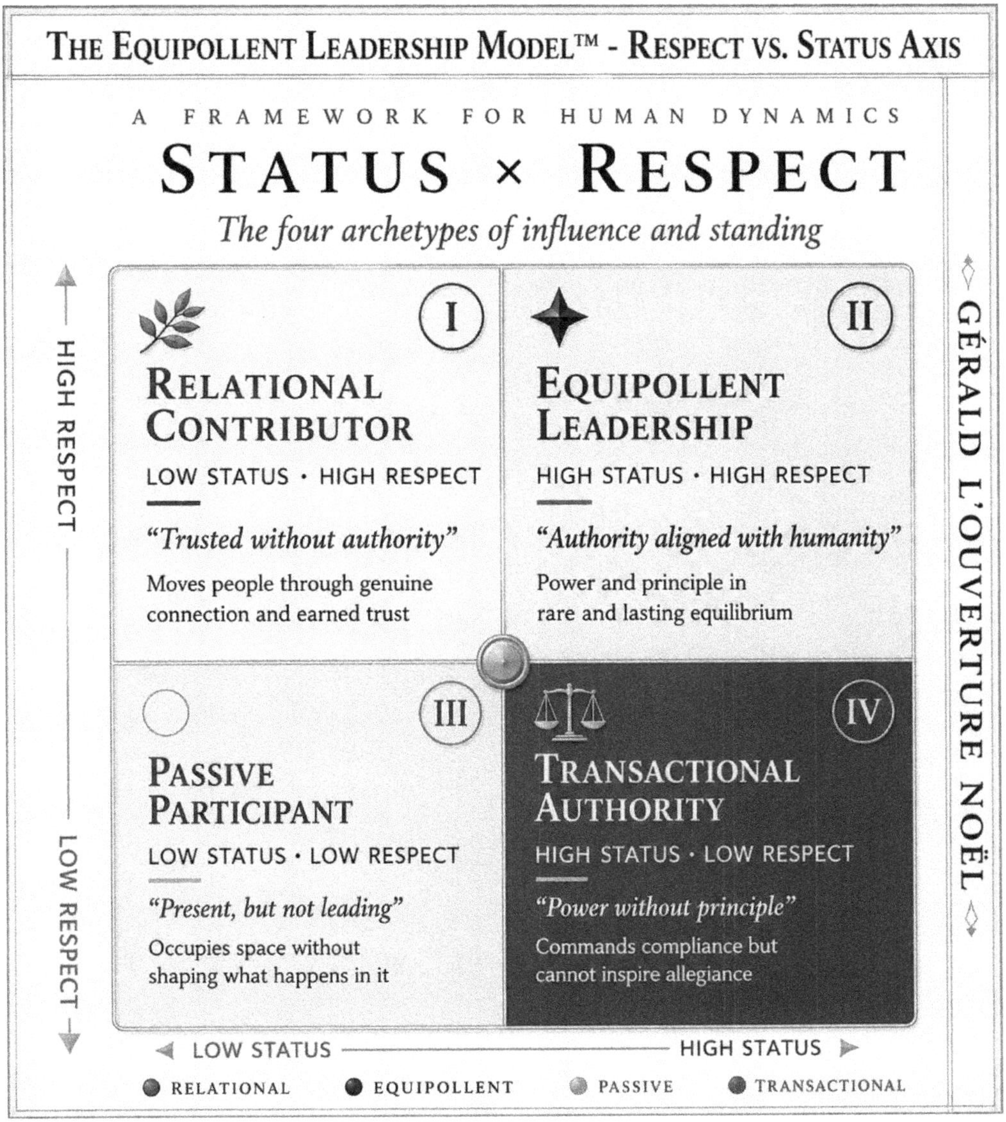

The model produces four distinct archetypes:

Relational Contributor (Quadrant I)
Low Status. High Respect.

Trusted without authority.

These are the people who move others through genuine connection and earned trust—

the bootblack who returned out of loyalty, not obligation.

They lead— without ever being named leaders.

Equipollent Leadership (Quadrant II)
High Status. High Respect.

Authority aligned with humanity.

Power and principle—held in rare and lasting equilibrium.

This is the standard the entire model is built toward—

and the rarest quadrant to occupy.

Passive Participant (Quadrant III)
Low Status. Low Respect.

Present—but not leading.

They occupy space without shaping what happens in it.

The danger here is not malice—

it is invisibility.

Transactional Authority (Quadrant IV)
High Status. Low Respect.

Power without principle.

Commands compliance—but cannot inspire allegiance.

This is the most common failure mode of senior leadership—

and the one this chapter examines most closely in the section that follows.

This model reinforces a foundational principle:

Status may grant you power—but only respect sustains leadership.

Status may position you above others—but it does not make you a leader.

People report to your title—but they follow your character.

Status defines where you stand—respect defines who you are.

When Leadership Fails — Respect Becomes Conditional

This principle was tested in one of the most defining environments of my career.

A leader—whom I refer to as Mr. Virus—introduced a culture not of leadership, but of division.

In meetings, he consistently prioritized full-time federal employees while bypassing me—

Despite my role as a Senior IT Project Manager and my tenure within the agency as a contractor, where my responsibilities and contributions remained integral to the mission.

The pattern was not incidental—it was consistent.

The disparity became more visible when another project manager—who joined nearly seven months after me—was elevated to Program Manager.

We held the same title.

We operated within the same structure.

Yet we were not treated the same.

Access shifted.

Visibility shifted.

Recognition shifted.

I was excluded—systematically.

This was not leadership.

It was hierarchy, selectively applied.

And in that environment, respect was no longer a principle—it was a variable.

Mr. Virus did not lose my respect because of authority.

He failed to earn it because of how he chose to use it.

I have come to believe this:

Project managers do not fail projects—at least, not most of the time.

Leadership fails project managers.

Without leadership support, even the most capable project manager becomes a scapegoat.

Accountability becomes misdirected.

And success, even when achieved, becomes unsustainable.

This is not criticism—it is a call for better leadership.

But accountability is not one-sided.

Project managers must still carry their responsibility:

to remain disciplined,

to stay productive,

and to maintain focus under pressure—even when the system around them does not.

Leadership Under Pressure — The True Test

Despite that environment, I made a decision:

I would not become what I was exposed to.

Even when I later operated within the CIO branch—

Serving as the bridge between leadership—

where proximity to authority could have justified retaliation—

I chose restraint.

I worked with him.

I held him accountable for reporting, performance, and delivery.

I engaged him as part of the system—not as an adversary.

Ironically, he reported into my function—yet not once did I use that position to diminish him.

Not once did I allow ego to replace principle.

Because leadership is not tested when conditions are favorable.

It is revealed when power is available—and restraint is chosen.

Leadership Is Identity — Not Behavior.

I pray daily for one thing:

To remain humble.

To remain respectful.

To remain grounded in who I am—regardless of where I stand.

Because leadership is not what you do.

It is who you are.

It is a constitution—one that applies universally, not selectively.

So—Are Leaders Born or Made?

Before answering that—

we must refine the question:

Where does leadership truly originate?

Leadership is not a fixed state.

It is a composition—

a convergence of identity

and the work of becoming.

Who you are is shaped early—
your personality,
your instincts,
your values.

Who you become is shaped over time—
through experience,
through adversity,
through choice.

This is where philosophy meets reality.

I have long studied the work of Sigmund Freud,
who argued that personality is formed
through the interaction of the id, ego, and superego.

While I challenge aspects of his framework—
particularly the absence of cultural influence—
his core premise remains powerful:

Our early experiences shape the foundation
of who we become.

You cannot eliminate the ego.

But you can refine it.

You can redirect it.

You can discipline it.

And that requires reflection—
especially of your childhood.

Because the leader you are today
is deeply connected
to the person you were then.

The Work of Becoming

Growth does not happen passively.

It demands intention.
It demands sacrifice.

As John C. Maxwell teaches
through the Law of Trade-Offs:
To gain something greater—
you must be willing to give something up.
This is where leadership becomes difficult.

And where it becomes real.

Change demands discomfort.

Transformation demands discipline.

Even B. F. Skinner demonstrated—
behavior is not accidental.

it is shaped
through reinforcement,
through repetition
through deliberate choice.

We are capable of change.

But we must choose it.

And what we choose—

repeatedly—

becomes who we are.

Because in the end—

What you do,

Consistently,

Defines who you become—

As nature is shaped through nurture.

Not intention.
Not potential.
Not belief.

Only what is done— consistently— becomes real.

My mother once told me:

"To make a difference,

you must first be different."

Choosing What to Emulate

I grew up in environments
where leadership was often corrupted—
where immorality
and disorder
were normalized.

But I made a decision:

I would not emulate
dysfunction.

I created my own internal scale—
what I call
a positron mindset—
choosing what was right,
not what was common.

Where others followed,
I questioned.

Where others conformed,
I resisted.

This is where I align
with Jean-Jacques Rousseau:

"Man is born free,
but everywhere he is in chains."

I chose not to remain
in those chains.

I challenged
the status quo.

And in doing so—
I ensured
that I was not a product
of my environment—
but a response to it.

The Leader I Choose to Be

The blueprint I leave behind is simple—but not easy:

Lead with respect.
Lead without hierarchy of human value.
Lead with awareness of your own shadow.

Lead as someone still becoming.

Because the greatest leaders are not those who arrive—

They are those who continue evolving.

So, am I a leader who was born—or made?

I am both.

The foundation was formed early—
through character,
values,
and perspective.

But the refinement—
the strength,
the discipline,
the clarity—
was forged through experience.

Through adversity.
Through environments
that tested everything I believed.

And like all great leaders—
I was shaped under pressure—
not destroyed by it.

If the leader within you feels distant—
there is only one place to begin:
Return
to where it was first formed.

Because wherever leadership was lost—
That is exactly
where it must be found again.
"He who influences the thought of his times
influences the times that follow"
—Elbert Hubbard

From Leadership to execution —where principles become practice

One does not need to be the deepest technical engineer to lead transformation.

It is time to remove that blindfold.

For too long, many have hesitated—believing that technical mastery alone is the prerequisite to lead technology-driven initiatives. It is not.

Because success in transformation does not belong to those who know the most—it belongs to those who can execute with structure, lead with clarity, and govern with discipline.

Migrations do not fail due to a lack of tools—they fail due to a lack of coordination, governance, and leadership.

This is where the leader in you steps forward—where leadership reveals itself, because leadership leads.

This is where true project management rises—not as an administrative function, but as the force that turns strategy into execution.

This is the principle I stand on:

Bridging discipline with technology—so complexity becomes clarity, and vision becomes delivery.

My strength—and my passion—has always been in that bridge.

As a certified Project Management Professional (PMP®) through the Project Management Institute (PMI®), this book is grounded in proven frameworks, governance models, and real-world execution practices—not theory alone.

Cloud Migration PM Bible™ is designed to serve as your operational guide—equipping you to lead, structure, and deliver successful infrastructure, application, and cloud migrations with confidence.

As one of my mentors told me at the age of 16—The virtue of knowledge is fundamentally structured upon three principles:

Knowledge.

Dare.

Boundary.

To possess knowledge is to have the courage to speak with clarity.

To dare is to express it with conviction.

And to understand its boundary is to know precisely when to stop. — RR

And now, we move beyond philosophy... beyond perception... and into execution—

From mindset to method. From vision to delivery.

Let us begin with Cloud Migration through the paradigm of Infrastructure.

CHAPTER 4

Migration Leadership Foundations

Understanding Modern Enterprise Migration

A migration is the controlled movement of systems, applications, services, or infrastructure from one environment to another—

While preserving business continuity, security, performance, and operational supportability.

But in modern enterprises, migration is rarely a standalone technical effort.

It is a coordinated business transformation.

Migrations are typically driven by broader organizational objectives:

Cloud adoption and platform modernization

Cost optimization and capital expense reduction

Data center exit and infrastructure consolidation

Cybersecurity enhancement and zero-trust enablement

Application modernization and SaaS adoption

Regulatory compliance and operational resilience

While these drivers may originate from different parts of the business, their success depends on one critical factor:

The ability to translate strategic intent into disciplined execution.

Organizations migrate for many reasons.

To reduce technical debt.

To improve scalability.

To strengthen security posture.

To adopt cloud-native capabilities.

To modernize legacy platforms.

The business case may be financial, strategic, operational, or regulatory.

But the outcome is always the same:

The environment must continue to operate—without disruption.

This is where complexity begins.

Because enterprise environments are not clean systems.

They are layered, interconnected, and often imperfect.

They contain:

Undocumented integrations

Legacy authentication mechanisms

Tightly coupled applications

Custom middleware and data flows

Fragile network dependencies

Vendor-controlled components

Operational procedures built over time—not always by design

Each of these elements introduces uncertainty.

And in migration, uncertainty is risk.

This is why migration leadership requires more than coordination.

It requires:

Architecture awareness — understanding how systems interact beyond documentation

Governance discipline — enforcing control across decisions, ownership, and escalation

Operational alignment — ensuring business, engineering, and support functions move together

Risk visibility — identifying what is unknown before it becomes a failure point

Because migration is not simply about moving systems.

It is about preserving the integrity of a living operating model while it is being transformed.

The challenge is not movement.

The challenge is control during movement.

Typical migration drivers include:

Cloud modernization and platform consolidation

Infrastructure refresh and end-of-life remediation

Security improvement and zero-trust enablement

Data center exit or facility consolidation

Application modernization and SaaS adoption

Business continuity, resilience, and disaster recovery improvement

But regardless of the driver—

the underlying requirement remains constant:

The system must remain stable while it is changing.

And that is where most migrations begin to fail.

Not because the strategy was wrong.

But because execution began before the system was fully understood.

This is the gap between intention and outcome.

Between planning and control.

Between movement—

and stability.

To close that gap, migration must be approached differently.

Not as a sequence of tasks—

But as a controlled system of execution.

That is the purpose of what follows— Foundations of Controlled Migration Execution™

Foundations of Controlled Migration Execution™

The Mindset, Structure, and Validation Discipline Behind Successful Migration

Migration does not fail because teams lack effort.

It fails because execution begins before understanding is complete.

And in enterprise environments, that mistake is rarely recoverable—because the system continues to move even when control is lost.

In enterprise environments—where infrastructure, applications, identity, data, and business operations intersect—migration is not a technical task.

It is a controlled transformation of a living system.

And control is never accidental.

It is designed.

This section defines the foundation of that control.

Not as theory.

But as an operational discipline.

Because in practice, migration success is not determined at cutover.

It is determined long before execution begins—

Through how well the system is understood, how clearly dependencies are mapped, how rigorously risks are evaluated, and how deliberately readiness is proven.

Controlled migration execution rests on three foundational conditions—the Three Foundations of Controlled Execution—which are distinct from, and precede, the Four Operational Pillars introduced later in this chapter:

1. Mindset — Thinking in Systems, Not Tasks

Migration cannot be managed as a checklist.

It must be understood as a system.

Every application interacts with infrastructure.

Every identity connects to access.

Every dependency introduces risk.

Every change impacts operations.

Without systems thinking, teams optimize locally—

But fail globally.

Controlled execution begins when the project manager stops asking:

"Are tasks complete?"

And starts asking:

"Is the system ready to operate in its new state?"

2. Structure — Designing Control Before Movement

Structure is the mechanism through which control is enforced.

Without structure, migration becomes reactive.

With structure, migration becomes predictable.

This includes:

Defined migration strategies (6R alignment)

Wave-based execution planning

Dependency mapping across systems and environments

Readiness gates before each transition

Clearly defined roles, ownership, and escalation paths

Structure ensures that movement is not based on urgency—

But on readiness.

Because in enterprise environments, speed without structure does not create efficiency.

It creates exposure.

3. Validation — Proving Readiness Through Evidence

Validation is the discipline that separates assumed readiness from proven readiness.

In uncontrolled environments, teams rely on confidence.

In controlled environments, teams rely on evidence.

Validation must occur across:

Infrastructure (connectivity, compute, network readiness)

Applications (functionality, performance, integration behavior)

Identity and access (authentication, authorization, policy enforcement)

Data integrity (consistency, completeness, accessibility)

Operational readiness (monitoring, alerting, support procedures)

If it is not validated—

It is not ready.

And if it is not ready—

It should not move.

These three pillars—Mindset, Structure, and Validation—form the conditions required for controlled execution.

Together, they transform migration from an event—

Into a disciplined system of delivery.

But even with these foundations in place—

execution is not guaranteed.

Because structure alone does not drive outcomes.

People do.

And how they think determines how they execute.

This is where the next layer begins.

Not just in process—

But in mindset.

This foundation defines what controlled migration requires.

But it does not yet define how leaders operate within it.

That is the difference between structure—

And leadership.

The Migration Mindset of Elite Project Managers

Elite migration project managers think beyond task completion.

They manage migrations as business-critical operating events.

That means they constantly ask:

Is the target environment truly ready?

Can the business absorb the change?

Is the rollback viable?

Can support teams sustain the environment after cutover?

Strong migration PMs do not rely on optimism.

They rely on evidence.

They drive dependency discovery early, enforce clear ownership, insist on validation criteria before execution, and ensure that risks are documented in language leadership can understand.

They also understand that timing matters:

A technically correct migration performed at the wrong business moment can still be a failure.

The migration mindset can be summarized in five leadership behaviors:

Think in systems

Plan in waves

Validate with evidence

Communicate with precision

Close with formal sign-off

Elite migration PMs operate with the following instincts:

Systems thinking — see the application, infrastructure, identity, data, and support ecosystem as one operating chain

Risk anticipation — assume hidden issues exist until proven otherwise and use discovery to expose them

Operational discipline — build repeatable gates, checklists, rehearsal steps, and stabilization windows

Decision-focused communication — translate technical realities into schedule, risk, cost, and business impact

Accountability for readiness — do not permit migration waves to proceed without evidence that teams, tools, and environments are prepared

Elite project managers do not ask:

"Can we migrate?"

They ask:

"Are we ready to migrate—proven by evidence across systems, dependencies, and operations?"

This mindset defines how elite project managers think.

But thinking alone does not create control.

Execution does.

And execution requires structure.

Not abstract structure—

but operational structure.

Structure that defines what must be proven, what must be controlled, and what must be sustained before, during, and after migration.

This is where mindset becomes measurable.

Where discipline becomes visible.

Where leadership becomes operational.

The behaviors described above must translate into concrete execution controls.

They must answer a simple question:

What must be true for a migration to be considered successful?

That answer is not theoretical.

It is operational.

It is defined through four pillars:

Validation

Risk Management

Rollback Strategy

Monitoring and Stabilization

These pillars do not replace mindset—

They operationalize it.

The Four Pillars of Successful Migration

Pillar 1 — Validation

Every successful migration relies on four operational pillars: Validation, Risk Management, Rollback Strategy, and Monitoring and Stabilization.

These pillars form the backbone of enterprise migration governance.

Validation ensures that the migrated system functions exactly as expected before the migration is considered successful.

A system coming online is not enough.

Validation proves that the system works.

It confirms that infrastructure, applications, identity, data, integrations, and user workflows all operate within acceptable thresholds—

not in isolation,

but as a complete, functioning system.

Validation must be designed before execution—

not improvised after cutover.

Mature teams define:

Success criteria

Evidence owners

Validation checkpoints

Formal sign-off authorities

in advance.

Because if validation is not planned—

it will not be trusted.

Validation must be performed across multiple layers of the system:

Infrastructure validation: CPU and memory utilization, storage availability, load balancing, routing, firewall paths, and overall system health

Application validation: service startup, configuration correctness, dependency verification, API responses, and transaction success

Security validation: authentication, RBAC, certificates, secrets, encryption, and log visibility

Data validation: database connectivity, integrity checks, replication state, and reconciliation

Business validation: user acceptance testing, critical workflow confirmation, and support readiness

Each layer represents a control point.

And each control point must be proven—

not assumed.

Because in enterprise migration:

Functionality without validation is uncertainty.

And uncertainty is risk.

Validation is not a phase.

It is a discipline.

It begins in planning, continues through execution, and extends into stabilization.

It defines whether the migration is ready—

and ultimately, whether it can be trusted.

Pillar 2 — Risk Management

Migration introduces operational, technical, business, security, and vendor-related risks.

In enterprise environments—especially in cloud migration—these risks are not edge cases.

They are constants.

Risk management does not begin the week before cutover.

It begins in discovery.

Because what is not identified early—

cannot be controlled later.

Mature project managers treat risk as a system—

not a list.

They understand that every dependency, every integration, and every assumption introduces potential failure points.

And in complex environments, those failure points are rarely isolated.

They are interconnected.

This is why risk management is not reactive.

It is predictive.

Mature PMs use structured mechanisms to surface risk early:

RAID logs

Readiness assessments

Dependency mapping

Environment and architecture reviews

Stakeholder workshops and technical deep dives

These are not administrative artifacts.

They are instruments of visibility.

Risk management becomes effective only when each material risk is fully defined and controlled.

That means every risk must have:

A clearly assigned owner

A defined impact statement

A documented mitigation plan

A measurable trigger condition

A viable contingency path

Without these elements, risk is not managed—

it is merely acknowledged.

Common migration risks include:

Hidden dependencies and undocumented integrations

Insufficient compute or storage capacity

Network latency or firewall misconfiguration

Identity federation failures or access gaps

Incomplete replication or data corruption

Vendor readiness gaps and maintenance window conflicts

But beneath these individual risks lies a deeper reality:

Every migration environment contains constraints.

Points where progress slows, breaks, or becomes dependent on a single variable.

If those constraints are not identified and addressed—

they will define the outcome of the migration.

Because in controlled migration:

Risk is not something to avoid.

It is something to expose—

so it can be controlled.

Pillar 3 — Rollback Strategy

Rollback is not failure.

It is control.
Every migration wave requires a predefined rollback strategy.

Rollback planning protects business continuity, service availability, and customer experience when the target state fails validation or introduces instability.

In migration, strategy defines direction.

But tactics define survival.

A strategy may define how a system moves forward.

Rollback defines how it returns—

safely,

deliberately,

and without disruption.

This is where many organizations fall short.

They define the forward path—

but neglect the reverse path.

They plan for success—

but not for controlled failure.

Rollback is not a sign of poor planning.

It is evidence of mature planning.

Because in controlled environments, success is not measured by avoiding failure—

It is measured by the ability to recover from it without impact.

Leadership confidence is not built on optimism.

It is built on recoverability.

When leadership knows that the organization can restore service quickly—

decisions become faster,

risk becomes manageable,

and execution becomes controlled.

Rollback strategies must be defined with the same rigor as forward execution. They are not theoretical options.

They are executable procedures.

This includes clearly defined rollback tactics such as:

DNS failback or traffic redirection

VM or infrastructure snapshot restoration

Database restore, replica failback, or point-in-time recovery

Re-deployment of previous application versions

Load balancer routing reversal or blue/green switchback

Each rollback path must be:

Tested where possible

Time-bound

Operationally understood by execution teams

Aligned with business tolerance for disruption

Because in enterprise migration:

If rollback is not executable—

it does not exist.

Pillar 4 — Monitoring & Stabilization

Go-live is not the finish line.

Stability is.

After migration, systems must be continuously observed during a defined stabilization period—often referred to as hypercare.

Because many issues do not surface in the first moments of go-live.

They emerge under real conditions:

Actual user behavior

Production transaction volume

Batch processing cycles

Time-dependent integrations

This is where migration is truly tested.

Not in controlled validation environments—

But in live operation.

Stabilization ensures that the environment is not only functional—

but sustainable.

During this period, engineering and support teams:

Monitor system behavior

Respond to anomalies

Compare performance against expected baselines

Confirm that the operating model can be maintained under real-world conditions

Key indicators observed during stabilization include:

CPU, memory, disk, and network metrics

Response times, error rates, and transaction failures

Authentication logs and access exceptions

Queue depth, batch processing, and integration health

Availability, uptime, and user-reported issues

Each signal represents a form of feedback.

And together, they answer a single question:

Can this system operate reliably beyond the moment of migration?

Because in enterprise environments:

A system that works at go-live—

but fails under sustained usage—

has not succeeded.

Stabilization is the phase where confidence is earned.

It is where assumptions are either confirmed—

or corrected.

It is where the organization determines whether the new state can be trusted as the new normal.

From Pillars to Execution

These pillars define what must be true for migration to succeed.

But they do not define when or how these conditions are achieved.

That requires structure.

Structure is what transforms principle into execution.

It defines when validation occurs.

It determines how risk is surfaced and controlled.

It ensures rollback is not theoretical—but executable.

It embeds monitoring and stabilization as part of delivery—not as an afterthought.

Without structure, these pillars remain isolated concepts.

With structure, they become a coordinated system of execution.

This is where migration moves from understanding—
to controlled delivery.

From intention—to outcome.

The next chapter introduces that structure in full.

PART III

The Migration Master Framework

How structure becomes the pillar of migration — the dual-phase model, the seven phases, and the 6R strategy.

CHAPTER 5

The Dual-Phase Migration Model (Foundation of the Migration Master Framework)

Why Structure Is the Pillar of Migration

Migration success is not defined by effort.

It is defined by structure.

In complex environments—where infrastructure, applications, data, security, and business operations intersect—

Migration cannot rely on urgency or assumption.

Without structure, even the most capable teams are forced into reactive execution, where dependencies are discovered too late, risks surface under pressure, and decisions are made without full visibility.

Structure is what creates control.

It ensures that:

The environment is understood before movement begins.

Dependencies are identified before they break.

Data is classified before it is exposed.

Risks are evaluated before they materialize.

Without structure, migration becomes unpredictable.

With structure, migration becomes deliberate.

A mature migration program does not begin with execution.

It begins with clarity.

And from that clarity—execution becomes controlled.

The Principles of Migration

Migration is often treated as a technical exercise.

It is not.

It is a structured discipline.

One that requires clarity, control, and deliberate execution.

Over time, I have found that successful migrations—regardless of size, complexity, or environment—consistently follow a set of underlying principles.

These principles are not optional.

They are what separate controlled execution from reactive delivery.

1. Structure Precedes Execution

Migration does not begin with movement.

It begins with understanding.

Without structure, execution becomes reactive.

With structure, execution becomes controlled.

2. What Is Not Understood Will Break

Every undiscovered dependency becomes a future incident.

Every unclassified dataset becomes a risk.

Every overlooked assumption becomes a disruption.

In complex environments, failure rarely comes from what is known.

It comes from what was never surfaced.

Discovery exists to expose that hidden reality—before it surfaces under pressure.

It is not a formality.

It is a control mechanism.

Discovery is not where migration begins. It is where failure is prevented.

3. Strategy Must Reflect Reality

Not every system should be treated the same.

Migration strategy must align with:

Technical constraints
Business priorities
Risk tolerance
Operational readiness

The wrong strategy—no matter how well executed—still leads to failure.

A well-executed wrong strategy is still failure—just delivered with confidence.

4. Migration Happens in Waves, Not Events

Large-scale migration is not a single action.

It is a sequence of controlled executions.

Waves reduce risk, create learning cycles, and improve outcomes over time.

Migration is not an event.
It is a controlled sequence of decisions, executed in waves.

5. Validation Defines Success

Migration is not complete at cutover.

It is complete when:

Systems perform as expected
Users can operate without disruption
Data integrity is preserved
Security and compliance remain intact

Execution without validation is assumption.

Cutover is not success.

Validation is.

6. Rollback Is a Requirement, Not a Backup Plan

Every migration must have a way back.

Without it, execution becomes risk exposure.

7. Stability Is the Final Milestone

Deployment marks movement.

Stability proves control.

Migration is only complete when the system proves it can operate reliably under real conditions.

"Go-live proves deployment.

Stability proves success."

Migration is not about moving systems.

It is about controlling change.

And control is only possible when structure exists from the very beginning.

Everything that follows in this framework is built on that foundation.

These principles define what must be true.

But they do not define how execution is structured.

To operationalize these principles, migration must be approached through a structured model.

Introducing the Dual-Phase Model

To simplify how migration should be approached, I use a foundational operating model:

Discovery → Implementation

This model separates understanding from execution.

It ensures that:

Decisions are based on evidence

Strategy reflects actual conditions

Execution follows structured preparation

This model does not replace the Migration Master Framework.

It simplifies it.

The detailed lifecycle—discovery, strategy selection, wave planning, readiness, validation, stabilization, and rollback—will be explored in the chapters that follow.

But at its core, all of it can be understood through two phases:

First, understand.

Then, execute.

The following model illustrates how this structure governs controlled migration execution.

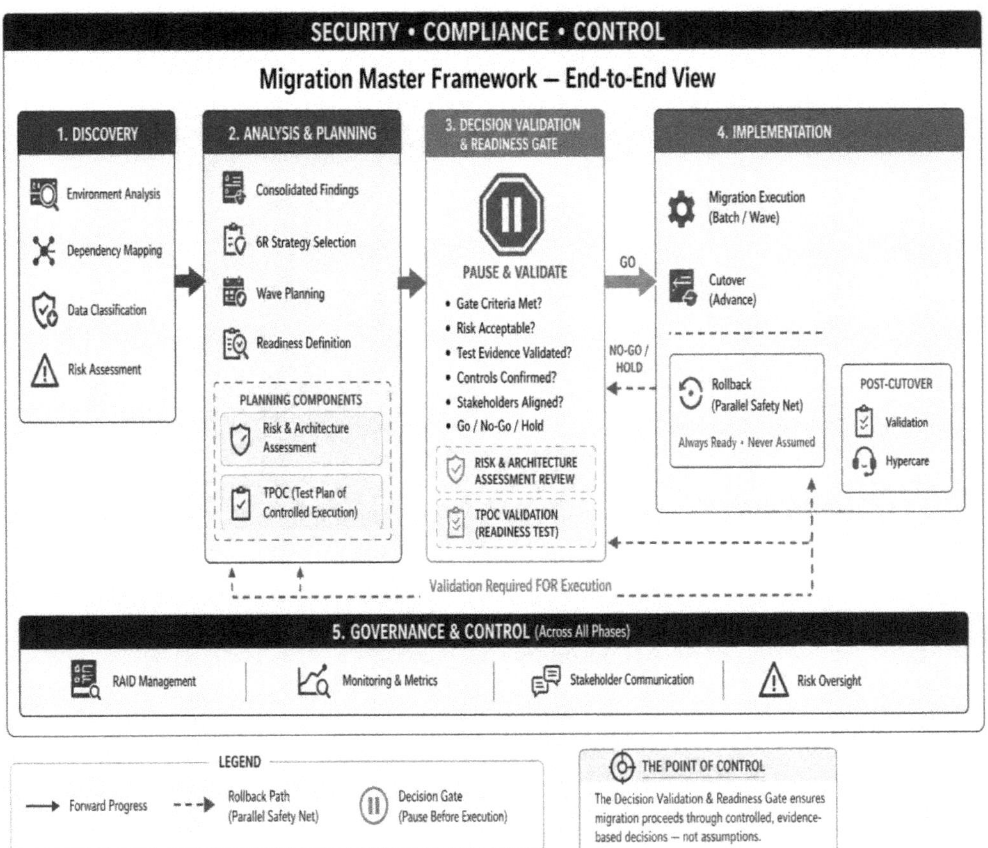

Let's now examine how each phase translates structure into controlled execution–shaping successful migration outcomes.

1. Discovery Phase — Understand Before You Move

The Discovery Phase establishes control before execution begins.

This is where organizations:

Analyze the environment

Identify dependencies

Classify data

Evaluate risk

These activities form the foundation of everything that follows.

Without them, migration becomes assumption-driven.

With them, migration becomes predictable.

"Discovery is where uncertainty is removed—before it becomes failure."

2. Analysis & Planning — Turning Insight Into Direction

Discovery alone does not execute migration.

It must be translated into decisions.

This is where organizations:

Select migration strategies (6R)

Define execution sequencing

Group workloads into waves

Establish readiness and control mechanisms

Planning bridges what is known with what must be done.

This is where migration becomes intentional.

Planning is the moment where knowledge becomes control.

3. Implementation Phase — Execute With Control

Implementation is where migration becomes real.

But in a structured model, execution is not reactive—it is controlled.

This phase includes:

Strategy execution

Wave-based migration

Cutover management

Validation and stabilization

Rollback protection

Each of these elements ensures that migration is not only completed—but completed safely.

Controlled execution is not about speed.

It is about predictability.

However, control is not established during execution alone.

It is determined in the moment between understanding and execution—

where decision must be validated before they are acted upon.

This is where many organizations lose control.

4. Decision Validation & Readiness Gate — The Point of Control

Between planning and execution, there is a moment that determines whether migration will remain controlled—or begin to drift.

This is that moment.

The Decision Validation & Readiness Gate is the point where planning is no longer accepted at face value.

It is examined, challenged, and confirmed before execution begins.

Because once execution starts, decisions become difficult to reverse.

What was theoretical becomes operational.

And what was assumed becomes exposed.

This phase exists to prevent that exposure.

It ensures that migration does not move forward based on confidence alone—but on validated direction.

At this stage, the organization does not ask, "Do we have a plan?"

It asks, "Is this plan ready to be executed?"

What makes this phase critical:

This is where control is either reinforced—or quietly lost.

This phase ensures that:

Migration strategies align with both technical reality and business intent.

Dependencies and sequencing are fully understood and accounted for.

Assumptions are identified and either validated or removed.

Rollback and contingency strategies are clearly defined.

Stakeholders are aligned on scope, risk, and execution approach.

Go/no-go criteria are established with clear accountability.

Planning creates direction.

Validation creates confidence.

Without this checkpoint, organizations move forward with decisions that have not been tested under scrutiny.

Gaps remain hidden.

Risks remain unchallenged.

And execution becomes an act of assumption.

This is where many migrations begin to lose control—not during execution, but just before it.

Because decisions were never truly validated.

The readiness gate is not a meeting.

It is a control mechanism.

It represents a deliberate pause—where execution is held back until clarity is achieved.

It forces the organization to confront one question:

Are we ready to proceed—based on evidence, not assumption?

If the answer is no, execution does not begin.

Because controlled migration is not defined by movement.

It is defined by discipline.

Principle

Execution does not begin when plans are created.

It begins when decisions are validated.

5. Risk & Architecture Assessment — The Last Point of Predictable Control

Before any system is tested in the cloud, its behavior must be understood by design.

This phase answers:

"Should this architecture even be attempted in the cloud?"

It evaluates:

Identity behavior

Network latency sensitivity

Stateful dependencies

Storage coupling

Integration patterns

Hardcoded assumptions

This phase does not test systems.

It predicts them.

Skipping this phase does not save time.

It converts predictable failure into expensive failure.

6. Technical Proof of Concept (TPOC) — Validation, Not Discovery

A Technical Proof of Concept is not where architecture is discovered.

It is where architecture is validated.

It answers:

"Now that we believe this should work—does it actually behave as expected?"

The correct role of TPOC:

Validate identity behavior

Confirm performance under real latency

Test integration reliability

Verify operational readiness

The distinction is critical:

Architecture Assessment → determines if it can work

TPOC → confirms that it does work

The TPOC should not be where we discover whether the architecture works.

It should confirm behavior we already predicted.

7. When TPOC Is Misused — The Collapse of Control

When architecture assessment is skipped, the TPOC becomes a diagnostic lab.

You will hear it first:

"Let's just try it and see what breaks"

"We'll figure it out during the POC"

Then you will see it:

Expanding scope

Constant redesign

Timeline instability

Then you will feel it:

Authentication failures

Performance collapse

Integration breakdown

These are not bugs.

They are architectural incompatibilities.

8. From Validation to Controlled Execution

Once architecture is validated, execution can begin with confidence.

This leads into:

Pilot migrations

Wave-based execution

Controlled cutover

Stabilization (hypercare)

Optimization

Once architecture is validated, execution begins with control—not assumption.

And control is only possible when:

systems are understood before movement

architecture is validated before execution

and decisions are based on evidence—not assumption

Migration is not controlled by how fast systems move.

It is controlled by how well they are understood—

how rigorously they are validated—

and how deliberately they are executed.

Everything that follows in this book builds on that discipline.

Failure Scenario — When Discovery Is Skipped

While the dual-phase model creates structure, it is equally important to understand what happens when that structure is ignored.

In many organizations, migration begins with urgency instead of clarity. Teams move directly into execution without fully understanding the environment, dependencies, or risks involved.

The result is not acceleration—it is instability.

Skipping discovery does not save time.

It shifts risk into execution—where it becomes more expensive, more visible, and more difficult to control.

"Skipping discovery does not accelerate migration.

It delays failure—into execution."

The following illustration demonstrates how skipping discovery transforms a controlled migration into a reactive and often chaotic process.

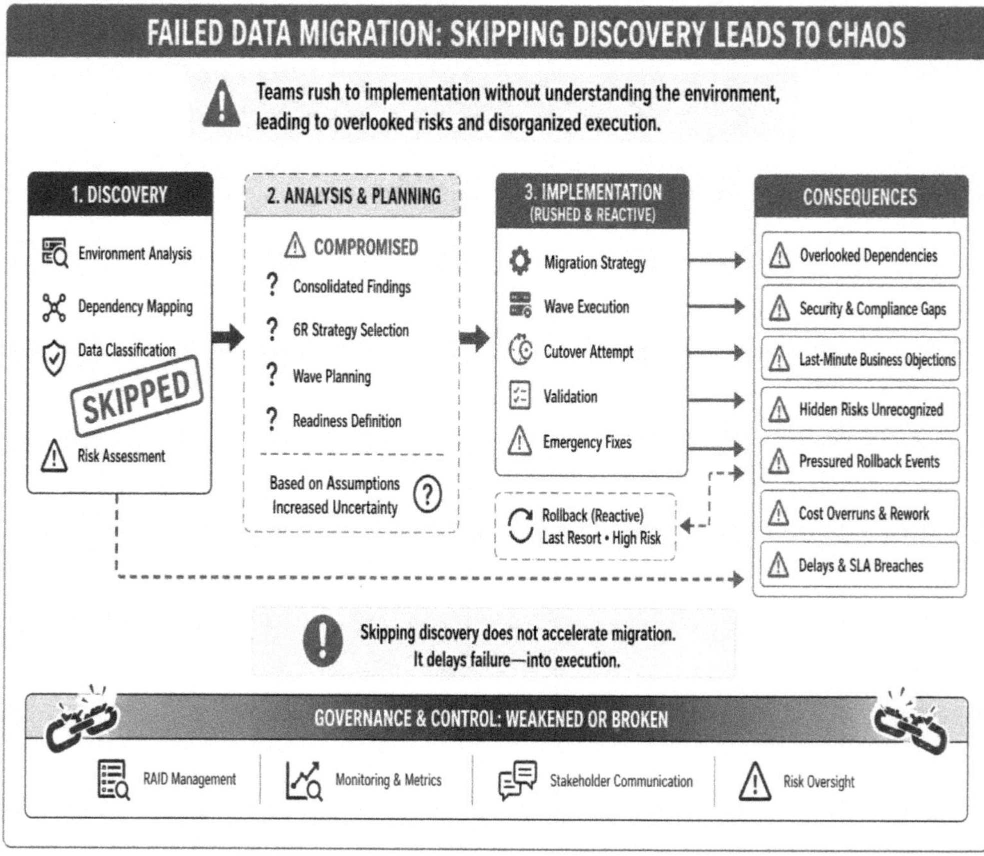

The Dual-Phase Migration Model is not a replacement for the framework.

It is the lens that makes the framework easier to understand.

It ensures that migration is approached with discipline:

Understand first.

Execute second.

Everything else in this book builds on that principle.

while the model defines how migration should be approached, it is equally important to understand where it fits within the broader enterprise landscape.

How the Migration Master Framework Comes Together

It is not designed to replace established enterprise frameworks nor designed to operationalize them.

Behind that simplicity sits a structured system.

The Migration Master Framework is not a collection of disconnected practices. It is a coordinated sequence of decisions and actions that build on one another.

Each component exists for a reason.

Each phase informs the next.

Each chapter that follows expands one part of this system:

The Seven Phases of Migration Execution define the full lifecycle

The 6R Framework determines how each workload should be migrated

Migration Wave Planning defines how execution is structured and controlled

Together, they form a complete delivery model—one that transforms migration from a series of tasks into a structured, repeatable system.

“Frameworks do not execute migrations.

Structured decisions do.”

At the enterprise level, organizations rely on multiple frameworks to govern technology, manage risk, secure systems, and deliver services.

These frameworks each serve a distinct purpose—

But they are rarely unified in execution.

This is where the Migration Master Framework becomes critical.

It acts as the execution bridge between governance, security, and delivery.

At a high level:

COBIT defines governance and control expectations.

NIST defines security and risk management practices.

ITIL defines service management and operational processes.

But none of these frameworks, on their own, provide a complete operating model for executing a large-scale enterprise migration from end to end.

The Migration Master Framework fills that gap.

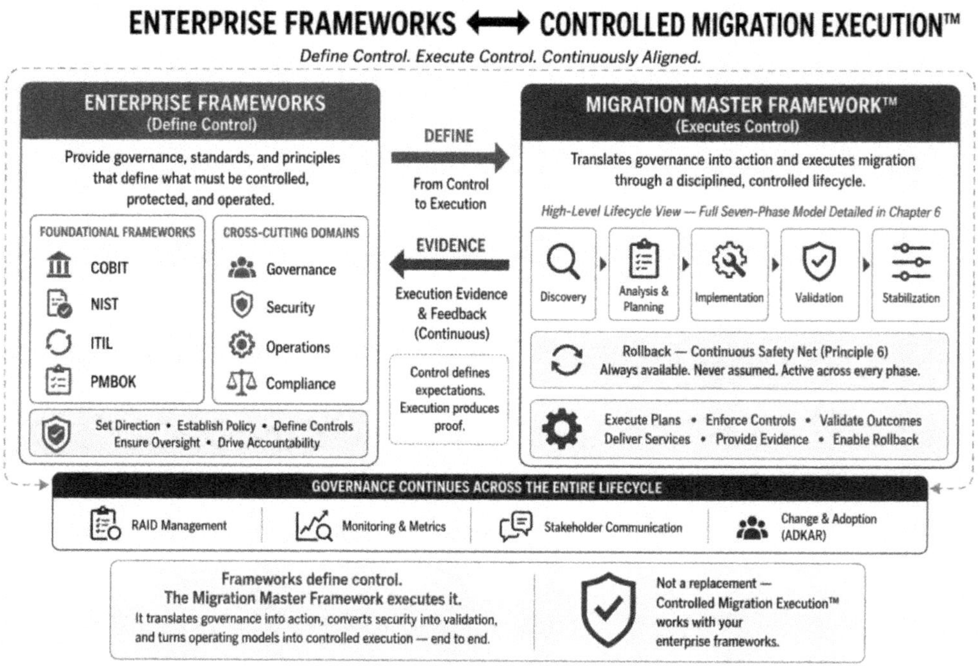

It translates governance into action.

It converts security requirements into validation.

It transforms operational models into controlled execution.

Within the Migration Master Framework:

Discovery Phase aligns with governance and risk identification.

Planning Phase aligns with control definition and architecture alignment.

Implementation Phase aligns with service execution and operational delivery.

Across the lifecycle:

Governance frameworks ensure what must be controlled.

Security frameworks ensure what must be protected.

Service frameworks ensure how systems must operate.

The Migration Master Framework ensures how everything is executed together.

But understanding where the framework fits is only the beginning.

To fully apply it, we must now examine how it comes together as a structured system.

CHAPTER 6

The Seven Phases of Migration Execution

Before we move forward, there is something that must be made clear.

Understanding migration phases is not what makes a program successful.

Execution does.

And execution is not clean.

It is where:

Assumptions break.

Dependencies surface.

Decisions must be made under pressure.

This chapter is where the Migration Master Framework moves beyond structure—and into reality.

Here, we will not only define each phase, but examine:

How each phase is actually executed.

What it looks like in real programs.

Where things fail in practice.

How a strong project manager maintains control when they do.

Because in real-world migration—

Control is not theoretical.

It is earned.

From Structured Theory to Controlled Execution in the Real World

The Migration Master Framework follows seven phases that together create a repeatable operational lifecycle.

But understanding the phases is not enough.

Execution is where migrations succeed—or collapse.

This chapter introduces not only what each phase is—but how it is executed in real environments, and what actually happens when things go wrong.

1. Discovery and Dependency Mapping

You cannot migrate what you do not understand.

How It Is Executed

This phase is not a checklist—it is an investigation.

A strong PM drives structured discovery across:

Application inventory (CMDB, SME interviews, system scans)

Infrastructure mapping (servers, VMs, storage, network paths)

Data flows (ingress/egress, batch jobs, APIs)

Identity & authentication dependencies (AD, Entra ID, service accounts)

Scheduled jobs (cron, Windows Task Scheduler, pipelines)

Hidden dependencies (hardcoded IPs, legacy integrations)

Execution Tactics:

Conduct multi-layer workshops (App + Infra + Security together)

Validate findings against real traffic/logs, not assumptions

Build a dependency map—not just a list

Real-World Simulation Scenario

A financial system is marked as "standalone."

During cutover testing, it fails.

Why?

Because:

It depended on a legacy SMTP relay for notifications.

That relay was not documented.

The relay was decommissioned during migration.

Result:

The system "worked"—but business workflows failed.

Discovery failures are not visible during planning.

They are revealed during execution.

2. Migration Strategy Selection (6R Framework)

Not all systems should be migrated the same way.

How It Is Executed

Each workload is evaluated across:

Business criticality

Technical complexity

Compliance/security requirements

Time constraints

Cost considerations

Then mapped to one of the 6Rs:

Rehost

Replatform

Refactor

Repurchase

Retain

Retire

Execution Tactics:

Do not let engineering default to "lift-and-shift everything"

Align strategy with future-state architecture—not current state

Document justification for each decision

Real-World Simulation Scenario

A legacy HR system is rehosted (lift-and-shift) to cloud.

Post-migration:

Performance degrades

Licensing model becomes more expensive

Security controls are misaligned

Why?

Because it should have been Repurchased (SaaS) instead of migrated.

A wrong strategy executed perfectly still leads to failure.

3. Migration Wave Planning

Execution is not one big move—it is controlled sequencing.

How It Is Executed

Systems are grouped into waves based on:

Dependency chains

Business criticality

Risk level

Testing capacity

Operational readiness

Execution Tactics:

Start with low-risk, low-dependency systems

Avoid mixing high-risk + high-dependency systems in the same wave

Define clear entry/exit criteria for each wave

Real-World Simulation Scenario

A program groups systems by department instead of dependencies.

During Wave 2:

System A migrates successfully

System B (same department) fails because it depends on System C (in Wave 4)

Result:

Execution becomes blocked. Timeline slips.

Control Principle

Poor wave planning creates artificial risk that did not previously exist.

4. Infrastructure Readiness

The target environment must be ready before anything moves.

How It Is Executed.

This phase ensures the landing zone is operational, not theoretical.

Includes:

Compute provisioning

Storage configuration

Network routing, DNS, firewalls

Identity and access (IAM, RBAC, MFA)

Logging and monitoring (Splunk, Datadog, CloudWatch, Azure Monitor, etc.)

Backup and recovery setup

Certificates and encryption

Execution Tactics:

Use a production readiness checklist

Validate connectivity end-to-end—not in isolation

Confirm monitoring visibility before migration begins

Real-World Simulation Scenario

Infrastructure is "ready" on paper.

After migration:

Applications are running

But no logs are being captured

Monitoring alerts are not configured

Result:

Failures occur silently.

Control Principle

Infrastructure readiness is not deployment—it is verification.

5. Validation and Testing

This is where assumptions are challenged.

How It Is Executed

Testing must cover:

Infrastructure validation (compute, network, storage)

Application functionality

Data integrity

Security controls

End-to-end business workflows

Execution Tactics:

Define test scenarios tied to business outcomes

Include real user workflows—not just technical tests

Validate authentication, authorization, and data access paths

Real-World Simulation Scenario

Application passes all technical tests.

But in production:

Users cannot log in

Why?

Authentication flow through the identity provider (such as Okta, Entra ID, or both in a federated configuration) was not validated end-to-end.

Control Principle

Passing tests does not mean the system works.

It means the tests were incomplete.

6. Monitoring and Stabilization (Hypercare)

Go-live is not the end—it is the beginning of validation under real conditions.

How It Is Executed

This phase ensures:

System performance meets expectations

Errors are identified and resolved quickly

Users can operate without disruption

Execution Tactics:

Establish hypercare window (typically 2–4 weeks for standard workloads; 4–12 weeks or longer for mission-critical platforms aligned to a business cycle—such as quarter-end close, fiscal year-end, or peak seasonal demand).

Daily review of:

Incidents

Performance metrics

User feedback

Dedicated war room / command center – Operational Handover (NOC Transition)

Stabilization is not complete until operational ownership is successfully transferred.

During hypercare, responsibility begins to shift from the migration team to the operations team (NOC).

Depending on the organization, this may be a Network Operations Center (NOC), application support team, SRE/DevOps function, or a managed service provider.

This includes:

Runbook validation

Monitoring and alert ownership

Incident response readiness

Knowledge transfer and shadowing

The transition is gradual—not immediate.

A successful migration is not defined by system availability alone—but by the ability of operations to sustain it independently.

A system is not truly migrated until it can operate independently under its designated operations team.

Real-World Simulation Scenario

Migration is declared "successful" immediately after go-live.

Within 48 hours:

Ticket volume spikes

Performance degrades under real load

Users adopt workarounds

Result:

Confidence in the migration drops.

Stability is not declared—it is observed over time.

7. Rollback and Risk Control

Control is defined by your ability to reverse failure.

How It Is Executed

Rollback is not a document—it is an active capability.

Includes:

Backout procedures

Data restoration plans

Traffic redirection strategy

Decision thresholds for rollback

Execution Tactics:

Define clear rollback triggers

Keep source environment operational until validation is complete

Rehearse rollback scenarios when possible

Real-World Simulation Scenario

A migration fails during peak hours.

Rollback plan exists—but:

Data has already been overwritten

DNS propagation delays recovery

Teams are unsure who makes the rollback decision

Result:

Extended outage.

If rollback is not executable under pressure, it does not exist.

Execution Is Where Control Is Proven

These seven phases are not independent steps.

They are a control system.

Each phase:

Reduces uncertainty

Validates assumptions

Prepares the next stage

When executed correctly, migration becomes:

Predictable

Controlled

Repeatable

When executed poorly, migration becomes:

Reactive

Fragile

High-risk

Migration is not about moving systems.

It is about controlling change—

phase by phase, decision by decision, under real-world pressure.

From Phases to Execution — Where It All Comes Together

Understanding each phase individually is necessary.

But migration does not happen in isolation.

It happens across time—under pressure—where decisions in one phase directly impact the next.

To fully understand how control is maintained, we now step into a real-world execution scenario.

End-to-End Migration Simulation

From Day 0 to Stabilization — How Controlled Execution Actually Happens

Frameworks define structure.

Execution reveals truth.

This simulation walks through a realistic enterprise migration scenario, showing how the seven phases operate in sequence, under pressure, and in real time.

Scenario Overview

A federal agency is migrating a critical financial application to a secure cloud environment.

Users: 2,500+

Dependencies: Identity provider, database cluster, batch jobs, external APIs

Constraints:

Must avoid business disruption

Must meet security compliance requirements

Limited migration window (weekend cutover)

Day 0 — Discovery Begins (Weeks Before Migration)

(Phase 1: Discovery and Dependency Mapping)

The program starts with what appears to be a "well-documented system."

It is not.

What Happens in Reality

CMDB shows:

3 application servers

1 database

Workshops reveal:

2 undocumented batch jobs

External API dependency

Legacy authentication fallback still active

Network logs uncover:

Hidden outbound traffic to a deprecated endpoint

What a Strong PM Does—

Forces cross-functional validation sessions

Requires evidence-based confirmation (logs, not opinions)

Builds a true dependency map

What Would Have Gone Wrong

Without this step:

Batch jobs fail silently

External integrations break post-cutover

Reality Check

Discovery is where unknown risk becomes visible.

Or remains hidden until failure.

Day 15 — Strategy Is Locked

(Phase 2: Migration Strategy Selection)

The team debates:

Rehost (fast, low effort)

Refactor (better long-term)

Repurchase (SaaS alternative)

Decision

Application tier → Rehost

Database → Replatform (managed service)

Legacy reporting module → Retire

What a Strong PM Does—

Forces alignment between:

Engineering

Security

Business owners

Documents why each decision was made

What Would Have Gone Wrong

If everything was lift-and-shift:

Database performance issues

Increased operational cost

Security misalignment

Reality Check

Strategy decisions are long-term commitments disguised as short-term choices.

Day 30 — Wave Planning Finalized

(Phase 3: Migration Wave Planning)

The system is scheduled for Wave 3.

Why not Wave 1?

Because:

It has moderate dependencies

Requires identity validation readiness

Needs lower-risk waves to validate the process first

What a Strong PM Does—

protects sequencing discipline.

Pushes back on business pressure to "move critical apps first"

Defines:

Entry criteria

Exit criteria

Rollback boundaries

What Would Have Gone Wrong

If migrated too early:

Unvalidated infrastructure

Immature process

Higher failure probability

Reality Check

Early success builds control.

Early failure destroys confidence.

Day 45 — Infrastructure Ready (On Paper vs Reality)

The environment is provisioned.
On paper, every domain shows green.
In practice, "provisioned" and "ready" are not the same thing.

What Happens in Reality

During validation:

Firewall rule missing → blocks API traffic

Monitoring dashboards exist—but no alert thresholds configured
Backup configured—but not tested

What a Strong PM Does—

Demands functional validation, not checklist completion.

Runs:

Connectivity tests

Failover simulations

Monitoring verification

What Would Have Gone Wrong

Silent failures

No alerting during incidents

False sense of readiness

Reality Check

"Ready" is the most dangerous word in migration if not verified.

This is the control gate the PM enforces before infrastructure is allowed to advance—each domain validated, each decision path defined.

The diagram below codifies that gate — five validation domains feeding a single Go / Conditional Go / No-Go decision point that governs whether infrastructure is cleared to advance into Phase 5.

This tells the reader what they're about to look at and why it's there.

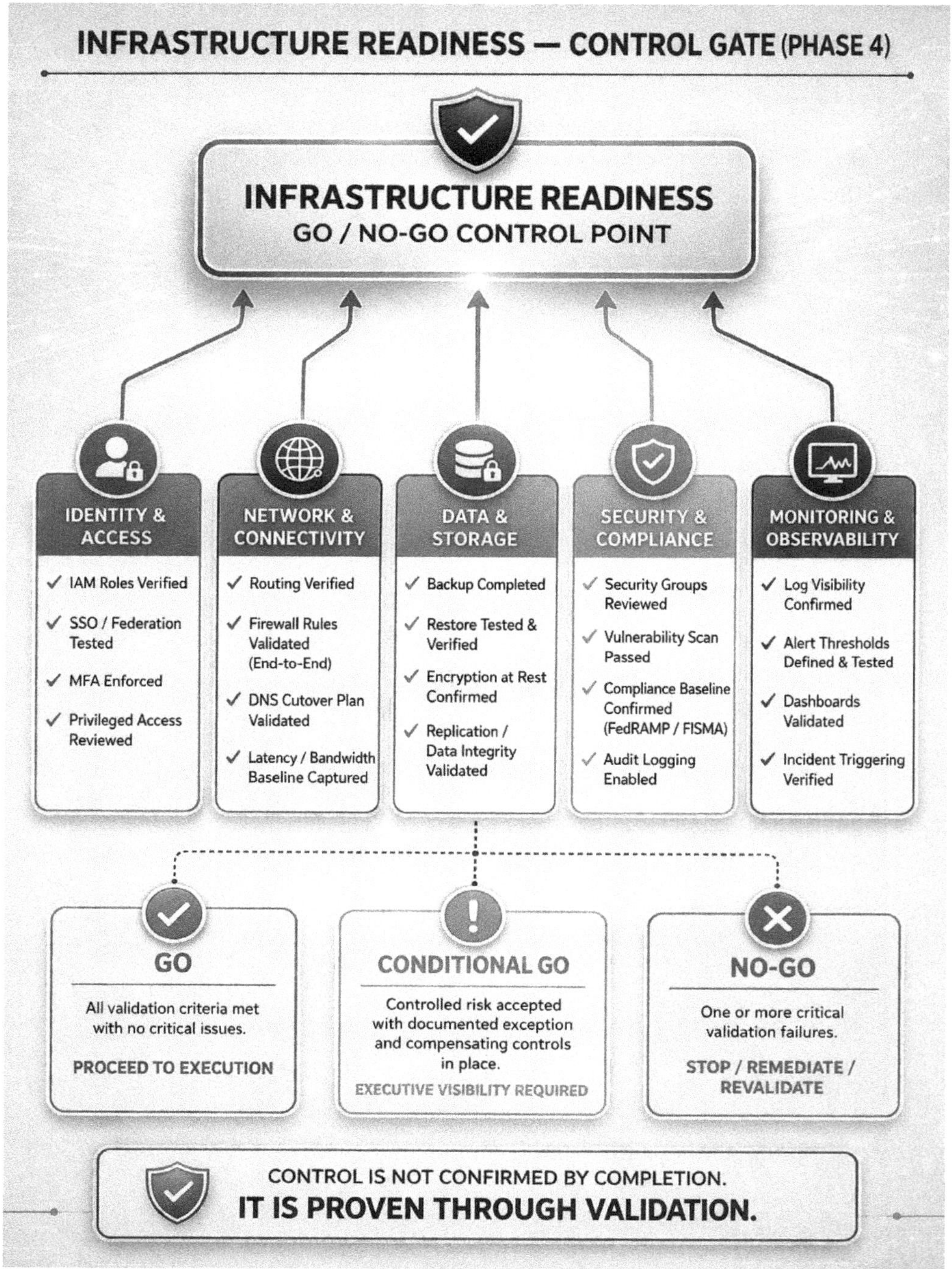

With the readiness gate cleared, the migration moves from preparation into proof. Phase 5 is where assumptions meet evidence — and where "ready" is either confirmed or exposed.

Reality Check

"Ready" is the most dangerous word in migration if not verified.

Day 55 — Testing Reveals the Truth

(Phase 5: Validation and Testing)

Testing begins.

Everything looks good—initially.

What Happens in Reality:

Functional tests pass

Infrastructure tests pass

But:

End-to-end test fails

Users cannot authenticate through SSO

Root Cause:

Token exchange misconfiguration between identity provider and application

What a Strong PM Does—

ensures business workflow testing—

not just technical validation.

Forces:

Identity validation

Data flow validation

Real user simulation

What Would Have Gone Wrong

Go-live failure

User lockout

Emergency rollback

Reality Check

Testing does not confirm success.

It exposes what was missed.

Day 60 — Cutover Weekend

(Execution + Rollback Readiness)

This is the moment where planning meets reality.

Cutover Timeline

Friday Night

Final data sync initiated

Change freeze activated

Teams enter war room

Saturday

Application migrated

Database switched to new environment

DNS updated

What Happens in Reality

Minor latency issues observed

One batch job fails due to path mismatch

What a Strong PM Does

Tracks:

Real-time metrics

Incident logs

Keeps rollback on standby—not abandoned

Critical Decision Point

System is degraded—but functional.

Do we:

Roll forward and fix?

Or rollback?

Decision

Roll forward with controlled fixes.

Reality Check

Cutover is not execution.

It is decision-making under pressure.

Day 61–75 — Hypercare and Stabilization

(Phase 6: Monitoring and Stabilization)

Now the real test begins.

What Happens in Reality

Ticket volume spikes in first 48 hours

Performance stabilizes after tuning

Users adapt to new system behavior

Hypercare Actions

Daily war room calls

Incident triage and prioritization

Performance monitoring:

CPU

Latency

Error rates

What a Strong PM Does—

maintains visibility.

Tracks:

Trends, not just incidents

Ensures:

No silent failures

No user abandonment

What Would Have Gone Wrong

Without hypercare:

Issues ignored

User confidence drops

Shadow IT/workarounds emerge

Reality Check

Stability is proven in production—not in testing.

Day 75 — Rollback Window Closes

(Phase 7: Rollback and Risk Control)

System is stable.

Metrics confirm:

Performance within SLA

No critical incidents

Business operations normal

Final Actions

Formal business sign-off

Rollback plan retired

Wave officially closed

What a Strong PM Ensures

Closure is:

Measured

Verified

Approved

A migration is not complete when systems move.

It is complete when risk is removed.

What This Simulation Proves

This is what real migration looks like:

Imperfect discovery

Debated strategy

Adjusted execution

Continuous validation

Controlled decision-making

The Truth Most Frameworks Do Not Show

Things will go wrong.

Assumptions will break.

Pressure will rise.

Murphy's Law—Anything that can go wrong will go wrong.

What Separates Success from Failure

Not tools.

Not technology.

Control.

What This Simulation Reveals

The seven phases are not steps.

They are a control system—operating continuously, not sequentially.

This is where most organizations fail.

They understand the phases.

But they fail to control the flow between them.

CHAPTER 7

Migration Strategy and the 6R Framework

Choosing the Right Path Before Execution Begins

Before any system is moved, a decision must be made.

Not how to migrate it.

Whether it should be migrated at all. And if so—how.

This is where many migration programs lose control.

Because strategy is often treated as a formality—rather than a decision that defines everything that follows.

In reality:

The wrong strategy creates unnecessary risk

The wrong strategy increases cost

The wrong strategy forces rework during execution

And most importantly—

The wrong strategy cannot be fixed by execution.

This chapter focuses on how to make that decision correctly.

Not just what the 6R strategies are—but:

When to use each strategy

How to evaluate workloads properly

What real-world conditions drive the decision

Where organizations commonly get it wrong

Because migration success is not determined during execution.

It is determined at the moment the strategy is chosen.

Real-World Scenario — Where Strategy Goes Wrong

A large enterprise begins a migration program with a clear mandate:

"Move everything to the cloud."

No further clarification is provided.

Engineering defaults to lift-and-shift (Rehost).

Months later:

Costs increase instead of decrease

Performance issues emerge

Legacy inefficiencies remain unchanged

Why?

Because the decision was never:

"What is the right strategy per workload?"

It was:

"How fast can we move everything?"

The result is not transformation.

It is relocation.

The 6R Framework — Strategic Decision Model

Organizations commonly use the 6R framework when deciding how to move workloads.

The strength of the 6R model is that it forces organizations to recognize that every workload requires a different decision.

A note on terminology and origin: the model traces back to Gartner analyst Richard Watson, who introduced the original 5R framework in 2011 (Rehost, Refactor, Revise, Rebuild, Replace).

AWS's Stephen Orban built on this work in 2016,

publishing the now-widely-cited *6 Strategies for Migrating Applications to the Cloud*,

which expanded the model to include Retain.

AWS later introduced a seventh strategy, *Relocate*, addressing hypervisor-level moves—

most commonly VMware Cloud on AWS scenarios—

where a virtualization platform is moved without

re-architecting workloads.

The principles in this chapter apply across the 5R, 6R, and 7R formulations.

The model used here remains the 6R,

as it is the most widely recognized standard across enterprise migration practice.

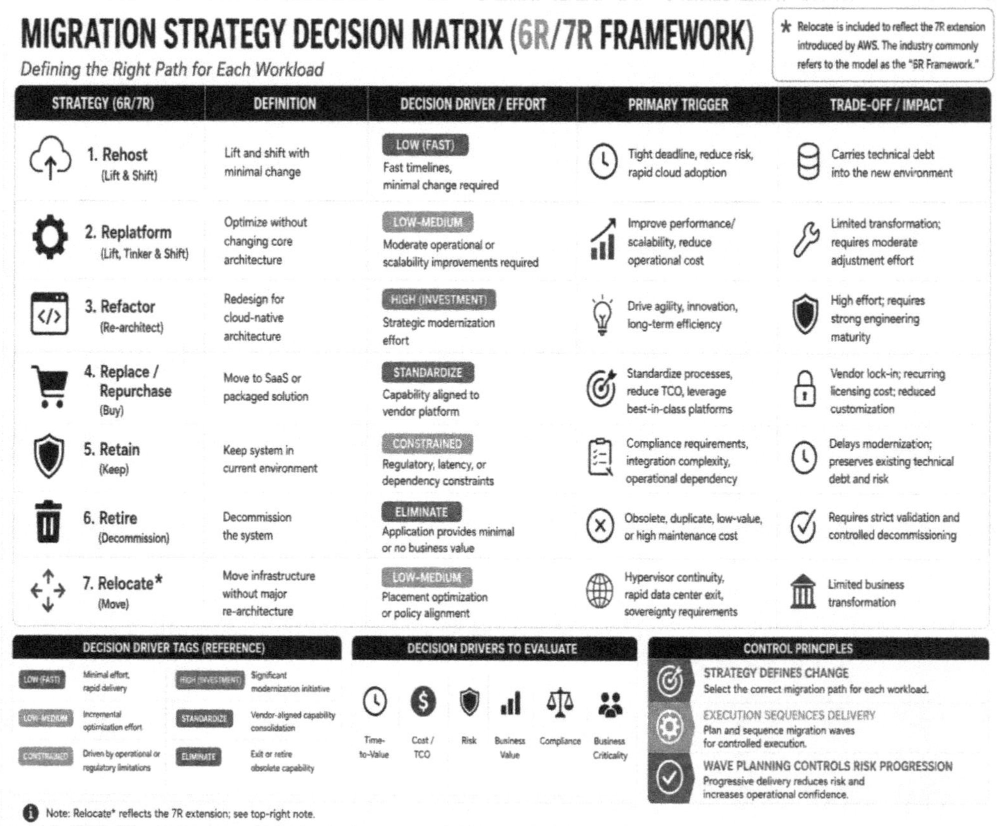

Migration Strategy Decision Matrix (6R Framework) — defining the right path for each workload.

Migration Strategy vs Execution Approach

Clarifying How Systems Move After Strategy Is Defined

Before going further, an important distinction must be made.

The 6R framework defines what will be done to a system.

It does not define how or when the system is moved.

That is determined by the execution approach.

This distinction is often misunderstood—

and when it is, migration programs lose control.

Understanding the Difference

At its core, migration control is defined by the relationship between strategy and execution.

Strategy answers what changes. Execution answers how—

and when—that change is introduced.

They are related, but they are not the same.

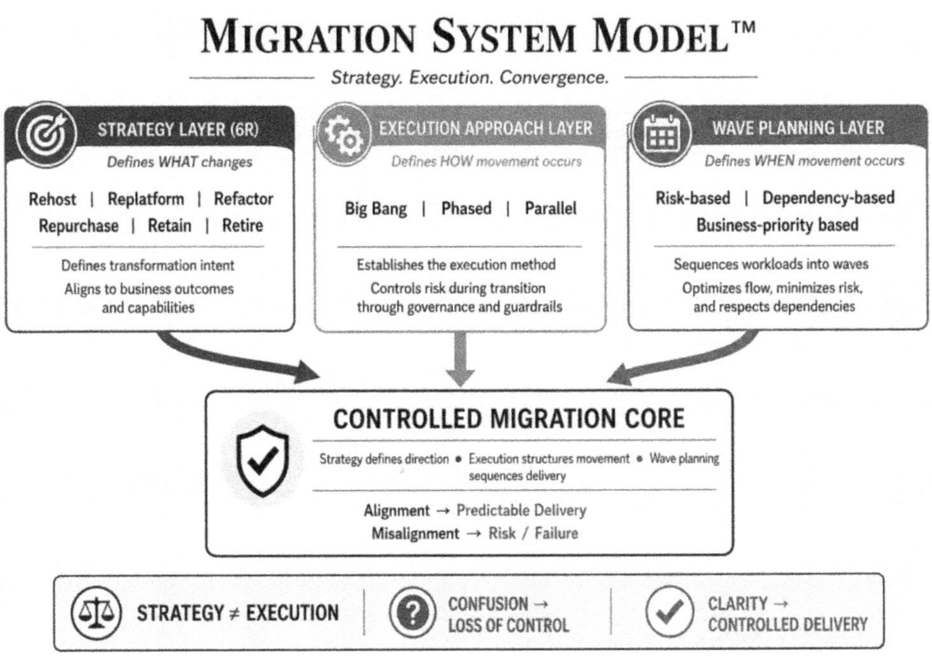

Migration System Model™ — defining direction (Strategy Layer / 6R) versus governing movement (Execution Approach Layer), converging on a Controlled Migration Core.

Simple Principle — The 6R framework defines the transformation strategy.

The execution approach defines how that strategy is carried out.

Wave planning defines when each workload moves and in what dependency-aware sequence. Together, they converge on controlled migration.

Why This Distinction Matters

If this separation is not clearly understood:

Rehost may be confused with Big Bang

Refactor may be assumed to require phased execution

Strategy and execution become incorrectly linked

Which leads to flawed planning.

Migration does not fail only because of poor strategy.

It also fails when the execution approach does not align with risk, dependencies, and operational realities.

How Strategy and Execution Work Together

Strategy and execution are not separate decisions made in sequence.

They operate as a single system.

The pattern is consistent: strategy sets the load—execution carries it.

Alignment is not a preference. It is a control mechanism.

In Practice

A Rehost strategy may tolerate a Big Bang approach—the system is not being fundamentally altered.

A Refactor strategy typically requires phased execution—the system is being redesigned and must be validated incrementally.

A Repurchase (SaaS) strategy often requires parallel execution—to ensure data integrity, user adoption, and process alignment.

The Relationship

Strategy drives complexity.

Execution approach absorbs that complexity.

When the two are aligned:

Risk is controlled

Execution is predictable

Outcomes are stable

When they are not:

Failures surface during cutover

Rollbacks become necessary

Confidence is lost

A simple strategy can tolerate aggressive execution.

A complex strategy requires controlled execution.

Migration Strategies — How to Apply Each Decision

Rehost (Lift-and-Shift)

Rehost is the fastest path when the organization needs speed, such as a data center exit or urgent infrastructure refresh.

The application is moved largely as-is, often from on-premises virtual machines to cloud-based virtual machines.

Rehost should not be confused with low risk.

Moving technical debt without redesign can preserve:

Hidden weaknesses

Manual operational patterns

Inefficient cost structures

When to Use:

Time-constrained migrations

Data center exits

Temporary stabilization strategies

Caution:

Data center exits with hard lease deadlines are also the most common scenario where Rehost gets locked in by deadline pressure—even when Replatform or

Refactor would be the right long-term answer. The decision must be made deliberately, not by default.

Where It Fails:

When used as a long-term solution

When cost optimization is expected immediately

When legacy architecture is fundamentally broken

Replatform

Replatform introduces limited optimization without redesigning the application.

Examples include:

Moving a self-managed database to a managed service

Adjusting storage and scaling configurations

Improving operational supportability

This approach balances speed with moderate improvement.

The project manager must coordinate platform-specific testing, as small changes in platform behavior can create compatibility issues.

When to Use:

Need for modest improvement without full redesign

Operational efficiency gains are desired

Time allows for controlled optimization

Where It Fails:

When deeper architectural problems exist

When mistaken for full modernization

Refactor (Re-Architect)

Refactor involves redesigning the application to take advantage of cloud-native capabilities.

This may include:

Microservices architecture

Containerization

Serverless compute

Managed messaging and integration patterns

This is the most transformative—and most demanding—strategy.

When to Use:

Strategic, business-critical applications

Long-term modernization initiatives

When engineering maturity is strong

Where It Fails:

When attempted without proper skills or planning

When timelines do not support transformation

When business value does not justify effort

Repurchase (SaaS Adoption)

Repurchase — sometimes referred to interchangeably as Replace — means adopting a SaaS or packaged solution instead of continuing with a custom or legacy system.

In many enterprises, this is the most practical option for non-differentiating capabilities.

However, the complexity shifts from technology to transformation.

The project manager must manage:

Business process redesign

Data migration

Identity integration

Reporting changes

End-user adoption

When to Use:

Commodity capabilities (HR, CRM, finance, etc.)

High maintenance legacy systems

Availability of mature SaaS solutions

Where It Fails:

When organizational change is underestimated

When data and integration complexity is ignored

Retain

Retain is a deliberate decision to keep a workload in its current environment.

This is often necessary due to:

Regulatory requirements

Latency constraints

Hardware dependencies

Unresolved technical dependencies

Retain is not avoidance—it is a strategic delay.

However, it must be controlled.

When to Use:

Constraints prevent safe migration

Dependencies are unresolved

Migration introduces more risk than value

Where It Fails:

When undocumented

When no future plan exists

When it becomes silent technical debt

Retire

Retire means the application is no longer needed and should be decommissioned.

This is one of the most overlooked—and most valuable—strategies.

Mature migration programs reduce cost significantly by eliminating unnecessary systems.

Retirement requires discipline.

This includes:

Business owner confirmation

Data retention and archival decisions

Interface shutdown sequencing

Support closure

When to Use:

Application provides little or no value

Redundant or replaced functionality exists

Maintenance cost exceeds benefit

Where It Fails:

When business validation is incomplete

When dependencies are not fully identified

Migration strategy is not about choosing how to move a system.

It is about deciding what that system should become.

Execution Approaches — How Systems Are Moved

Migration execution typically follows one of three approaches:

Big Bang

Phased (Wave-Based) Migration

Parallel (Dual-Run) Migration

Each approach

manages risk

differently.

Big Bang Migration

A Big Bang migration

moves a system—

or multiple systems—

at once,

in a single

cutover event.

There is little

to no coexistence

between old

and new environments.

When It Applies:

Tightly coupled systems

Limited ability to run environments in parallel

Business requires immediate transition

Trade-Off:

High risk if failure occurs

Limited rollback flexibility

High pressure during cutover

Because everything

changes

at once.

Real-World Simulation — Big Bang Under Pressure

During a Streamwide voicemail

platform upgrade,

the organization made the decision

to execute

a full Big Bang migration.

The objective

was clear:

Move the entire Streamwide platform

from a physical server environment

to a cloud-based infrastructure—

within a single weekend

cutover window.

There would be:

No phased transition.

No parallel environment.

No gradual fallback.

Everything would move at once.

Execution Begins:

The migration window began late Friday night.

All systems were brought down in sequence.

Data was migrated.

Infrastructure was provisioned.

Services were brought online

in the cloud environment.

At first, everything appeared stable.

Then the issue surfaced.

Failure Emerges

Both authentication flows
and inter-service registration
between components
began to fail—
intermittently.

Voicemail services
were not consistently
connecting—

Call routing dependencies
became unstable—

What initially appeared to be a minor
configuration issue—
quickly revealed itself as a deeper problem:
an incompatibility in service communication
between the migrated platform components.

Specific protocol-level detail is omitted here for confidentiality—the lesson, however, applies regardless of the underlying technology.

At that moment,

the risk became clear.

This was not a contained failure.

This was a platform-wide impact.

The Decision Point

With users expected back online

within hours,

the team had two options:

Continue troubleshooting under pressure

Execute the rollback plan

Because a rollback strategy

had been prepared

and validated,

the decision was made

quickly.

The system was rolled back to the original environment.

Service was restored.

Business impact was avoided.

What Made the Difference

The failure itself was not the defining moment.

The response was:

The rollback plan existed—and was executable

The team was aligned and decisive

The issue was contained before business hours

The presence of international vendors added another layer of complexity.

Teams across time zones—

from Europe to the United States—

worked in parallel,

coordinating in real time

to diagnose and stabilize the environment.

There was no pause.

Only execution.

The issue was later identified, corrected, and revalidated.

A subsequent migration attempt succeeded.

This time—with deeper insight into system dependencies and behavior under real conditions.

As one of my colleagues said once:

"With IT, we can place the world inside a bottle."

That statement reflected the reality of the moment.

Despite the pressure, there was confidence.

Because the team was prepared.

Because the system was understood.

And because every issue that surfaced was met with immediate action.

Lesson from the Scenario

Big Bang migration is not inherently flawed.

But it is unforgiving.

It demands:

Complete readiness

Proven rollback capability

Real-time coordination

Decisive leadership

Because when everything moves at once—

There is no margin for uncertainty.

Phased / Wave-Based Migration

Phased migration moves systems gradually—

in controlled groups

(waves).

Each wave is validated

before the next begins.

This is the most common—

and most controlled—

approach in enterprise environments.

When It Applies:

Complex environments with dependencies

Need for risk reduction and validation

Large-scale transformation programs

Trade-Off:

Longer timelines

Requires strong coordination across waves

Parallel (Dual-Run) Migration:

Parallel migration runs both old and new
environments
simultaneously
for a defined period.

This allows comparison,
validation,
and fallback
before full cutover.

When It Applies:

High-risk or mission-critical systems

Regulatory or audit-sensitive environments

Situations requiring zero or near-zero disruption

Trade-Off:

Increased cost
(running two environments)

Data synchronization complexity

Operational overhead

Critical Clarification:

Execution approaches—

are independent of the 6R strategies.

For example:

Rehost can be executed as Big Bang or Phased

Refactor is often phased—but not always

Repurchase (SaaS) may require parallel validation

Strategy defines what changes.

Execution approach defines how risk is managed.

Connecting Back to the Framework:

Wave-based migration aligns directly with:

Migration Wave Planning (Chapter 9)

Controlled execution and validation

Progressive risk reduction

This is why most mature programs avoid Big Bang—
unless absolutely necessary.

If phased migration is the execution approach—
wave planning is the structure
that makes it controllable.

Migration Wave Planning

Structuring Phased Execution with Precision

Once the migration strategy has been selected
and the execution approach has been defined—
the next question
becomes operational:

How should the movement actually be sequenced?

This is where migration wave planning becomes critical.

Wave planning is not an administrative exercise.

It is one of the most surgical decisions in migration execution.

A wave determines not only when a system moves—
but what risk moves with it,
what dependencies must move around it,
and how much disruption
the organization is prepared to absorb
at a given point in time.

In mature migration programs,
wave planning is shaped by more than

technical readiness alone.

It must reflect:

The structure of the environment

Dependency relationships across systems

Business criticality

Organizational risk appetite

Testing capacity

Support readiness

Vendor and operational constraints

A technically simple application

may still belong in a later wave—

if it depends on a high-risk identity service,

a shared database platform,

or a business process

that cannot tolerate early disruption.

This is why wave planning must be strategic.

It is not enough to know what will be migrated.

It is not enough to know how it will be migrated.

A successful program

must also determine
in what order
migration should occur—
and under what conditions
each wave
is allowed to proceed.

When designed properly,
migration waves reduce disruption,
create learning cycles,
validate the migration model incrementally,
and protect the organization from introducing unnecessary risk too early.

When designed poorly—
they create artificial failure.

Because in phased migration, sequencing is not logistics.

It is control.

Operationalizing Wave Planning

Large organizations do not migrate everything at once.

They organize workloads into migration waves.

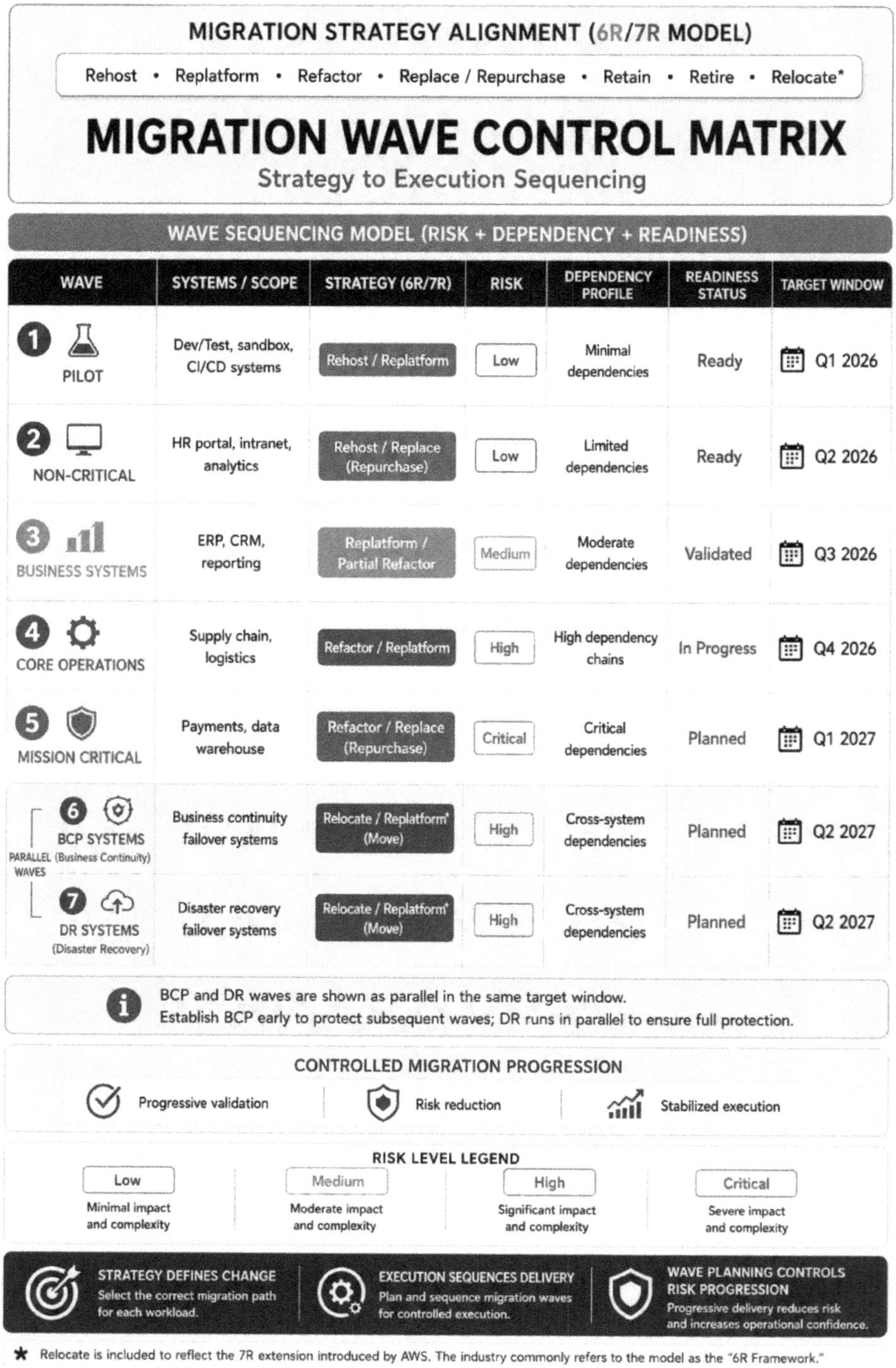

MIGRATION STRATEGY ALIGNMENT (6R/7R MODEL)

Rehost • Replatform • Refactor • Replace / Repurchase • Retain • Retire • Relocate*

MIGRATION WAVE CONTROL MATRIX

Strategy to Execution Sequencing

WAVE SEQUENCING MODEL (RISK + DEPENDENCY + READINESS)

WAVE	SYSTEMS / SCOPE	STRATEGY (6R/7R)	RISK	DEPENDENCY PROFILE	READINESS STATUS	TARGET WINDOW
1 PILOT	Dev/Test, sandbox, CI/CD systems	Rehost / Replatform	Low	Minimal dependencies	Ready	Q1 2026
2 NON-CRITICAL	HR portal, intranet, analytics	Rehost / Replace (Repurchase)	Low	Limited dependencies	Ready	Q2 2026
3 BUSINESS SYSTEMS	ERP, CRM, reporting	Replatform / Partial Refactor	Medium	Moderate dependencies	Validated	Q3 2026
4 CORE OPERATIONS	Supply chain, logistics	Refactor / Replatform	High	High dependency chains	In Progress	Q4 2026
5 MISSION CRITICAL	Payments, data warehouse	Refactor / Replace (Repurchase)	Critical	Critical dependencies	Planned	Q1 2027
PARALLEL WAVES: 6 BCP SYSTEMS (Business Continuity)	Business continuity failover systems	Relocate / Replatform* (Move)	High	Cross-system dependencies	Planned	Q2 2027
PARALLEL WAVES: 7 DR SYSTEMS (Disaster Recovery)	Disaster recovery failover systems	Relocate / Replatform* (Move)	High	Cross-system dependencies	Planned	Q2 2027

BCP and DR waves are shown as parallel in the same target window.
Establish BCP early to protect subsequent waves; DR runs in parallel to ensure full protection.

CONTROLLED MIGRATION PROGRESSION

Progressive validation | Risk reduction | Stabilized execution

RISK LEVEL LEGEND

Low — Minimal impact and complexity
Medium — Moderate impact and complexity
High — Significant impact and complexity
Critical — Severe impact and complexity

STRATEGY DEFINES CHANGE — Select the correct migration path for each workload.
EXECUTION SEQUENCES DELIVERY — Plan and sequence migration waves for controlled execution.
WAVE PLANNING CONTROLS RISK PROGRESSION — Progressive delivery reduces risk and increases operational confidence.

★ Relocate is included to reflect the 7R extension introduced by AWS. The industry commonly refers to the model as the "6R Framework."

Migration Wave Control Matrix — strategy-to-execution sequencing across waves. Note: the two Disaster Recovery rows shown at the bottom (BCP and DR) represent successive waves; treat the second row as Wave 7.

Wave Planning — Controlled Execution Through Sequencing

Wave planning reduces operational disruption.

It creates learning cycles.

It allows lower-risk systems to validate the migration model—before critical platforms are moved.

Wave Composition Should Consider:

System criticality
Dependency chains
Environment readiness
Testing capacity
Business calendars
Vendor constraints
Support availability

A technically simple application may still belong in a later wave—if it depends on a high-risk identity or data service.

A practical wave model often begins with internal or low-risk tools.

Then progresses to moderate systems with controlled integrations.

And concludes with high-criticality business platforms—once the organization has proven the method.

Execution Discipline

Do not separate tightly coupled upstream and downstream systems—without an explicit integration plan.

Do not place a high-volume production system in the first wave—unless there is a compelling business reason.

Use rehearsal migrations and cutover runbooks—to strengthen later waves.

Wave Governance

Treat each wave as a mini-program.

With its own readiness review.

Cutover plan.

Validation checklist.

And formal sign-off.

Execution Alignment

At this point, the relationship becomes clear:

Strategy determines the treatment.

Execution approach determines the method of movement.

Wave planning determines the sequence—through which that movement is safely carried out.

This structure is not theoretical—it operates as a unified migration system model.

Strategy,

execution,

and sequencing operate together as a single system.

Its practical application is realized through structured wave planning.

Wave planning is not an abstract concept—it is the mechanism through which execution is structured in practice.

Execution is structured through controlled sequencing.

This is where sequencing becomes control.

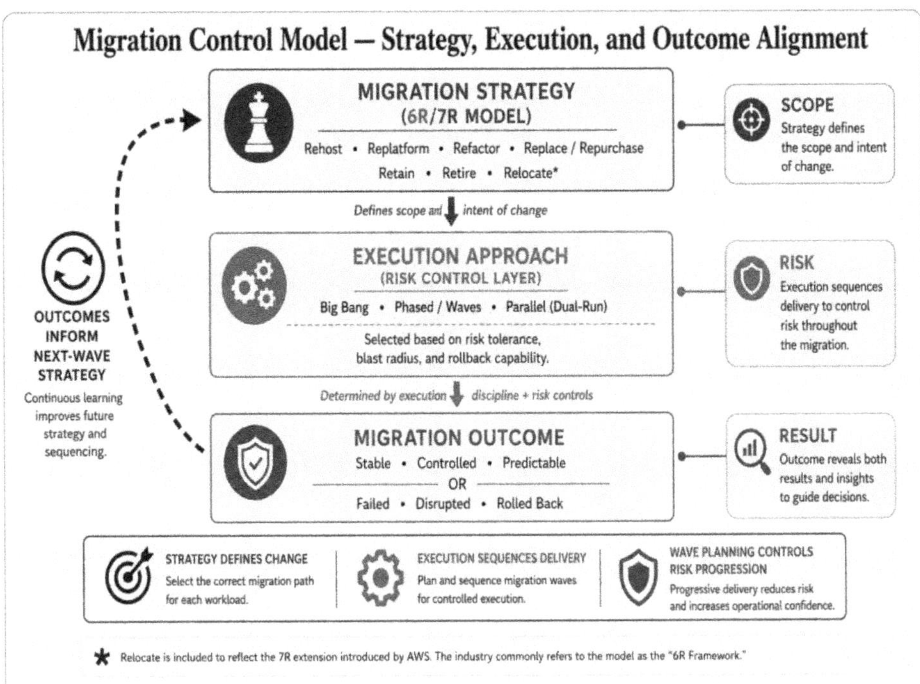

Migration Control Model — Strategy, Execution, and Outcome Alignment.

While wave planning defines how execution is structured in practice, the migration model can ultimately be reduced to three governing forces.

Strategy Defines Outcome

Migration strategy is not about selecting an option from a list.

It is about defining the future state of the system.

Every decision made here shapes:

Cost

Risk

Performance

Operational complexity

Long-term sustainability

Execution does not correct strategy.

It exposes it.

Strategy and Execution in Practice

What ultimately matters is not the selection of strategy alone—

but how that decision is carried through execution.

Because in real-world migration programs—

decisions do not exist in isolation.

They are tested under pressure.

They are exposed during cutover.

They are validated—or broken—by execution.

You are not simply selecting a migration strategy.

You are defining:

What changes

How that change is introduced into the environment

And how risk is controlled throughout that transition

This is the difference between structured migration programs and reactive ones.

In structured programs:

Strategy is intentional

Execution is controlled

Outcomes are predictable

In reactive programs:

Strategy is assumed

Execution is improvised

Outcomes are uncertain

Migration success is not defined by strategy alone.

It is defined by how strategy and execution approach work together under real-world conditions.

Because strategy defines direction.

Execution determines survivability.

PART IV

Migration Architecture

The infrastructure layers that must be validated before any system moves.

CHAPTER 8

The 10 Infrastructure Layers That Must Be Validated

Establishing What Exists Before Declaring Success

We often declare victory before reaching the finish line—because we anticipate the outcome before it is fully proven.

In infrastructure, that instinct does not apply.

Systems do not operate on anticipation.

They operate on what is real, what is validated, and what is proven.

There is only what has been tested—and what has been proven under real conditions.

Before any migration can be considered successful, a fundamental question must be answered:

What, exactly, has been proven to work?

Why Infrastructure Validation Is Non-Negotiable

Every migration touches a set of foundational infrastructure layers.

These layers do not operate independently—they function as an interconnected system.

If even one layer is partially validated:

Hidden defects remain

Dependencies fail under load

Security gaps are introduced

Recovery becomes uncertain

This is where many migration programs lose control.

Not because systems failed to move—

But because they were never fully proven.

Migration success is not defined by system availability.

It is defined by complete validation across the entire infrastructure stack.

What Must Be Validated — The 10 Infrastructure Layers

A complete validation model spans ten critical layers. Each must be verified with ownership, evidence, and defined success criteria.

1. Compute

Servers, virtual machines, containers

CPU and memory utilization

Autoscaling behavior

Service state and runtime stability

2. Storage

Disk volumes and mount points

Object storage and capacity thresholds

Data persistence and integrity

Backup alignment and restore capability

3. Network

DNS resolution and routing paths

Load balancers and traffic distribution

Subnets, firewall rules, and security groups

Latency and connectivity behavior

4. Identity and Access Management (IAM)

Directory services and federation

Single Sign-On (SSO) and federation (SAML, OIDC)

Multi-Factor Authentication (MFA) enforcement and policy

Role-Based Access Control (RBAC)

Service accounts and privileged access

5. Database / Data Platform

Connectivity and query execution

Schema compatibility

Replication and failover behavior

Data integrity and performance

6. Application Services

Web and application tiers

Configuration variables and environment settings

Background jobs and processing tasks

API functionality and response behavior

7. Security Controls

Certificates and secret management

Encryption (at rest and in transit)

Endpoint protection and policy enforcement

Logging and audit enforcement

8. Monitoring and Observability

Logs, alerts, and dashboards

Telemetry and tracing

Incident visibility and escalation

9. Integration Services

Message queues and ETL pipelines

Vendor integrations and external interfaces

Internal APIs and batch dependencies

10. Backup and Disaster Recovery

Backup integrity and recovery points

Replication across environments

Failover readiness

Runbook accuracy and execution capability

How Validation Must Be Performed

Validation is not a checkbox.

It is a controlled process.

The Project Manager does not execute every validation activity—but is accountable for ensuring that validation is complete, structured, and defensible.

Validation is not sustained by responsibility alone—it is sustained through structure.

To ensure that validation is consistent, repeatable, and defensible across all infrastructure layers, it must operate as a controlled system.

That system is defined through three conditions of proof—ownership, evidence, and exit criteria.

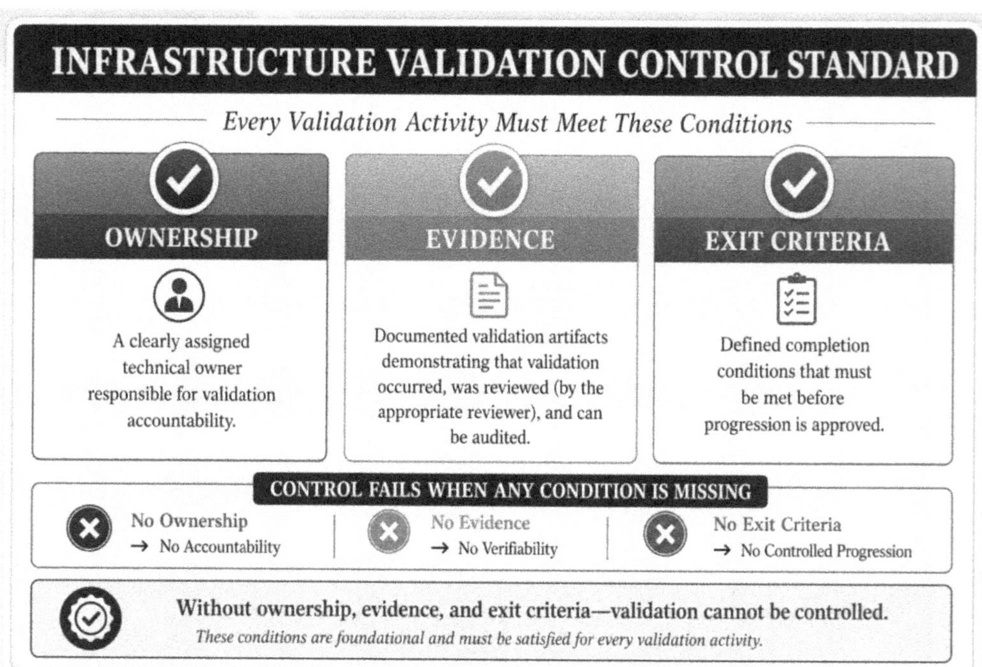

This standard establishes the foundation of validation.

But validation is not only defined by what must exist alone—it is governed by how it is executed.

To move from definition to execution, validation must be structured as a controlled sequence.

This is where validation becomes operational—not as individual checks, but as a coordinated control system.

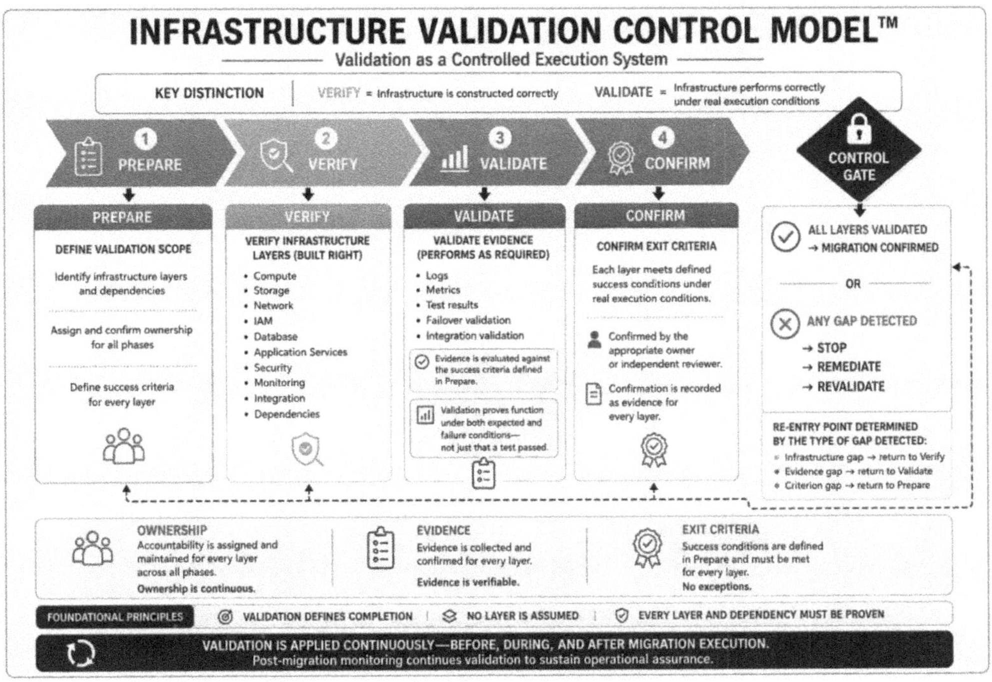

This model reinforces a critical truth:

Validation is not performed in isolation.

It is executed as a coordinated control system—where every layer, every dependency, and every condition must be proven before success is declared.

Validation Is Not Binary

Validation is not:

"The system is up"

"The test passed"

It is:

"This layer has been proven to function under expected and failure conditions."

Validation is not confined to a single moment in time.

It is applied continuously—before, during, and after migration execution.

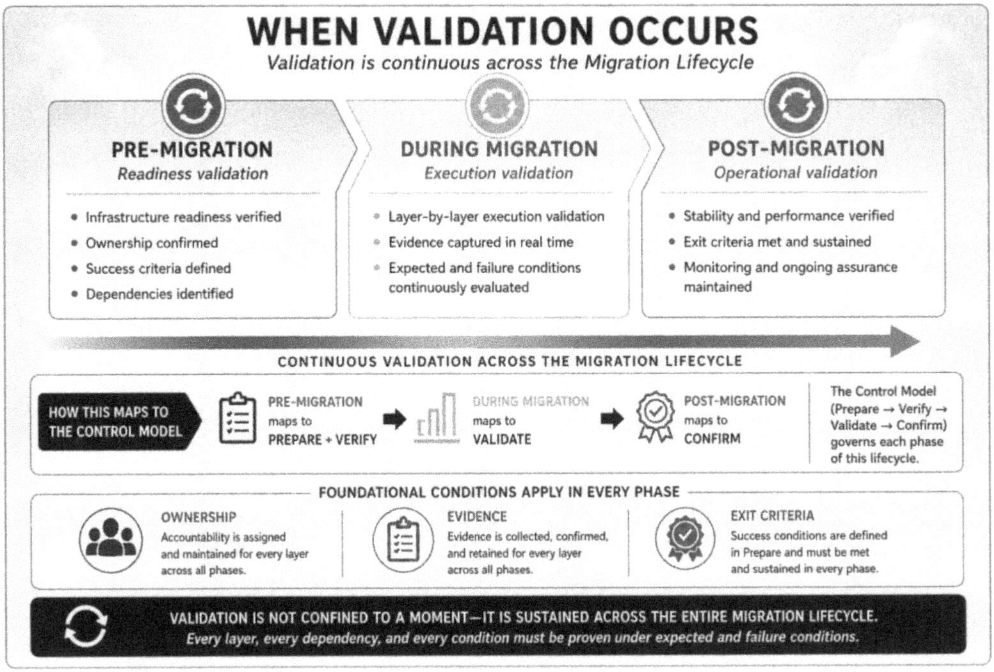

This continuity ensures that validation is not reactive—but sustained across the entire migration lifecycle.

Validation is not a phase.

It is a control discipline.

Where Organizations Get This Wrong

Most organizations validate what is visible:

Application access

User authentication

Basic functionality

But fail to validate what is critical:

Integration paths

Failover mechanisms

Observability coverage

Dependency behavior under stress

This creates a false sense of completion.

Because what is working is not always what is proven.

Dependency Mapping and System Integration Awareness

Understanding What Connects the System You Just Validated

Validation confirms that each layer functions.

Dependency mapping confirms that the system functions as a whole.

Because in enterprise environments, systems do not operate in isolation.

They operate through relationships.

And it is those relationships—not the individual components—that most often fail.

Why Dependency Mapping Is Critical

A migration can appear successful:

Applications are online

Users can authenticate

Infrastructure is stable

But still fail—because something outside the system boundary was not accounted for.

A downstream report breaks.

An upstream API times out.

A service account loses access to a hidden dependency.

These failures are not caused by migration errors.

They are caused by incomplete visibility.

Where Organizations Get This Wrong

Most organizations:

Rely on outdated diagrams

Assume CMDB accuracy

Focus only on direct system dependencies

And overlook:

Indirect integrations

Scheduled processes

Identity relationships

Vendor-side dependencies

This creates a dangerous assumption:

The system is assumed to be self-contained.

It is not.

What Dependency Mapping Must Include

Dependency mapping is not limited to application diagrams.

It must capture the full operational ecosystem:

Infrastructure dependencies

(compute, network paths, storage access)

Application dependencies

(services, APIs, internal components)

Data dependencies

(databases, warehouses, pipelines, file transfers)

Identity dependencies

(Okta, Entra ID, service accounts, tokens)

Vendor dependencies

(third-party APIs, SaaS platforms)

Operational dependencies

(monitoring, logging, backup, ticketing)

Business process dependencies

(reports, workflows, scheduled jobs)

How Dependency Mapping Is Executed

Dependency mapping is not a documentation exercise.

It is an investigation.

Because most dependencies are:

Not documented

Not visible in diagrams

Not captured in CMDBs

Execution Approach

A structured mapping process requires:

Cross-functional workshops

(Application, Infrastructure, Network, DB, Security, Support, Business SMEs)

Validation against real system behavior

(logs, traffic flows, authentication paths, job execution)

Iterative refinement

(initial maps are always incomplete)

What This Produces

The output is not a static diagram.

It is a working control artifact used to:

Sequence migration waves

Define testing scope

Shape maintenance windows

Identify integration risks

Expose rollback dependencies

Real-World Simulation — Failure Due to Missing Dependency Awareness

During a migration of a healthcare reporting platform, all core systems were successfully moved to the cloud:

Application services were operational

Database connections were stable

Users accessed dashboards without issue

The migration was declared successful.

What Was Missed

A nightly batch process responsible for generating compliance reports depended on:

A legacy on-prem file share

A scheduled job running outside the application environment

A service account tied to the old domain

None of these dependencies were captured in the migration plan.

What Happened

Within 48 hours:

Compliance reports stopped generating

Regulatory deadlines were missed

Investigation revealed the batch job could no longer access the required file share

The Reality

The system was working.

The process was broken.

What This Scenario Proves

Migration success is not defined by:

System readiness

Application functionality

Infrastructure validation

It is defined by:

Complete awareness of how systems interact beyond their boundaries

Control Principle — Systems Fail at the Edges

Failures rarely occur at the center of systems.

They occur at the edges:

Between systems

Across environments

Through integrations

Within dependencies

Validation proves that components work.

Dependency mapping proves that the system works together.

And in migration—

What breaks is not what you see.

It is what you did not map.

Infrastructure Health Checks

The Final Confirmation That the Environment Is Truly Stable

There is a moment after every migration where everything appears quiet.

No alerts.

No escalations.

No visible failures.

And someone in the room says:

"We're good."

That moment is dangerous.

Because silence is not proof.

Stability is not assumed.

It is verified.

And what appears healthy on the surface can still be failing underneath.

After systems have been migrated,

after validation has been performed,

and after dependencies have been mapped,

a final question remains:

What proves that the environment is truly stable—not simply not failing yet?

When migration leaders refer to infrastructure health checks, they are not asking whether a system is running.

They are asking whether the entire hosting foundation is operating correctly, consistently, and under real conditions.

Infrastructure health checks represent the final layer of proof that the system is stable, the environment is resilient, and the platform can sustain real-world usage.

Application testing can pass.

Users can log in.

Systems can respond.

And still fail—hours or days later.

Because infrastructure weaknesses are often hidden beneath application behavior, triggered only under load, and revealed only over time.

This is why health checks exist.

To prove that the foundation—not just the application—is stable.

Infrastructure health checks validate the operational integrity of the environment across all layers:

This validation model can be visualized as a unified control structure:

Infrastructure Health Check Validation Model

Ensuring Infrastructure Stability Before Production

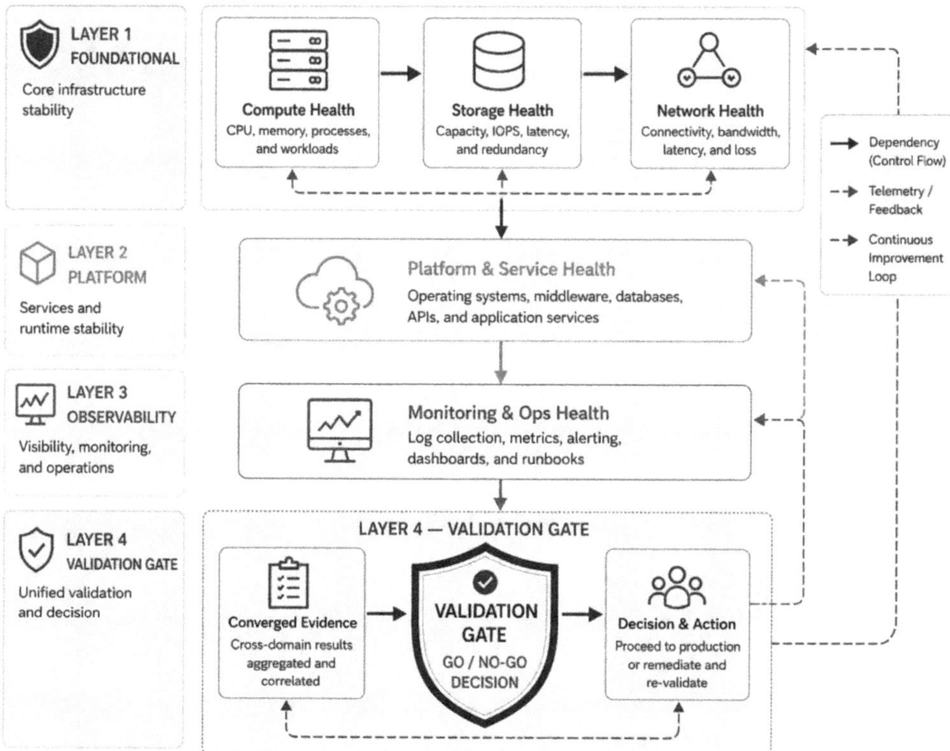

PROVING RESILIENCE AFTER MIGRATION

#	VALIDATION AREA	WHAT WE VALIDATE	SUCCESS CRITERIA (EXAMPLES)	METHOD	TARGET	PASS / FAIL*
1	Compute (CPU & Memory Stability)	Sustained resource utilization and performance stability	• Avg CPU ≤ 70% over 24 hours • Memory utilization ≤ 75% • No resource saturation events	Monitoring, performance metrics	24 Hours	✓
2	Storage (Data Integrity & Backup)	Data integrity and backup/restore effectiveness	• Checksum match 100% • Backup job success rate = 100% • Restore test completed successfully	Integrity checks, backup reports, restore test	Daily	✓
3	Network (Security & Performance)	Network performance, security posture, and access controls	• Latency within baseline • Packet loss < 1% • No critical security findings	Network tests, security scans, flow logs	24 Hours	✓
4	Platform & Service Stability	Platform components, services, and dependencies	• All critical services healthy • Dependency checks pass • No error budget exhaustion	Health checks, synthetic tests, dependency maps	24 Hours	✓
5	Monitoring & Ops (Alerts & Incident Readiness)	Alerting accuracy, coverage, and incident response readiness	• All P1 / P2 alerts fire in test • Alert noise within acceptable limits • Runbooks validated and accessible	Alert tests, simulation, runbook validation	Before Go-Live	✓

** Example post-validation state for illustration purposes.*

→ Dependency (Control Flow) ⇢ Telemetry / Feedback ⇢ Continuous Improvement Loop

STRATEGY DEFINES CHANGE
Choose the right path for each workload.

EXECUTION SEQUENCES DELIVERY
Plan and sequence waves for controlled delivery.

WAVE PLANNING CONTROLS RISK PROGRESSION
Progressive delivery reduces risk and builds confidence.

This model validates the health of critical infrastructure domains and proves resvtesilience after migration before proceeding to production.

Each layer represented above must be validated not independently but—but as part of a continuously operating system.

Compute Health:

Server and VM operational state

Container readiness

CPU and memory thresholds

Core services running consistently

Storage Health:

Disk utilization and mount points

Throughput and performance (IOPS)

Backup integrity

Replication status

Network Health:

DNS resolution

Routing and connectivity

Firewall and security group enforcement

Load balancer behavior and latency

Platform and Service Health:

IAM roles and permissions

Certificates and secret validity

Middleware and service availability

Autoscaling and platform behavior

Monitoring and Operational Health:

Logs flowing correctly

Alerts triggering as expected

Dashboards reflecting real conditions

Incident response hooks active

Validation proves that systems work.

Health checks prove that systems remain stable under real conditions.

During a cloud migration of an enterprise application platform, all validation checkpoints were successfully completed:

Applications passed functional testing

Users authenticated without issue

APIs responded correctly

The migration was declared successful.

Infrastructure health checks, however, were not fully enforced.

CPU thresholds were not monitored under peak load.

Autoscaling rules were misconfigured.

Monitoring alerts were not fully validated.

Within 72 hours of go-live:

System performance degraded under increased user traffic

Application latency increased significantly

Autoscaling failed to trigger correctly

Users experienced slow response times.

Support tickets increased.

Emergency remediation was required.

The system was working.

But the environment was not stable.

Migration success is not defined by successful deployment, functional validation, or user access.

It is defined by sustained operational stability after go-live.

Infrastructure health checks answer the final question:

Can this environment sustain real-world conditions—without failure?

A migration is not successful because systems are live.

It is not successful because tests passed.

It is successful only when the environment proves it can operate, sustain, and recover under real conditions.

PART V

Governance and Delivery Control

Risk, RAID, rollback, and the governance cadence that holds execution under pressure.

CHAPTER 9

Risk Management and RAID Governance

Governance and Delivery Control

Migration programs do not fail because of technology alone—they fail because of a lack of control.

As complexity increases across infrastructure, applications, security, and dependencies, the ability to govern execution with clarity and discipline becomes the defining factor between success and failure.

Governance is not bureaucracy—it is visibility, accountability, and control applied consistently across the lifecycle of delivery.

Delivery control ensures that decisions are not reactive, risks are not hidden, and progress is not assumed—it is measured, validated, and actively managed.

At its core, governance and delivery control provide three essential capabilities:

Clarity — Leadership understands exactly where the program stands

Accountability — Ownership is defined and enforced across all workstreams

Control — Risks, dependencies, and execution are actively managed—not discovered too late

This chapter introduces four foundational artifacts that operationalize governance and delivery control in migration programs:

Understanding RAID Categories — A Common Language for Control

The RAID framework categorizes
the four critical elements required
to manage migration programs.

Risks —

potential future events.

Assumptions —

conditions believed to be true.

Issues —

active problems requiring resolution.

Dependencies —

relationships across systems and teams.

A note on convention:

This book uses the
Risks / Assumptions / Issues / Dependencies definition—

which is the most common
in cloud and infrastructure migration practice.

Some PRINCE2-influenced organizations use:

Risks / Actions / Issues / Decisions instead.

Both are valid—

what matters is consistency
within a single program.

Real-World Intervention — Restoring Control Through Structure

During a Microsoft 365 implementation,

risks were actively identified
across multiple workstreams.

Security concerns were raised.

Identity dependencies were noted.

Operational gaps were discussed.

But nothing moved.

There was:

No ownership.

No mitigation path.

No escalation model.

No cross-functional alignment.

Each team assumed
someone else was responsible.

The result was predictable:

Confusion.

Delay.

Exposure.

To restore control,

a structured Risk Workshop was introduced.

In a single working session:

All risks were consolidated
into one forum.

Each risk was clearly defined
and validated.

Ownership was assigned immediately.

Mitigation actions were documented.

Escalation paths were established.

What changed was not the risk.

What changed was control.

From that point forward:

Risks became visible.

Ownership became enforceable.

Execution became accountable.

This is the difference
between tracking risk—

and managing it.

Understanding RAID is foundational—

but execution requires
structured tracking,

ownership,

and governance.

That structure becomes meaningful
only when it is translated
into a live governance mechanism.

The following RAID Log transforms
these concepts into actionable
delivery control.

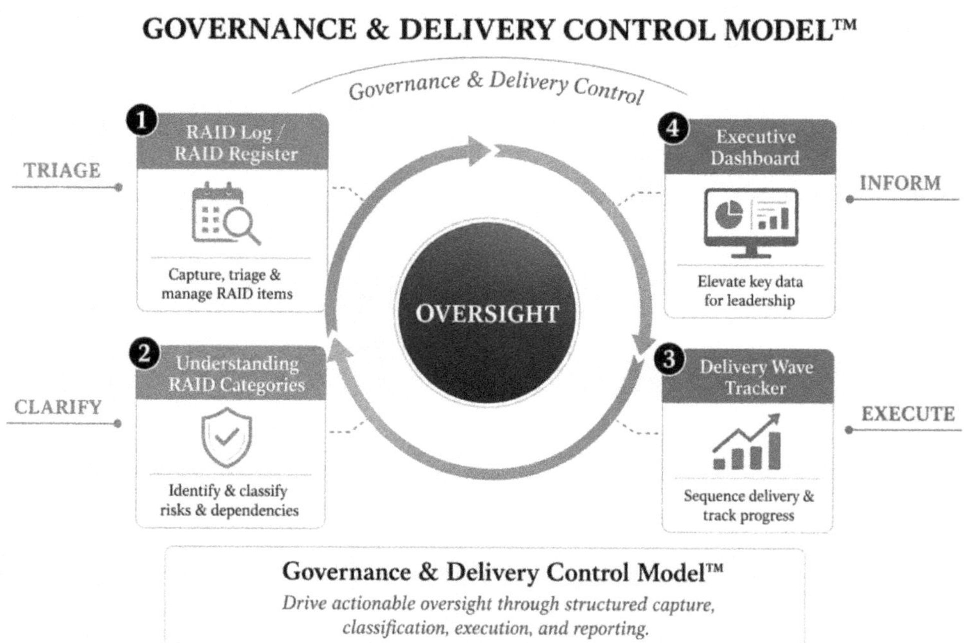

This model turns abstract delivery risk into something visible, owned, and manageable.

A well-structured RAID log includes:

Description

Impact

Mitigation strategy

Owner

Timeline

Status

Escalation thresholds

This ensures that risks are not
simply recorded—
but actively governed across the
migration lifecycle.

Governance Cadence — Control Through Rhythm

A RAID log without cadence is ineffective.

Control requires rhythm:

Weekly reviews during standard phases

Daily reviews during cutover and stabilization

At these stages, risk exposure increases—and response time must decrease.

Cadence ensures:

Risks are not forgotten

Issues are not delayed

Dependencies are not overlooked

With cadence established, governance can move from broad delivery control to focused risk exposure management.

Migration Risk Log — Focused Risk Control Within RAID

While the RAID log captures the full spectrum of delivery variables, risk-specific tracking requires a more focused lens.

The Migration Risk Log isolates risk into a dedicated control view.

Purpose: Capture, triage, and actively manage risk exposure across all migration phases.

Structure:

Risk

Impact

Mitigation

Owner

Status

When risk is separated into a focused view, leadership can govern exposure more quickly and more precisely.

RISK REGISTER

This register captures key risks identified for the cloud migration program.

RISK	IMPACT	MITIGATION STRATEGY	OWNER	STATUS
Data loss during migration cutover	HIGH	Real-time replication with validated snapshots prior to cutover. Recovery Point Objective (RPO) + 10 minutes.	Data Engineering Lead	IN PROGRESS
Extended downtime exceeding SLA	HIGH	Parallel-run strategy (72 hours) with tested rollback procedures before each wave.	Platform Architect	OPEN
Network latency post-cloud migration	MEDIUM	Pre-migration benchmarking, CDN optimization, load balancing adjustments, and 30-day monitoring.	Infrastructure Team	COMPLETE
Third-party license incompatibility	MEDIUM	Full license audit, vendor renegotiation, and cloud-compatible replacements secured.	Procurement	COMPLETE
Skill gaps in cloud platform	LOW	Structured training program with certification targets and hypercare support.	HR / L&D	PLANNED
Security & compliance gaps	HIGH	Security gates enforced per wave, penetration testing, and IAM validation.	CISO / Security Lead	PLANNED

STATUS KEY: COMPLETE IN PROGRESS PLANNED BLOCKED

This enables leadership to:

Focus on high-impact exposure

Track mitigation progress

Make faster decisions

Once risk is visible and actively controlled, execution itself must be made equally visible.

Migration Wave Tracker

Execution Visibility Across the Program

Migration occurs in waves—not all at once.

The Migration Wave Tracker provides visibility into:

Sequencing

Risk distribution

Execution progress

Dependencies

Execution visibility is most effective when sequencing and exposure can be seen together in one view.

Migration Wave Tracker

Tracks the progression of migration waves, including scope, risk level, phase, and current status.

WAVE	SYSTEMS / SCOPE	RISK LEVEL	PHASE	STATUS
Wave 1 — Pilot	Dev/Test, CI/CD, monitoring, sandbox	LOW	Phase 1	COMPLETE
Wave 2 — Non-Critical	HR portal, intranet, analytics, reporting tools	LOW	Phase 2	COMPLETE
Wave 3 — Business Systems	ERP, CRM, finance, collaboration tools	MEDIUM	Phase 3	COMPLETE
Wave 4 — Core Operations	Supply chain, logistics, inventory systems	HIGH	Phase 4	IN PROGRESS
Wave 5 — Mission Critical	Payments, data warehouse	HIGH	Phase 5	PLANNED
Wave 6 — DR / BCP	Disaster recovery, business continuity systems	HIGH	Phase 6	PLANNED

STATUS KEY: COMPLETE · IN PROGRESS · PLANNED · BLOCKED

It answers a critical question:

Where is risk concentrated across the migration timeline?

A disciplined cadence is weekly review for normal phases and daily review during cutover windows or hypercare/post cutover.

Once execution visibility is established across the program, that same visibility must be translated into leadership decision-making.

Executive Dashboard From Data to Decision

Executives do not need detail.

They need clarity.

The Executive Dashboard translates delivery into:

Schedule status

Financial health

Risk exposure

Operational indicators

Business impact

For leadership, governance must be reduced to a view that supports rapid understanding and informed action.

Its purpose is simple:

To enable informed decision-making.

Clarity—not volume—drives decisions.

There is beauty in simplicity.

Governance Artifact Summary

A Unified Control System

These artifacts are not independent.

They operate as a unified system:

RAID Log → Captures all delivery variables
Risk Log → Focuses on high-impact risk
Wave Tracker → Visualizes sequencing and exposure
Executive Dashboard → Enables leadership decisions

The full structure of governance is not theoretical.

It operates as a continuous control system across the migration lifecycle.

To fully understand how these artifacts work together, the governance model can be visualized as a single integrated control system.

GOVERNANCE CONTROL SYSTEM™

From Risk Identification to Sustained Control

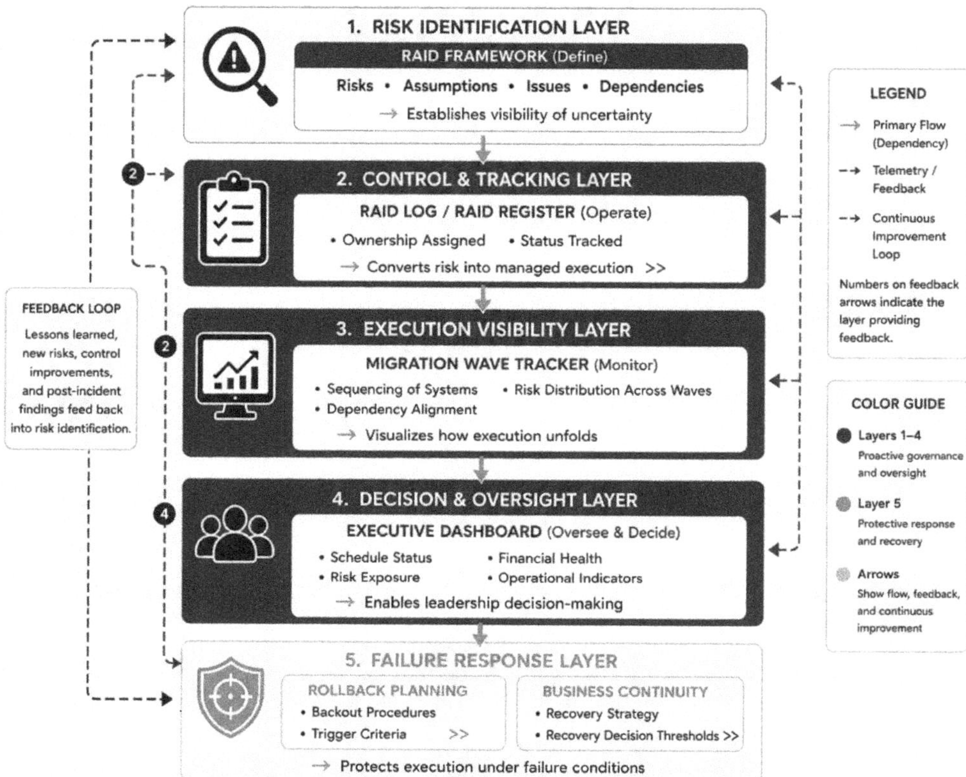

GOVERNANCE OUTCOME CHAIN (End-to-End Flow)

RISK Identify uncertainty → **CONTROL** Manage and track → **VISIBILITY** Monitor execution in motion → **DECISION** Lead with confidence → **RESPONSE** Act and recover → **STABILITY** Maintained continuously

GOVERNANCE IS NOT REPORTING – IT IS CONTROL IN MOTION.

GOVERNANCE ROLES & ACCOUNTABILITY (RACI)

ROLE	KEY RESPONSIBILITIES
Steering Committee	Sets direction, approves decisions, and removes escalations
Risk Owner	Owns risks, updates status, and manages mitigations
Wave Lead	Executes wave plan, tracks dependencies, and reports progress
Technical Lead	Validates technical health, resolves issues, and ensures stability
Operations Lead	Monitors environment, manages alerts, and coordinates response

GOVERNANCE CADENCE (RHYTHM OF CONTROL)

CADENCE	FOCUS	PARTICIPANTS	KEY OUTPUT
Daily Standup	Execution status, blockers, immediate risks	Wave Leads, Tech & Ops Leads	Daily actions, updated risk status
Weekly RAID Review	RAID log review, risk trends, mitigation progress	Risk Owners, Wave Leads, Steering Rep	Updated RAID, decisions, risk closures
Monthly Steering Review	Performance, risk exposure, financial health	Steering Committee, Program Leads	Strategic decisions, policy updates
Event-Driven Escalation	Threshold breaches, critical incidents	Escalation Matrix	Incident response, decisions, communication

ESCALATION PATHS
(When Thresholds Are Breached)

① Threshold Breach (Severity: Sev 1 / 2 / 3)
↓
② Alert Generated (Automated)
↓
③ Operations Lead Notified (Severity-Based)
↓
④ Risk Owner Engaged (Severity-Based)
↓
⑤ Steering Committee Escalation (If Needed)
↓
⑥ Decision & Action Executed
↓
⑦ Post-Event Review & Update RAID

Sev 1 (Critical) Sev 2 (High) Sev 3 (Medium)

GOVERNANCE CONTROL KPIs (Examples – Mapped to Layers)

- % Risks with Mitigation Plan ≥ 90% (Layer 1)
- RAID Action Closure Rate ≥ 95% (Layer 2)
- Issue Closure Within SLA ≥ 90% (Layer 3)
- Mean Time to Respond (MTTR) ≤ 4 Hours (Layer 5)
- Control Effectiveness Trend Improving (Layer 4)
- Successful Waves Delivered On Plan (Outcome)

This model illustrates how governance evolves from risk identification to sustained operational control–ensuring that execution remains visible, accountable, and controlled at every stage.

This model illustrates how governance evolves from risk identification to sustained operational control—ensuring that execution remains visible, accountable, and controlled at every stage.

Together, they create:

Visibility → Accountability → Control

Risk Must Be Actively Managed

Risk does not disappear because it is documented.

It disappears when it is:

Owned

Acted upon

Tracked

Resolved

Unmanaged risk becomes:

Delay

Failure

Escalation

Managed risk becomes—Controlled execution

Risk is not dangerous because it exists—it is dangerous when it is unmanaged.

Rollback Planning and Business Continuity

Failure Response as a Controlled Strategy

If risk management identifies what could go wrong—

rollback planning defines what happens when it does.

Risk without response is exposure.

Rollback planning is the mechanism that converts risk awareness into operational resilience.

To understand how this operates in practice, rollback must be viewed as a structured control flow—not a reactive action.

This control flow can be visualized as a structured response model—from active execution through failure, rollback, investigation, and controlled resumption.

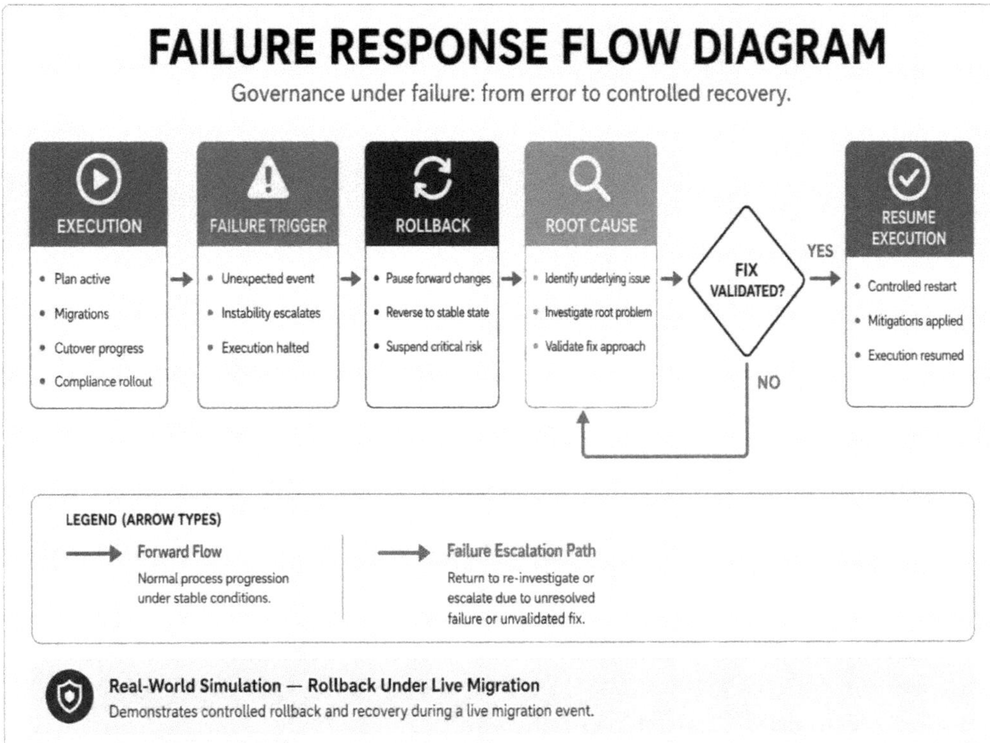

This model reinforces a critical principle: failure is not the end of execution—it is a governed transition point within it.

It is not a contingency.

It is a designed outcome of governance.

Failure Is Not an Exception—It Is a Condition to Be Engineered For

In technology transformations, especially in cloud and infrastructure migrations, one truth remains constant:

Not everything will go as planned.

Dependencies behave differently in production.

Latency surfaces under real load.

Authentication flows fail under edge conditions.

Data behaves unpredictably at scale.

Failure is not rare.

It is expected.

The difference between stable programs and failed ones is not the absence of failure—

It is the presence of a controlled response.

Rollback Planning as a Strategic Control Layer

Rollback planning is not a technical afterthought.

It is a strategic control layer within governance.

It answers a critical question:

What is our controlled path back when forward execution introduces unacceptable risk?

Without this answer, execution becomes irreversible—and risk becomes unmanaged.

Rollback planning ensures that:

Execution remains reversible

Risk remains bounded

Decisions remain controlled under pressure

This is where governance proves its value—not when things go right, but when they don't.

What Rollback Planning Actually Requires

Effective rollback planning is precise, structured, and time-bound.

It is not:

"We'll fix it"

"We'll troubleshoot in real time"

"Engineering will handle it"

These are reactions—not strategies.

A true rollback strategy includes:

1. Technical Reversal Design

Step-by-step backout procedures

System state restoration sequencing

Configuration reversion logic

Traffic redirection (DNS, routing, load balancers)

2. Data Protection Strategy

Verified backups and snapshots

Replication checkpoints

Data reconciliation approach post-rollback

Recovery Point Objective (RPO) alignment

3. Decision Thresholds (Go / No-Go)

Defined failure conditions

Performance degradation thresholds

Security or compliance triggers

Business impact tolerances

4. Time-Bound Execution Windows

Rollback decision time-boxes

Cutover window constraints

Viability windows for reversal

Expiration point where rollback is no longer safe

5. Ownership and Accountability

Named rollback decision authority

Technical execution owners

Business escalation points

Cross-functional alignment (Infra, App, Security, Business)

6. Communication Control

Executive notification triggers

Stakeholder communication templates

Real-time status updates during rollback

Alignment between technical and business messaging

Integration with Cutover Planning

Rollback does not exist separately from execution.

It is embedded directly into the cutover plan.

Every migration execution must define:

Rollback checkpoints

Validation gates

Decision points

Reversal steps aligned to each stage

A cutover plan without rollback is not a plan.

It is a one-way action.

And one-way execution in complex systems is uncontrolled risk.

Real-World Simulation — Rollback Under Live Migration Conditions

During a live SID (Security Identifier) migration for the State of Georgia—the process of preserving and remapping Active Directory object identities when moving users, groups, and computers across domains—systems were transitioned from DHS to the Board of Health across multiple clinics during active working hours.

The migration required strict continuity.

Clinical operations such as WIC could not tolerate disruption.

The environment included:

Active Directory (users, groups, computers)

Endpoints and file shares

Network dependencies and clinic-level systems

As part of the migration strategy, Zscaler (ZIA) was scheduled for decommissioning to transition network control and access.

The initial execution appeared successful.

Zscaler services were removed.

Systems transitioned as expected.

Connectivity remained stable.

But shortly after:

Zscaler Client Connector (ZCC) began reinstalling automatically across endpoints.

Before validation could be completed, the agent reappeared—reapplying policies and interfering with the migration state.

At that moment, execution could not safely continue forward.

This was no longer a migration step.

It was a failure condition.

What Happened Next

Without a controlled rollback strategy, teams would have:

Continued troubleshooting in production

Introduced instability across endpoints

Risked disruption to live clinical environments

Instead, the decision was made to roll back execution to a controlled state.

This allowed the team to:

Pause forward migration activities

Reassess the root cause

Prevent cascading impact across systems

The investigation revealed:

ZCC was being reinstalled through policy assignments—driven by endpoint management platform controls (Microsoft Intune / Endpoint Manager) and lingering configuration enforcement.

The issue was not the uninstall itself.

It was the control mechanism behind redeployment.

The Resolution

The team shifted from reactive troubleshooting to structured control:

Microsoft administrative guidance (SOP) was consulted

Policy assignments were identified and removed at the source

Device synchronization was forced

A scripted uninstall process was executed to fully remove ZCC

Once control of deployment behavior was restored:

ZCC reinstall loops stopped

Endpoint state stabilized

Migration execution resumed safely

The Impact

This issue introduced a delay of nearly three days.

Not because the problem was complex—

But because the control mechanism was not initially understood.

What This Proves

Nothing in the original plan accounted for this exact failure scenario.

And yet:

The migration did not fail.

Because rollback existed.

Rollback created:

Time to think

Space to investigate

Control over execution

Without rollback, this would have resulted in:

Endpoint instability

Policy conflicts

Operational disruption across clinics

The Deeper Lesson

Nothing is easy—

Until you understand how to do it.

And in migration:

Understanding often happens after execution begins.

Rollback is what allows you to survive that gap.

And when that control does not exist, the consequences become immediately visible.

The Cost of Not Having a Rollback Strategy

When rollback is not defined:

Teams hesitate under pressure

Decisions become delayed or emotional

Recovery becomes improvised

Business impact increases exponentially

What could have been a controlled reversal becomes:

Extended downtime

Data inconsistency

Loss of stakeholder confidence

This is not a technical failure.

This is a governance failure.

Rollback as Part of Business Continuity

Rollback planning is not just about systems.

It is part of business continuity strategy.

It ensures that:

Operations can be restored within acceptable timelines

Critical services remain available or recoverable

Business disruption is minimized

Rollback and business continuity must be aligned:

Technical recovery supports business priorities

Decision thresholds reflect operational impact

Recovery timelines match SLA expectations

This alignment ensures that recovery is not just technical—

It is operationally meaningful.

Control Principle — Execution Must Be Reversible

Execution is not considered controlled unless it can be reversed.

Rollback planning enforces this principle.

It ensures that:

Every forward action has a defined fallback

Every risk has a response path

Every failure has a controlled outcome

This is the difference between:

Execution with confidence—and execution with exposure.

Failure does not break systems.

Uncontrolled failure does.

Migration Monitoring and Stabilization

Proving That the System Holds Under Real Conditions

If rollback defines how we recover from failure—

Monitoring and stabilization define how we ensure the system holds under real-world conditions.

Stability Is Not Proven at Go-Live

There is a moment after every migration where systems are live, users can access applications, and initial validation appears successful.

This is often where organizations declare success.

This is also where many migrations begin to fail.

Because a system being live does not mean it is stable.

It means only that it has not failed yet.

Why Monitoring and Stabilization Are Non-Negotiable

Structured testing validates expected behavior.

Real-world usage exposes actual behavior.

Under real conditions:

Load patterns change

User behavior varies

Dependencies activate differently

Latency emerges across systems

Edge cases surface

These conditions cannot be fully replicated in testing environments.

They can only be observed in production.

This is why monitoring and stabilization are not optional.

They are the final validation layer of the migration.

What Monitoring and Stabilization Actually Do

Monitoring and stabilization begin the moment the new environment is live.

Their purpose is to:

Verify sustained performance under real operating conditions

Detect issues that structured testing could not reveal

Ensure system behavior aligns with business expectations

Prevent minor defects from becoming major incidents

This phase transforms migration from:

"It works"

To

"It holds under pressure"

Hypercare — Controlled Operational Oversight

Hypercare is not extended support.

It is a controlled operational state.

A temporary mode where:

Support coverage is elevated

Incident response is accelerated

Reporting cycles are shortened

Change control is tightened

This is where stabilization is actively governed—not passively observed.

This stabilization discipline can be visualized as a controlled system—where monitoring, response, validation, and operational ownership work together to prove stability over time.

Each layer of this model represents a control point—ensuring that stability is validated across system behavior, user experience, and operational readiness.

This model reinforces a critical truth: stabilization is not a passive waiting period—it is an active control phase in which system behavior must be continuously verified before success is declared.

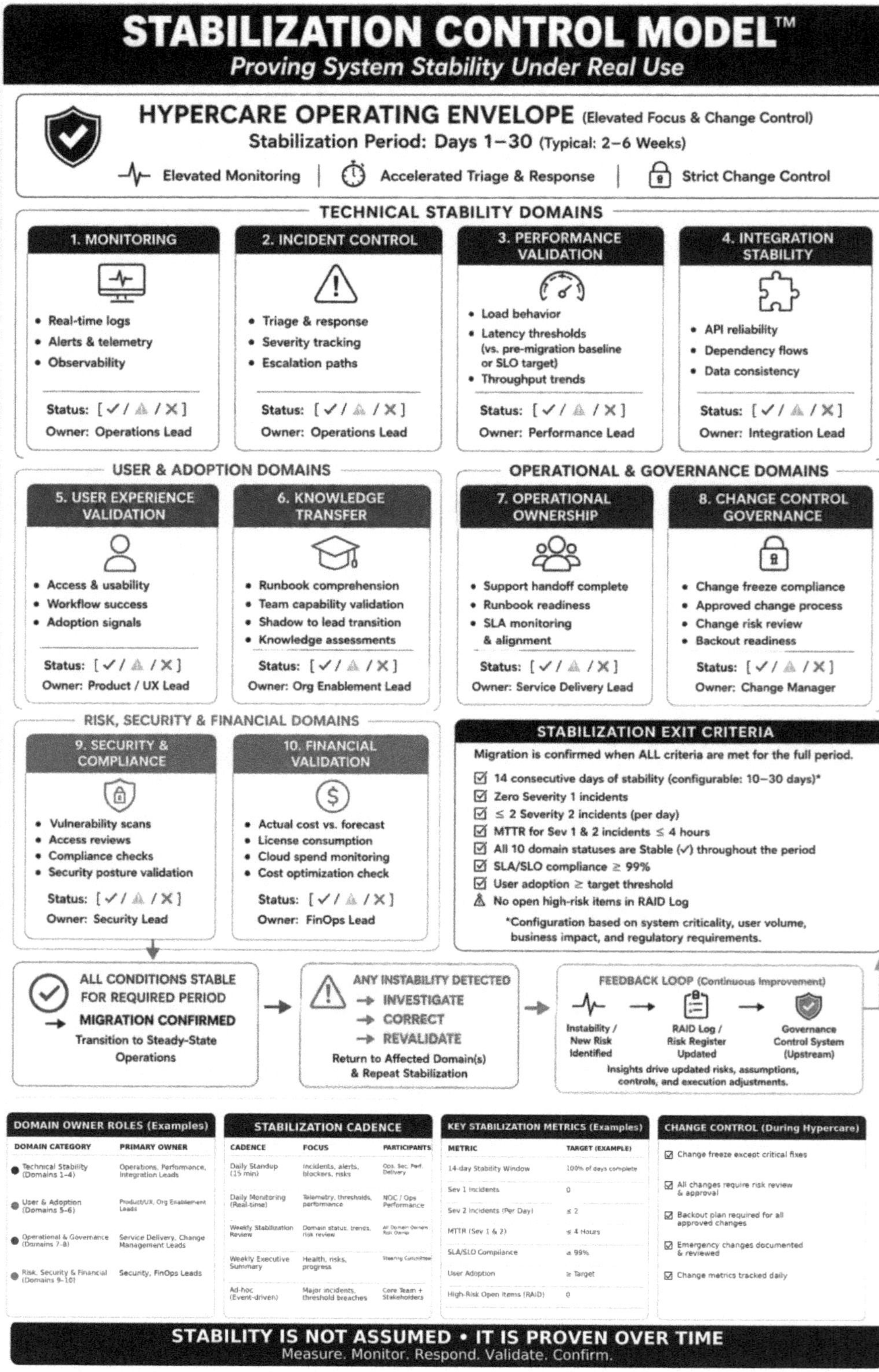
STABILIZATION CONTROL MODEL™
Proving System Stability Under Real Use
HYPERCARE OPERATING ENVELOPE (Elevated Focus & Change Control)
Stabilization Period: Days 1–30 (Typical: 2–6 Weeks)
Elevated Monitoring | Accelerated Triage & Response | Strict Change Control
TECHNICAL STABILITY DOMAINS
1. MONITORING
• Real-time logs
• Alerts & telemetry
• Observability
Status: [✓ / ⚠ / ✗]
Owner: Operations Lead
2. INCIDENT CONTROL
• Triage & response
• Severity tracking
• Escalation paths
Status: [✓ / ⚠ / ✗]
Owner: Operations Lead
3. PERFORMANCE VALIDATION
• Load behavior
• Latency thresholds (vs. pre-migration baseline or SLO target)
• Throughput trends
Status: [✓ / ⚠ / ✗]
Owner: Performance Lead
4. INTEGRATION STABILITY
• API reliability
• Dependency flows
• Data consistency
Status: [✓ / ⚠ / ✗]
Owner: Integration Lead
USER & ADOPTION DOMAINS
5. USER EXPERIENCE VALIDATION
• Access & usability
• Workflow success
• Adoption signals
Status: [✓ / ⚠ / ✗]
Owner: Product / UX Lead
6. KNOWLEDGE TRANSFER
• Runbook comprehension
• Team capability validation
• Shadow to lead transition
• Knowledge assessments
Status: [✓ / ⚠ / ✗]
Owner: Org Enablement Lead
OPERATIONAL & GOVERNANCE DOMAINS
7. OPERATIONAL OWNERSHIP
• Support handoff complete
• Runbook readiness
• SLA monitoring & alignment
Status: [✓ / ⚠ / ✗]
Owner: Service Delivery Lead
8. CHANGE CONTROL GOVERNANCE
• Change freeze compliance
• Approved change process
• Change risk review
• Backout readiness
Status: [✓ / ⚠ / ✗]
Owner: Change Manager
RISK, SECURITY & FINANCIAL DOMAINS
9. SECURITY & COMPLIANCE
• Vulnerability scans
• Access reviews
• Compliance checks
• Security posture validation
Status: [✓ / ⚠ / ✗]
Owner: Security Lead
10. FINANCIAL VALIDATION
• Actual cost vs. forecast
• License consumption
• Cloud spend monitoring
• Cost optimization check
Status: [✓ / ⚠ / ✗]
Owner: FinOps Lead
STABILIZATION EXIT CRITERIA
Migration is confirmed when ALL criteria are met for the full period.
☑ 14 consecutive days of stability (configurable: 10–30 days)*
☑ Zero Severity 1 incidents
☑ ≤ 2 Severity 2 incidents (per day)
☑ MTTR for Sev 1 & 2 incidents ≤ 4 hours
☑ All 10 domain statuses are Stable (✓) throughout the period
☑ SLA/SLO compliance ≥ 99%
☑ User adoption ≥ target threshold
⚠ No open high-risk items in RAID Log
*Configuration based on system criticality, user volume, business impact, and regulatory requirements.
ALL CONDITIONS STABLE FOR REQUIRED PERIOD
→ MIGRATION CONFIRMED
Transition to Steady-State Operations
ANY INSTABILITY DETECTED
→ INVESTIGATE
→ CORRECT
→ REVALIDATE
Return to Affected Domain(s) & Repeat Stabilization
FEEDBACK LOOP (Continuous Improvement)
Instability / New Risk Identified → RAID Log / Risk Register Updated → Governance Control System (Upstream)
Insights drive updated risks, assumptions, controls, and execution adjustments.
DOMAIN OWNER ROLES (Examples)
DOMAIN CATEGORY | PRIMARY OWNER
Technical Stability (Domains 1–4) | Operations, Performance, Integration Leads
User & Adoption (Domains 5–6) | Product/UX, Org Enablement Leads
Operational & Governance (Domains 7–8) | Service Delivery, Change Management Leads
Risk, Security & Financial (Domains 9–10) | Security, FinOps Leads
STABILIZATION CADENCE
CADENCE | FOCUS | PARTICIPANTS
Daily Standup (15 min) | Incidents, alerts, blockers, risks | Ops, Sec, Perf, Delivery
Daily Monitoring (Real-time) | Telemetry, thresholds, performance | NOC / Ops Performance
Weekly Stabilization Review | Domain status, trends, risk review | All Domain Owners, Risk Owner
Weekly Executive Summary | Health, risks, progress | Steering Committee
Ad-hoc (Event-driven) | Major incidents, threshold breaches | Core Team + Stakeholders
KEY STABILIZATION METRICS (Examples)
METRIC | TARGET (EXAMPLE)
14-day Stability Window | 100% of days complete
Sev 1 Incidents | 0
Sev 2 Incidents (Per Day) | ≤ 2
MTTR (Sev 1 & 2) | ≤ 4 Hours
SLA/SLO Compliance | ≥ 99%
User Adoption | ≥ Target
High-Risk Open Items (RAID) | 0
CHANGE CONTROL (During Hypercare)
☑ Change freeze except critical fixes
☑ All changes require risk review & approval
☑ Backout plan required for all approved changes
☑ Emergency changes documented & reviewed
☑ Change metrics tracked daily
STABILITY IS NOT ASSUMED • IT IS PROVEN OVER TIME
Measure. Monitor. Respond. Validate. Confirm.

That verification must be structured, visible, and continuously measured.

What Must Be Monitored

Effective stabilization requires disciplined, structured visibility.

During hypercare:

Use a daily stabilization dashboard

Track incident count, severity, and response time

Identify recurring defects and patterns

Separate authentication and access issues from application defects

Monitor system performance under peak conditions

Validate integration behavior under load

And most critically:

Do not close the migration wave until:

Support teams confirm operational ownership

Business stakeholders confirm usability

System behavior remains stable over time

The Risk of Skipping Stabilization

Many organizations rush through this phase.

They assume:

"No major issues means success"

"Users can log in, so we're done"

This creates a dangerous gap.

Because instability rarely appears immediately.

It emerges:

Hours later

Days later

Under load

Across integrations

Within edge conditions

Skipping stabilization does not remove risk.

It delays its visibility.

Real-World Reality — Where Migrations Actually Break

Most migration failures do not occur during execution.

They occur after.

When:

Monitoring is incomplete

Alerts are misconfigured

Ownership is unclear

Issues are not triaged quickly

What appears as a successful migration becomes:

Performance degradation

Recurring incidents

User dissatisfaction

Loss of confidence

This is not an execution failure.

This is a stabilization failure.

Control Principle — Stability Must Be Proven Over Time

A system is not stable because it is operational.

It is stable because it continues to operate correctly under real conditions.

Monitoring and stabilization enforce this principle.

They ensure that:

Performance is sustained

Issues are detected early

Behavior is understood

Risk is continuously managed

This is where migration shifts from:

Execution

To

Operational control

Final Signature Anchor

A system that works is not enough.

A system that holds is what defines success.

Transition — From Stabilization to Adoption

Migration does not end when systems stabilize.

At this stage:

Performance is validated

Monitoring is active

The environment is technically sound

From an engineering perspective, the migration may appear complete.

But from a business perspective—

The most critical phase is just beginning.

A stable system does not guarantee a successful migration.

If:

Users do not adopt the new environment

Teams do not operate effectively within it

The organization reverts to legacy behaviors

Then the migration has not truly succeeded.

Stabilization confirms that the system works.

Adoption determines whether the organization moves forward.

This is where migration shifts from execution to transformation.

CHAPTER 10

The PRE-MORTEM Risk Discovery Framework™

A Structured Failure-First Model for Proactive Risk Identification and Mitigation

Most projects do not fail at the moment of collapse.

They fail quietly—long before execution begins.

Risks go unnoticed.

Assumptions go unchallenged.

Dependencies remain unvalidated.

By the time failure becomes visible, the cost of correction is higher, options are fewer, and control is already weakening.

This is the gap the PRE-MORTEM Risk Discovery Framework™ is designed to close.

Rather than waiting for risk to materialize, this framework forces risk to reveal itself early enough for action to be taken.

It is not a pessimistic exercise.

It is a control mechanism.

And in complex migration, infrastructure, and enterprise transformation programs, control begins long before execution.

Why This Framework Matters

Traditional risk identification often starts from the assumption that the plan is fundamentally sound and that risk is something to be documented as it appears.
But risk rarely announces itself politely.

It hides inside:

optimistic planning

incomplete dependency visibility

untested assumptions

weak cross-functional alignment

unchallenged confidence in execution readiness

That is why many programs appear well planned on paper and still fail in practice.

The issue is not that risk was absent.

The issue is that risk was not surfaced early enough, deeply enough, or honestly enough.

The PRE-MORTEM Risk Discovery Framework™ addresses that problem directly by reversing the mental model.

Instead of asking:

"What risks do we think might happen?"

it asks:

"The initiative has failed. What caused it?"

That shift is profound.

Because once failure is assumed, honesty becomes easier, hidden dependencies surface faster, and teams begin to think in terms of control rather than hope.

From Concept to Execution

The concept of the pre-mortem was originally introduced by Gary Klein as a way to imagine failure in advance and identify its likely causes before work proceeds. The technique is grounded in what Daniel Kahneman later termed prospective hindsight—the act of mentally projecting forward to a known failure and reasoning backward to its causes.

That concept is powerful.

But in many organizations, it remains informal:

A workshop

A brainstorming exercise

A one-time conversation

A risk discussion disconnected from delivery artifacts and governance

The PRE-MORTEM Risk Discovery Framework™ extends that original concept into a formal, repeatable methodology integrated with enterprise execution.

It moves pre-mortem thinking from:

A discussion → to a methodology

An exercise → to a governance mechanism

An idea → to an execution driver

This is what makes the framework valuable.

It does not stop at identifying failure.

It converts failure thinking into planning discipline, risk visibility, mitigation structure, and delivery control.

Framework Definition

The PRE-MORTEM Risk Discovery Framework™ is a proactive risk management model that simulates project failure in advance to systematically uncover hidden risks, challenge assumptions, and embed mitigation strategies into execution plans before work begins.

Unlike traditional risk identification approaches, this framework is:

Structured

Repeatable

Integrated with delivery artifacts

Aligned with executive governance

It is not merely about identifying what could go wrong.

It is about revealing what would otherwise remain invisible until it is too late.

We do not wait for risk to emerge—we force it to reveal itself.

Where It Applies

The PRE-MORTEM Framework™ is most effective where failure is costly, disruptive, or unacceptable.

It is especially valuable in:

Cloud migrations

Infrastructure transformations

Cybersecurity initiatives

Enterprise system implementations

Pre-cutover and go-live validation

It can be applied:

At project initiation

During planning phases

Before major milestones

Prior to production cutover

The more complex the initiative, the more valuable this framework becomes.

Because complexity increases hidden interdependencies.

And hidden interdependencies are where many failures begin.

What It Produces

When executed properly, the framework generates outcomes that are immediately useful to delivery governance. It produces:

An enhanced and more realistic risk register

A validated assumption log

A structured mitigation strategy

Cutover risk scenarios

Executive-level risk summaries

Risk-informed project planning

These are not theoretical outputs.

They are working control artifacts that shape readiness, sequencing, governance reviews, contingency planning, and execution decisions.

Most Teams Prepare for Success. High-Performing Teams Prepare for Failure.

Most teams prepare for success.

They build plans around how work is supposed to unfold, assuming alignment, stability, and cooperation.

They focus on:

milestones

timelines

deliverables

readiness claims

execution optimism

They ask:

How do we get there?

But they often avoid asking:

What could prevent us from getting there?

That is where fragility begins.

Because success and failure are not opposites.

Failure is often embedded inside success assumptions long before either outcome becomes visible.

High-performing teams take a different approach.

They prepare for failure.

Not because they expect to fail—but because they understand that every complex initiative contains:

Hidden risks

Fragile assumptions

Unseen dependencies

Points of misalignment

They ask:

Where will this fail—and how do we control it before it does?

This is not pessimism.

It is strategic realism.

When failure is anticipated:

Surprises are reduced

Decisions are faster

Mitigation is stronger

Teams remain in control

Failure loses much of its power when it is expected early enough to be governed.

This is exactly where the PRE-MORTEM Framework™ fits.

It operationalizes that philosophy.

Instead of hoping nothing goes wrong, it forces everything that could go wrong to surface early.

The P.R.E.M.O.T. Model™

The Operational Engine of the PRE-MORTEM Framework

The PRE-MORTEM Framework™ is executed through the P.R.E.M.O.T. Model™, which turns failure-first thinking into a structured sequence of discovery and control.

P — Project Failure Simulation

The process begins with a clear and intentional premise:

“The project has failed. What happened?”

This reframing disrupts optimism bias and gives teams permission to think critically, candidly, and without constraint.

The scope of the simulation may focus on:

The full project

A specific phase

A cutover event

A go-live milestone

The goal is not drama.

The goal is disciplined imagination grounded in operational reality.

R — Risk Brain Dump

Each participant independently documents possible causes of failure.

This step should be conducted silently before group discussion to:

eliminate groupthink

encourage candid thinking

surface individual insight

expose risks that might otherwise remain unspoken

Participants are encouraged to identify:

risks

assumptions

unknown variables

dependencies

weak points in readiness

This stage is deliberately broad.

At this point, capture matters more than refinement.

E — Expose & Share

Risks are then shared in a structured round-robin format.

The rules here matter:

no interruption

no filtering

no judgment

no immediate debate

All inputs are captured centrally.

This is where visibility begins.

Not every risk raised will become critical.

But every risk raised creates a chance for control.

M — Map & Cluster Risks

Once risks are exposed, they are grouped into meaningful domains to enable structured analysis. Typical categories include:

Technical (infrastructure, cloud, security)

Operational (runbooks, cutover readiness, support model)

Organizational (stakeholder alignment, resourcing, readiness)

Vendor / Third-party

Compliance / Regulatory

External dependencies

This stage transforms raw input into structured insight.

Patterns emerge here.

Clusters reveal concentration.

And concentration reveals where execution is most vulnerable.

O — Order & Prioritize

Not all risks deserve equal attention.

This stage introduces prioritization discipline using methods such as:

Likelihood × Impact scoring

MoSCoW classification (Must / Should / Could / Won't)

RED Lens filtering for critical exposure

This ensures attention is directed toward what truly threatens execution, rather than what merely sounds concerning.

Prioritization is where risk discovery begins to influence real planning.

T — Treat & Track

This is where discovery becomes governance.

Identified risks are converted into execution artifacts, including:

Mitigation strategies

Contingency plans

Assigned ownership

Tracking mechanisms

These outputs are then integrated into:

RAID logs

Project schedules

Governance reporting

Cutover runbooks

Without this step, the pre-mortem remains insight.

With this step, it becomes control.

Integration into Delivery

The PRE-MORTEM Framework™ does not operate in isolation. It is designed to strengthen the broader delivery model by:

Supporting risk management practices

Strengthening cutover readiness

Enhancing executive visibility

Aligning with governance cadence

That is what makes it foundational to risk assessment.

It complements the RAID-driven governance model you have already established, but it does something earlier and more surgical:

It reveals what the RAID log will need to govern.

RAID manages visible risk.

PRE-MORTEM helps make hidden risk visible first.

This is the key relationship.

The PRE-MORTEM Framework™ does not replace governance.

It strengthens governance by improving the quality, realism, and depth of what enters it.

The full structure of this framework can be visualized as a failure-first control model that integrates risk discovery directl into execution, governance, rollback strategy, and stabilization.

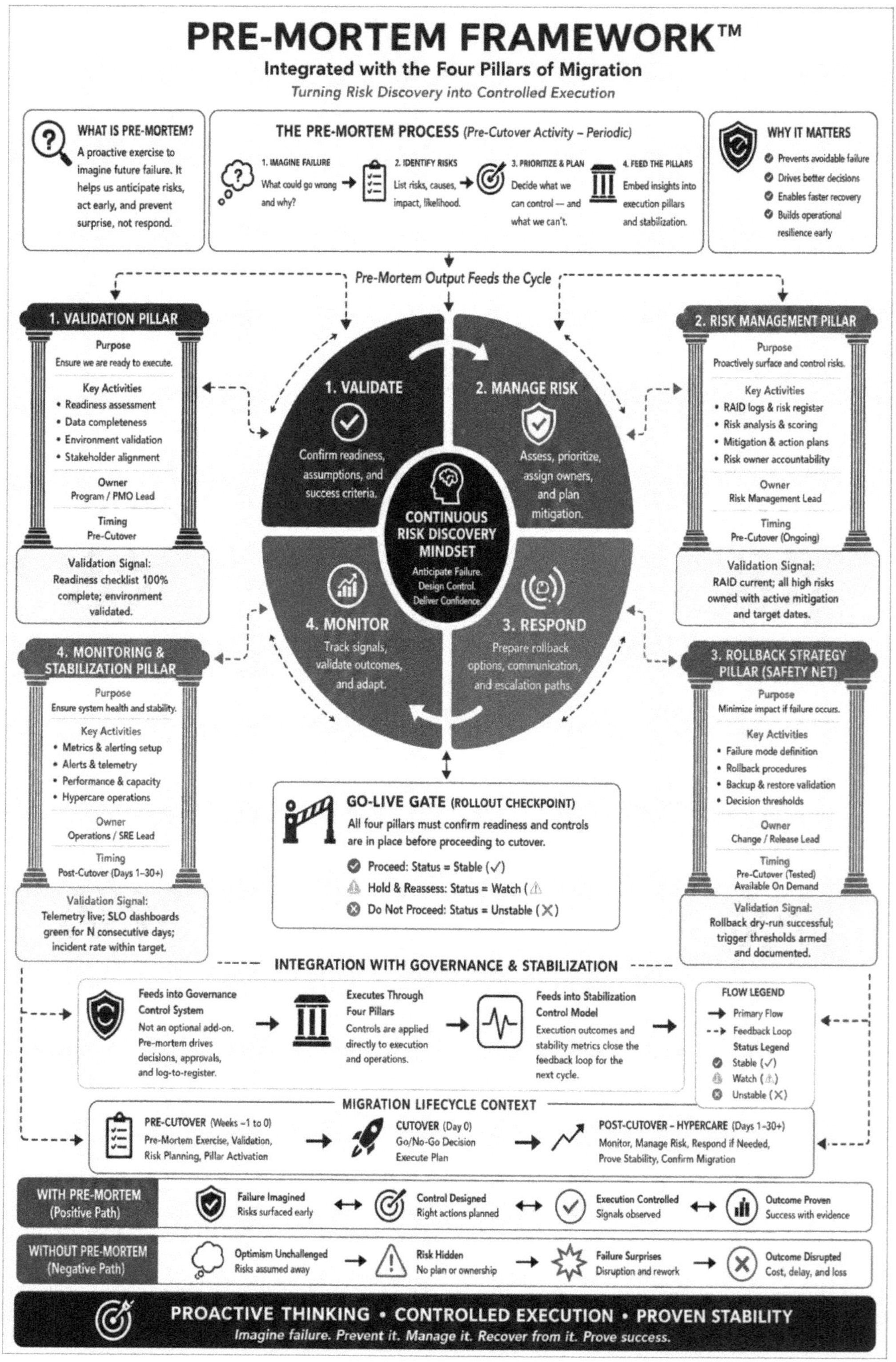
PRE-MORTEM FRAMEWORK™
Integrated with the Four Pillars of Migration
Turning Risk Discovery into Controlled Execution
WHAT IS PRE-MORTEM?
A proactive exercise to imagine future failure. It helps us anticipate risks, act early, and prevent surprise, not respond.
THE PRE-MORTEM PROCESS (Pre-Cutover Activity – Periodic)
1. IMAGINE FAILURE
What could go wrong and why?
2. IDENTIFY RISKS
List risks, causes, impact, likelihood.
3. PRIORITIZE & PLAN
Decide what we can control — and what we can't.
4. FEED THE PILLARS
Embed insights into execution pillars and stabilization.
WHY IT MATTERS
Prevents avoidable failure
Drives better decisions
Enables faster recovery
Builds operational resilience early
Pre-Mortem Output Feeds the Cycle
1. VALIDATION PILLAR
Purpose
Ensure we are ready to execute.
Key Activities
• Readiness assessment
• Data completeness
• Environment validation
• Stakeholder alignment
Owner
Program / PMO Lead
Timing
Pre-Cutover
Validation Signal:
Readiness checklist 100% complete; environment validated.
1. VALIDATE
Confirm readiness, assumptions, and success criteria.
2. MANAGE RISK
Assess, prioritize, assign owners, and plan mitigation.
CONTINUOUS RISK DISCOVERY MINDSET
Anticipate Failure. Design Control. Deliver Confidence.
4. MONITOR
Track signals, validate outcomes, and adapt.
3. RESPOND
Prepare rollback options, communication, and escalation paths.
2. RISK MANAGEMENT PILLAR
Purpose
Proactively surface and control risks.
Key Activities
• RAID logs & risk register
• Risk analysis & scoring
• Mitigation & action plans
• Risk owner accountability
Owner
Risk Management Lead
Timing
Pre-Cutover (Ongoing)
Validation Signal:
RAID current; all high risks owned with active mitigation and target dates.
4. MONITORING & STABILIZATION PILLAR
Purpose
Ensure system health and stability.
Key Activities
• Metrics & alerting setup
• Alerts & telemetry
• Performance & capacity
• Hypercare operations
Owner
Operations / SRE Lead
Timing
Post-Cutover (Days 1–30+)
Validation Signal:
Telemetry live; SLO dashboards green for N consecutive days; incident rate within target.
3. ROLLBACK STRATEGY PILLAR (SAFETY NET)
Purpose
Minimize impact if failure occurs.
Key Activities
• Failure mode definition
• Rollback procedures
• Backup & restore validation
• Decision thresholds
Owner
Change / Release Lead
Timing
Pre-Cutover (Tested)
Available On Demand
Validation Signal:
Rollback dry-run successful; trigger thresholds armed and documented.
GO-LIVE GATE (ROLLOUT CHECKPOINT)
All four pillars must confirm readiness and controls are in place before proceeding to cutover.
Proceed: Status = Stable (✓)
Hold & Reassess: Status = Watch (⚠)
Do Not Proceed: Status = Unstable (✕)
INTEGRATION WITH GOVERNANCE & STABILIZATION
Feeds into Governance Control System
Not an optional add-on. Pre-mortem drives decisions, approvals, and log-to-register.
Executes Through Four Pillars
Controls are applied directly to execution and operations.
Feeds into Stabilization Control Model
Execution outcomes and stability metrics close the feedback loop for the next cycle.
FLOW LEGEND
Primary Flow
Feedback Loop
Status Legend
Stable (✓)
Watch (⚠)
Unstable (✕)
MIGRATION LIFECYCLE CONTEXT
PRE-CUTOVER (Weeks –1 to 0)
Pre-Mortem Exercise, Validation, Risk Planning, Pillar Activation
CUTOVER (Day 0)
Go/No-Go Decision
Execute Plan
POST-CUTOVER – HYPERCARE (Days 1–30+)
Monitor, Manage Risk, Respond if Needed, Prove Stability, Confirm Migration
WITH PRE-MORTEM (Positive Path)
Failure Imagined
Risks surfaced early
Control Designed
Right actions planned
Execution Controlled
Signals observed
Outcome Proven
Success with evidence
WITHOUT PRE-MORTEM (Negative Path)
Optimism Unchallenged
Risks assumed away
Risk Hidden
No plan or ownership
Failure Surprises
Disruption and rework
Outcome Disrupted
Cost, delay, and loss
PROACTIVE THINKING • CONTROLLED EXECUTION • PROVEN STABILITY
Imagine failure. Prevent it. Manage it. Recover from it. Prove success.

This model makes one thing clear: pre-mortem thinking is not an isolated exercise—

It is a continuous control mechanism that connects risk discovery to validation, governance, execution, and operational stability.

Why This Framework Elevates Execution

Most teams prepare for success.

High-performing teams prepare for failure.

At first glance, that sounds ironic.

Why prepare for failure if the goal is success?

Because success is not the absence of failure.

It is the management of failure before it happens.

That is the deeper contribution of this framework.

It gives teams:

A structured way to challenge optimism

A disciplined way to uncover hidden risk

A repeatable method for turning failure scenarios into mitigation strategies

A governance-ready mechanism for integrating discovery into delivery

This is how teams move from:

Fragile planning → resilient planning

Reactive firefighting → controlled execution

Confidence alone → confidence with evidence

Control Principle — Failure Must Be Simulated Before It Can Be Controlled

The strongest plans are not the ones built only around how work should succeed.
They are the ones that have already examined how work could fail.

The PRE-MORTEM Risk Discovery Framework™ enforces this principle.

It makes failure thinkable before it becomes visible.

And by making failure thinkable, it makes control possible.

Most teams prepare for success.

High-performing teams prepare for failure.

Because when failure is expected, it can be managed.

And when it is managed, it no longer dictates the outcome.

PART VI

Organizational Change Management

Why most migrations fail due to people, not technology — and how adoption is engineered into the work.

CHAPTER 11

Why Most Migrations Fail Due to People, Not Technology

Many migration programs fail for reasons that have nothing to do with technology.

Systems are deployed successfully.

Environments are stabilized.

Architectures are modernized.

And yet—disruption follows.

Users struggle to perform their work.

Support teams are unprepared to troubleshoot.

Business units experience slowdowns, confusion, or resistance.

Leaders question whether the migration delivered its intended value.

The issue is not that the migration failed technically.

The issue is that the organization was not prepared to move with it.

Migration is often treated as a technical event—planned, executed, and completed once systems are live.

But migration is not just a system transition.

It is an organizational shift.

It changes how people work, how teams operate, how support functions respond, and how the business moves forward.

When that shift is not managed deliberately, even a technically successful migration can fail in practice.

This is where most migration strategies fall short.

They focus heavily on delivery—systems, infrastructure, data, and execution.

But they overlook adoption—how people understand, accept, and operate within the new environment.

Delivery moves the system.

Adoption moves the organization.

To successfully navigate this gap, change management must be approached as a structured discipline—not an afterthought.

It requires:

Clear communication aligned to business outcomes

Stakeholder engagement before and during migration

Role-based training and operational readiness

Support structures that extend beyond cutover

Reinforcement mechanisms that sustain the change

Without these elements, organizations revert to familiar behaviors—even when better systems are in place.

This chapter introduces a structured approach to managing adoption in migration programs.

It begins by establishing the role of change management as a parallel discipline to migration delivery.

It then introduces two complementary models:

The Prosci Change Management Framework, which defines how organizations prepare for, manage, and reinforce change at scale

The ADKAR Model, which explains how individuals adopt change through awareness, desire, knowledge, ability, and reinforcement

Together, these models provide a complete view of change:

From organizational alignment

To individual adoption

To sustained transformation

Migration success is not achieved at cutover.

It is achieved when the organization moves forward—confidently, consistently, and without reverting back.

Delivery enables change.

Adoption makes it permanent.

Change Management & Adoption in Migration Programs (Using ADKAR)

If migration delivery ensures that systems are moved successfully, adoption ensures that the organization is able to use what has been delivered.

This distinction is often overlooked.

In many migration programs, success is measured by technical completion—

Systems deployed, environments stabilized, and platforms modernized.

But these milestones only represent one dimension of success.

True success is realized when the organization operates effectively in the new environment.

This section establishes the role of change management as a parallel discipline to migration delivery and introduces adoption as a structured capability that must be intentionally designed and executed.

Why Adoption Determines Migration Success

Migration programs are often judged by technical milestones—systems moved, environments stabilized, platforms modernized.

But technical completion does not equal success.

A migration is only successful when:

Users adopt the new environment

Teams operate effectively within it

The organization sustains the change over time

Without adoption, even the most well-executed migration will fail to deliver its intended value.

This is where change management becomes essential.

Delivery vs. Adoption — Two Different Disciplines

Migration delivery and change adoption operate in parallel but serve different purposes.

Delivery (Migration Master Framework)

Focuses on systems, data, architecture, and execution

Adoption (Change Management)

Focuses on people, behavior, and sustained usage

One delivers the change.

The other ensures the change is actually used.

These disciplines should be aligned—but not confused.

Introducing ADKAR as a Supporting Model

One of several models' organizations may use to support adoption is the ADKAR® model, developed by Prosci®.

ADKAR provides a structured approach to understanding how individuals move through change.

It focuses on five key elements:

Awareness — Do people understand why the change is necessary?

Desire — Do they want to support the change?

Knowledge — Do they know how to change?

Ability — Can they perform in the new environment?

Reinforcement — Is the change sustained over time?

ADKAR does not manage the migration itself—it supports how people adopt what has been delivered.

Applying ADKAR in Migration Programs

ADKAR is most effective when applied alongside migration efforts—not embedded within them.

1. Awareness — Establishing the "Why"

Before or during early migration phases:

Communicate the purpose of the migration

Highlight risks of staying in the current state

Align messaging with business outcomes (security, scalability, compliance)

Without awareness, resistance begins early—even before execution starts.

2. Desire — Gaining Buy-In

Adoption depends on willingness, not just instruction, and that requires human connection.

How do we build desire? It is rhetorical.

Leadership needs to engage stakeholders early in the discussion

Address concerns (job impact, workflow disruption, learning curve)

Position benefits at the individual and team level

Desire is often the most underestimated—and most critical—component.

3. Knowledge — Enabling the Transition

Once direction is clear:

Provide training materials

Develop runbooks and user guides

Prepare support teams and operational staff

Knowledge ensures people understand what to do—but not yet how well they can do it.

4. Ability — Executing in the New Environment

This is where adoption becomes real:

Hands-on usage

Troubleshooting capability

Real-world execution under live conditions

Ability is proven through performance—not training completion.

5. Reinforcement — Sustaining the Change

After go-live:

Monitor adoption metrics

Enforce new processes and controls

Provide ongoing support and feedback loops

Without reinforcement, organizations revert to legacy behaviors.

That alone answers the question: migration fails not because technology fails, but because leadership fails to remove the old habit.

People are the most trainable beings.

The core principles behind operant conditioning, formalized by B. F. Skinner and grounded in the broader behavioral tradition that includes Pavlov, are not limited to animals—they apply to human behavior as well and help explain how patterns are formed, repeated, and sustained.

Behavior follows reinforcement.

If old behaviors are not actively replaced, they will return.

This is where the law of tradeoff applies: something of lower value must be intentionally replaced with something of higher value.

Without that exchange—without reinforcement—change does not sustain.

This is not theory—it is observable behavior.

What is reinforced is repeated.

What is not reinforced is forgotten.

Human behavior is shaped through reinforcement.

When a new system is introduced but old behaviors remain easier, familiar, or unchallenged, users will revert.

Adoption occurs only when the new behavior is consistently reinforced and supported.

Key Principle — Separation of Concerns

It is important to maintain a clear boundary:

The Migration Master Framework governs how systems are delivered.

ADKAR supports how people adopt that delivery.

Blending the two can create confusion and dilute execution clarity.

Keeping them separate preserves the strength of both.

When to Use ADKAR (and When Not To)

ADKAR is most valuable when:

The migration significantly impacts users or workflows

Organizational change is required across teams

Adoption risk is high

It is less critical when:

Changes are purely backend with minimal user impact

Adoption is automatic or enforced by system design

Not every migration requires formal change management—but many benefit from it.

A migration becomes sustainable

only when the organization can operate

in the new state without resistance,

confusion,

or regression.

It is achieved when the organization moves forward—

confidently,

consistently,

and without reverting back.

Delivery enables change.

Adoption makes it permanent.

Prosci® Change Management Framework

While adoption occurs at the individual level, successful transformation requires structure at the organizational level.

Change must be coordinated, communicated, and reinforced across teams, functions, and leadership layers.

Without this structure, even well-designed adoption efforts become fragmented, inconsistent, and difficult to sustain.

The Prosci Change Management Framework provides a practical model for managing change at scale—

Ensuring that stakeholders are aligned, communication is structured, and adoption is reinforced throughout the migration lifecycle.

While ADKAR explains how individuals adopt change, the Prosci framework defines how organizations structure and govern that change at scale.

Prosci organizes change management into three broad stages:

Prepare the organization

Manage the change

Reinforce the change

In migration programs, this provides a practical structure for aligning sponsors, managers, users, and support teams before, during, and after go-live.

Prepare the Organization

Prepare the Organization means establishing the conditions required for change before execution begins.

This includes:

Identifying impacted groups (stakeholder and user analysis)

Sponsor alignment

Impact assessment

Assessing adoption risk

Defining the change story

Planning communication and training (Training strategy)

At this stage, the organization builds clarity before disruption occurs.

Manage the Change

Managing the change means guiding people through the transition as the migration progresses:

Executing the communication plan

Equipping managers to support their teams (manager coaching)

Delivering training

Help desk readiness

Role-based training

Monitoring adoption signals

Responding to resistance

This is the active management layer of organizational transformation, because it is intentionally communicated and deliberately guided. That fulfills the why.

Reinforce the Change

Reinforcement ensures the organization does not drift back to old behaviors after go-live.

Adoption metrics

Sustaining new behaviors

Ticket trend review

Lessons learned

Refresher training

Closing gaps

Celebrating progress

Preventing reversion to old workarounds

Leadership reinforcement

Without reinforcement, the change may be implemented—but not sustained. This is what we call leadership in execution.

The ADKAR® Adoption Model

If organizational change defines the structure of transformation, individual adoption determines whether that transformation is realized.

Change does not happen at the system level—it happens at the individual level.

Each user, operator, and support team member must transition from the old way of working to the new.

The ADKAR model translates adoption into measurable conditions that can be actively managed during migration.

It defines five essential elements required for successful change:

Awareness — Understanding Why the Change Is Necessary

People understand why the migration is happening and why staying in the old state is no longer viable.

In migration programs, awareness answers the first and most important question:

Why are we changing at all?

Without awareness, users interpret migration as disruption rather than progress.

Desire — Willingness to Support and Participate in the Change

Stakeholders and users are willing to support and participate in the change.

Desire cannot be mandated.

It must be influenced through trust, relevance, and clear benefit.

In practice, desire grows when people understand how the migration improves their environment, protects the business, or reduces future pain.

Knowledge — Knowing How to Operate in the New Environment

Users, managers, and support teams know what to do in the new environment.

This includes:

Process understanding

Tool familiarity

Role-specific expectations

Support procedures

Knowledge prepares people for the transition, but does not yet confirm readiness under real conditions.

Ability — Demonstrating Performance in Real-World Conditions

People can successfully perform the work after go-live with the tools and support provided.

Ability is where theoretical readiness becomes operational reality.

It is demonstrated through:

Hands-on use

Successful task completion

Problem resolution

Performance under real-world conditions

This is why training alone is never enough.

Reinforcement — Sustaining the Change Over Time

It is what turns change into permanence.

It includes:

Leadership reinforcement

Support follow-through

Monitoring adoption signals

Correcting regressions

Maintaining accountability for the new state

Without reinforcement, adoption decays.

These elements provide a practical framework for ensuring that adoption is not assumed—but achieved.

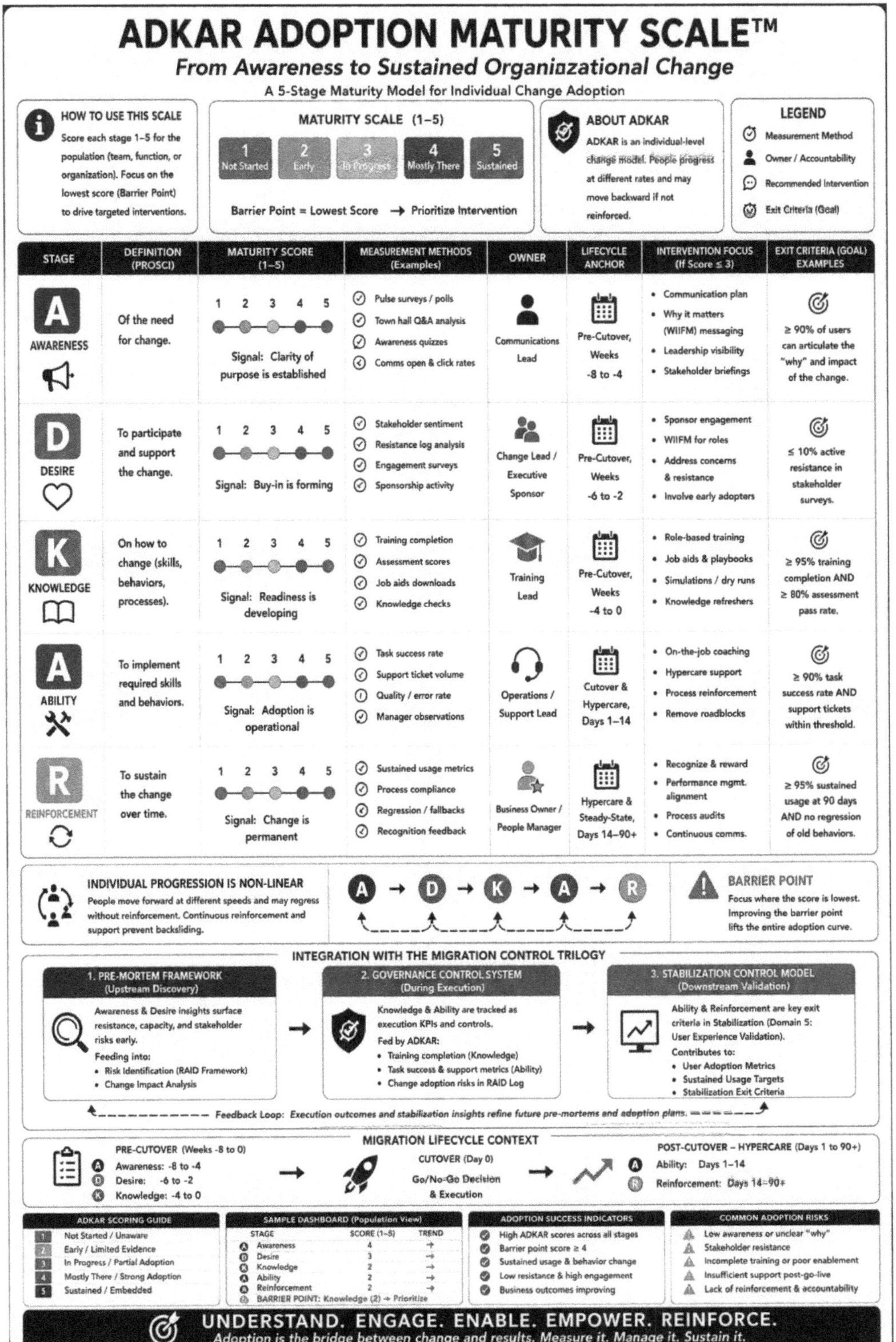
ADKAR ADOPTION MATURITY SCALE™
From Awareness to Sustained Organiozational Change
A 5-Stage Maturity Model for Individual Change Adoption
HOW TO USE THIS SCALE
Score each stage 1–5 for the population (team, function, or organization). Focus on the lowest score (Barrier Point) to drive targeted interventions.
MATURITY SCALE (1–5)
1 Not Started
2 Early
3 In Progress
4 Mostly There
5 Sustained
Barrier Point = Lowest Score → Prioritize Intervention
ABOUT ADKAR
ADKAR is an individual-level change model. People progress at different rates and may move backward if not reinforced.
LEGEND
Measurement Method
Owner / Accountability
Recommended Intervention
Exit Criteria (Goal)
STAGE
DEFINITION (PROSCI)
MATURITY SCORE (1–5)
MEASUREMENT METHODS (Examples)
OWNER
LIFECYCLE ANCHOR
INTERVENTION FOCUS (If Score ≤ 3)
EXIT CRITERIA (GOAL) EXAMPLES
A AWARENESS
Of the need for change.
1 2 3 4 5
Signal: Clarity of purpose is established
Pulse surveys / polls
Town hall Q&A analysis
Awareness quizzes
Comms open & click rates
Communications Lead
Pre-Cutover, Weeks -8 to -4
Communication plan
Why it matters (WIIFM) messaging
Leadership visibility
Stakeholder briefings
≥ 90% of users can articulate the "why" and impact of the change.
D DESIRE
To participate and support the change.
1 2 3 4 5
Signal: Buy-in is forming
Stakeholder sentiment
Resistance log analysis
Engagement surveys
Sponsorship activity
Change Lead / Executive Sponsor
Pre-Cutover, Weeks -6 to -2
Sponsor engagement
WIIFM for roles
Address concerns & resistance
Involve early adopters
≤ 10% active resistance in stakeholder surveys.
K KNOWLEDGE
On how to change (skills, behaviors, processes).
1 2 3 4 5
Signal: Readiness is developing
Training completion
Assessment scores
Job aids downloads
Knowledge checks
Training Lead
Pre-Cutover, Weeks -4 to 0
Role-based training
Job aids & playbooks
Simulations / dry runs
Knowledge refreshers
≥ 95% training completion AND ≥ 80% assessment pass rate.
A ABILITY
To implement required skills and behaviors.
1 2 3 4 5
Signal: Adoption is operational
Task success rate
Support ticket volume
Quality / error rate
Manager observations
Operations / Support Lead
Cutover & Hypercare, Days 1–14
On-the-job coaching
Hypercare support
Process reinforcement
Remove roadblocks
≥ 90% task success rate AND support tickets within threshold.
R REINFORCEMENT
To sustain the change over time.
1 2 3 4 5
Signal: Change is permanent
Sustained usage metrics
Process compliance
Regression / fallbacks
Recognition feedback
Business Owner / People Manager
Hypercare & Steady-State, Days 14–90+
Recognize & reward
Performance mgmt. alignment
Process audits
Continuous comms.
≥ 95% sustained usage at 90 days AND no regression of old behaviors.
INDIVIDUAL PROGRESSION IS NON-LINEAR
People move forward at different speeds and may regress without reinforcement. Continuous reinforcement and support prevent backsliding.
A → D → K → A → R
BARRIER POINT
Focus where the score is lowest. Improving the barrier point lifts the entire adoption curve.
INTEGRATION WITH THE MIGRATION CONTROL TRILOGY
1. PRE-MORTEM FRAMEWORK (Upstream Discovery)
Awareness & Desire insights surface resistance, capacity, and stakeholder risks early.
Feeding into:
Risk Identification (RAID Framework)
Change Impact Analysis
2. GOVERNANCE CONTROL SYSTEM (During Execution)
Knowledge & Ability are tracked as execution KPIs and controls.
Fed by ADKAR:
Training completion (Knowledge)
Task success & support metrics (Ability)
Change adoption risks in RAID Log
3. STABILIZATION CONTROL MODEL (Downstream Validation)
Ability & Reinforcement are key exit criteria in Stabilization (Domain 5: User Experience Validation).
Contributes to:
User Adoption Metrics
Sustained Usage Targets
Stabilization Exit Criteria
Feedback Loop: Execution outcomes and stabilization insights refine future pre-mortems and adoption plans.
MIGRATION LIFECYCLE CONTEXT
PRE-CUTOVER (Weeks -8 to 0)
Awareness: -8 to -4
Desire: -6 to -2
Knowledge: -4 to 0
CUTOVER (Day 0)
Go/No-Go Decision & Execution
POST-CUTOVER – HYPERCARE (Days 1 to 90+)
Ability: Days 1–14
Reinforcement: Days 14–90+
ADKAR SCORING GUIDE
1 Not Started / Unaware
2 Early / Limited Evidence
3 In Progress / Partial Adoption
4 Mostly There / Strong Adoption
5 Sustained / Embedded
SAMPLE DASHBOARD (Population View)
STAGE SCORE (1–5) TREND
Awareness 4 →
Desire 3 →
Knowledge 2 →
Ability 2 →
Reinforcement 2 →
BARRIER POINT: Knowledge (2) → Prioritize
ADOPTION SUCCESS INDICATORS
High ADKAR scores across all stages
Barrier point score ≥ 4
Sustained usage & behavior change
Low resistance & high engagement
Business outcomes improving
COMMON ADOPTION RISKS
Low awareness or unclear "why"
Stakeholder resistance
Incomplete training or poor enablement
Insufficient support post-go-live
Lack of reinforcement & accountability
UNDERSTAND. ENGAGE. ENABLE. EMPOWER. REINFORCE.
Adoption is the bridge between change and results. Measure it. Manage it. Sustain it.

Operationalizing ADKAR in Migration Programs

A migration PM can operationalize ADKAR by mapping each impacted group to the communications, training, coaching, access, and reinforcement actions needed before cutover and during hypercare.

That means:

Ensuring awareness before technical disruption begins

Building desire before resistance hardens

Delivering knowledge before new workflows are expected

Confirming ability during early live usage

Reinforcing the change before cutover and during hypercare

ADKAR provides a practical lens for evaluating whether the organization is truly moving with the migration—or merely being pushed through it.

Together, these models ensure that migration is not only delivered successfully—but adopted, sustained, and embedded into how the organization operates.

PART VII

Migration Leadership and Communication

Executive reporting, communication matrix, and the cross-functional governance that keeps stakeholders aligned.

CHAPTER 12

Executive Reporting and Migration Metrics

Migration success is not driven by execution alone.

It is driven by clarity.

And clarity is created through communication.

Communication is the protagonist for project success.

It is the mechanism through which:

Alignment is maintained

Risk is surfaced

Decisions are accelerated

Accountability is enforced

Without communication, even well-structured programs begin to drift.

With it, complex migrations remain coordinated, visible, and controlled.

Executives do not need detail.

They need clarity.

They need to understand the state of the program quickly, confidently, and without ambiguity.

Across migration programs, leadership is consistently focused on five core questions:

Are we on schedule?

Are we within budget?

What risks could affect delivery?

Is the solution stable?

Is the organization realizing business value?

Effective executive reporting answers these questions directly.

The most effective dashboards combine:

Milestone status

Financial health

Top risks

Operational indicators

Benefits realization

All presented using:

Simple RAG (Red, Amber, Green) status

Clear trend indicators

Concise commentary

The goal is not to report activity.

The goal is to enable decisions.

EXECUTIVE METRIC FRAMEWORK™

Executive Summary Layer for Migration Success

Aligning Stakeholders, Reporting, and Decision-Making in Migration

METRIC CATEGORY	WHAT LEADERSHIP WANTS TO KNOW	KEY METRICS & THRESHOLDS (Examples)	SAMPLE DASHBOARD VALUES (Current)	STATUS (RAG)	REPORTING CADENCE	OWNER (Accountability)
1. SCHEDULE PERFORMANCE	Are milestones on track? • Milestone completion • Schedule variance • Critical path status	• Schedule Performance Index (SPI) ≥ 0.95 • Milestone slip ≤ 5 days • % Critical path tasks on track ≥ 90%	SPI: 0.96 Milestone Slip: +2 days Critical Path On Track: 92%		Weekly Steering	Program / PMO Lead
2. FINANCIAL HEALTH	Is spend controlled? • Cost performance • Burn rate • Forecast accuracy	• Cost Performance Index (CPI) ≥ 0.95 • Burn rate vs. forecast within ±5% • Forecast variance ≤ ±5%	CPI: 0.97 Burn Rate Variance: -2% Forecast Variance: -1.2%		Monthly Steering	FinOps Lead / Finance Partner
3. RISK EXPOSURE	What could derail delivery? • Top risks • Issue aging • Dependencies	• Open Sev 1 risks: 0 • Open Sev 2 risks: ≤ 3 • Issue aging > 14 days: ≤ 5 • Blocked dependencies: 0	Open Sev 1: 0 Open Sev 2: 2 Issues > 14 Days: 3 Blocked dependencies: 0		Weekly Steering	Risk Management Lead
4. OPERATIONAL STABILITY	Is the environment reliable? • Uptime & availability • Incident impact • Delivery stability	• Uptime ≥ 99.9% • MTTR (Mean Time To Recover) ≤ 4 hrs • Incidents Sev 1: 0 / Sev 2: ≤ 2 • Deployment success rate ≥ 95%	Uptime: 99.97% MTTR: 2.1 hrs Sev 1: 0 | Sev 2: 1 Deploy Success: 96%		Weekly Steering	Operations / SRE Lead
5. BUSINESS VALUE	Did the migration create value? • Value realization • Benefits vs. business case • ROI / payback	• Benefits realized vs. plan ≥ 85% • Cost savings vs. business case ≥ 80% • ROI trend: Positive • Payback period ≤ Target	Benefits Realized: 88% Cost Savings: 82% ROI Trend: Positive Payback: On Track		Monthly Steering	Business Sponsor / Value Owner
6. PEOPLE & ADOPTION	Are people adopting the change? • Adoption level • Training completion • Resistance level	• ADKAR Overall Score ≥ 3.5 / 5 • Training completion ≥ 95% • Active resistance ≤ 10% • Usage vs. target ≥ 90%	ADKAR Score: 3.8 / 5 Training Completion: 96% Active Resistance: 7% Usage vs Target: 91%		Weekly Steering	Change Lead / People Manager
7. QUALITY	Is quality maintained? • Defects & incidents • SLA adherence • Test & release quality	• Defect escape rate ≤ 5% • SLA compliance ≥ 98% • Sev 1 defects post-release: 0 • Test pass rate ≥ 95%	Defect Escape Rate: 3.2% SLA Compliance: 98.6% Sev 1 Defects: 0 Test Pass Rate: 96%		Weekly Steering	QA Lead / Quality Manager
8. COMPLIANCE & ASSURANCE	Are we compliant and in control? • Control effectiveness • Audit & findings • Regulatory posture	• Critical controls effective ≥ 95% • High audit findings: 0 open • Policy compliance ≥ 98% • Regulatory issues: 0	Critical Controls: 97% High Audit Findings: 0 Policy Compliance: 98.5% Regulatory Issues: 0		Monthly Steering	Compliance Lead / Audit Partner

STATUS (RAG): On Track (Meets Threshold) · At Risk (Near Threshold) · Off Track (Below Threshold)

BARRIER POINT = Lowest scoring category. Focus here to lift the entire adoption and performance curve.

AUDIENCE MAP – WHO CARES ABOUT WHAT?

STEERING COMMITTEE	CFO	CIO / CTO	BUSINESS SPONSOR	COO / OPERATIONS	CHANGE LEADER
All 8 Categories (Enterprise View)	Financial Health Business Value Compliance	Operational Stability Risk Exposure Quality	Schedule Performance Business Value People & Adoption	Operational Stability Schedule Performance Quality	People & Adoption Schedule Performance Risk Exposure

INTEGRATION WITH THE MIGRATION CONTROL TRILOGY + ADKAR

1. PRE-MORTEM FRAMEWORK (Upstream Discovery)

Surfaces risks, resistance, capacity, and stakeholder concerns early.

Feeds Metrics:
- Risk Exposure (Category 3)
- People & Adoption (Category 6)

→ **2. GOVERNANCE CONTROL SYSTEM (During Execution)**

Executes controls and tracks performance.

Feeds Metrics:
- Schedule (Category 1)
- Financial (Category 2)
- Risk (Category 3)
- People & Adoption (Category 6)

→ **3. STABILIZATION CONTROL MODEL (Downstream Validation)**

Proves stability and validates outcomes during Hypercare.

Feeds Metrics:
- Operational Stability (Category 4)
- Quality (Category 7)
- Business Value (Category 5)

→ **4. ADKAR ADOPTION MATURITY SCALE (Human Change Adoption)**

Measures individual adoption maturity and change sustainment.

Feeds Metrics:
- People & Adoption (Category 6)
- Business Value (Category 5)

→ **5. EXECUTIVE METRIC FRAMEWORK (Executive Summary Layer)**

Aggregates signals for leadership visibility and decisions.

Feeds Decisions:
- Go / No-Go
- Investment
- Mitigation
- Operating
- Change

FEEDBACK LOOP: Lessons learned and updated risks flow upstream to refine pre-mortems, controls, and adoption plans.

METRICS DRIVE DECISIONS

GO / NO-GO DECISIONS (Schedule & Risk)
- Cutover readiness
- Scope adjustments
- Dependency resolution

INVESTMENT DECISIONS (Financial & Value)
- Budget reallocation
- Benefit realization focus
- ROI / payback tracking

MITIGATION DECISIONS (Risk & Quality)
- Risk treatment
- Quality issue resolution
- Escalation management

OPERATING DECISIONS (Operational & Quality)
- Support scaling
- Performance tuning
- Problem management

CHANGE DECISIONS (Adoption & People)
- Communication strategy
- Training / enablement focus
- Reinforcement actions

MIGRATION LIFECYCLE CONTEXT

PRE-CUTOVER (Weeks -8 to 0)
Focus: Planning, Readiness, Training, Risk Discovery

→ **CUTOVER** (Day 0)
Focus: Execution, Go/No-Go, Stabilization Kickoff

→ **HYPERCARE** (Days 1 to 30+)
Focus: Stability, Adoption, Performance, Issue Resolution

→ **STEADY-STATE** (Days 30+ to 90+)
Focus: Value Realization, Optimization, Sustainment

INFORM. ALIGN. DECIDE. ACT.

Executive metrics are not status updates. They are decision enablers.

Program Communication Matrix

Communication must be intentional.

It cannot be left to chance or personality.

A structured communication model ensures that:

The right stakeholders receive the right information

At the right time

In the right format

From the right owner

A strong communication matrix answers five essential questions:

Who needs the information?

Why do they need it?

How often do they need it?

How will it be delivered?

Who is responsible for delivering it?

This structure transforms communication from informal updates into a controlled delivery mechanism.

This communication structure can be visualized as a control system—

Where reporting, stakeholder alignment, governance, and decision flow operate together to ensure execution remains coordinated and visible.

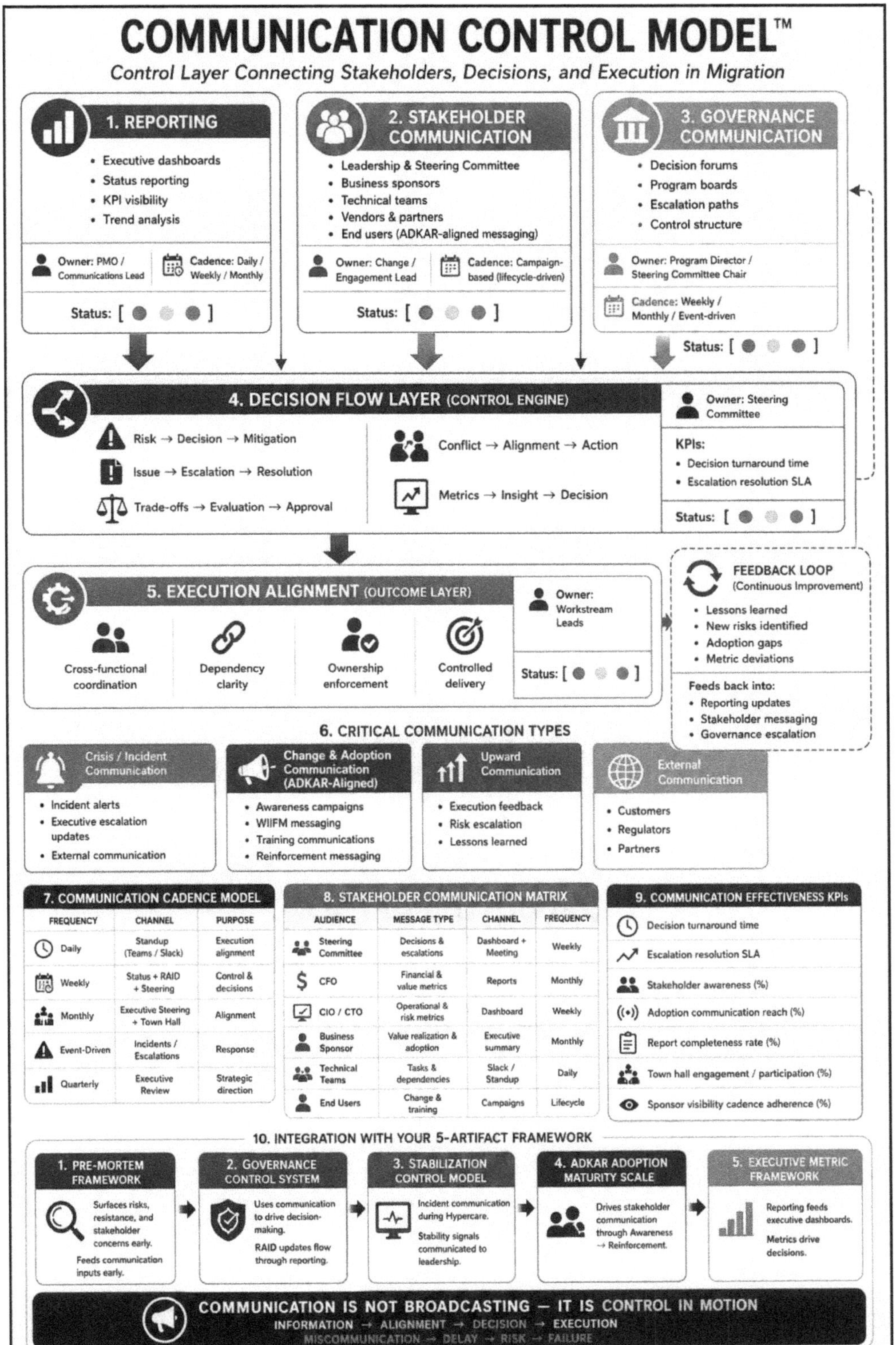
COMMUNICATION CONTROL MODEL™
Control Layer Connecting Stakeholders, Decisions, and Execution in Migration
1. REPORTING
Executive dashboards
Status reporting
KPI visibility
Trend analysis
Owner: PMO / Communications Lead
Cadence: Daily / Weekly / Monthly
Status:
2. STAKEHOLDER COMMUNICATION
Leadership & Steering Committee
Business sponsors
Technical teams
Vendors & partners
End users (ADKAR-aligned messaging)
Owner: Change / Engagement Lead
Cadence: Campaign-based (lifecycle-driven)
Status:
3. GOVERNANCE COMMUNICATION
Decision forums
Program boards
Escalation paths
Control structure
Owner: Program Director / Steering Committee Chair
Cadence: Weekly / Monthly / Event-driven
Status:
4. DECISION FLOW LAYER (CONTROL ENGINE)
Risk → Decision → Mitigation
Issue → Escalation → Resolution
Trade-offs → Evaluation → Approval
Conflict → Alignment → Action
Metrics → Insight → Decision
Owner: Steering Committee
KPIs:
Decision turnaround time
Escalation resolution SLA
Status:
5. EXECUTION ALIGNMENT (OUTCOME LAYER)
Cross-functional coordination
Dependency clarity
Ownership enforcement
Controlled delivery
Owner: Workstream Leads
Status:
FEEDBACK LOOP (Continuous Improvement)
Lessons learned
New risks identified
Adoption gaps
Metric deviations
Feeds back into:
Reporting updates
Stakeholder messaging
Governance escalation
6. CRITICAL COMMUNICATION TYPES
Crisis / Incident Communication
Incident alerts
Executive escalation updates
External communication
Change & Adoption Communication (ADKAR-Aligned)
Awareness campaigns
WIIFM messaging
Training communications
Reinforcement messaging
Upward Communication
Execution feedback
Risk escalation
Lessons learned
External Communication
Customers
Regulators
Partners
7. COMMUNICATION CADENCE MODEL
FREQUENCY | CHANNEL | PURPOSE
Daily | Standup (Teams / Slack) | Execution alignment
Weekly | Status + RAID + Steering | Control & decisions
Monthly | Executive Steering + Town Hall | Alignment
Event-Driven | Incidents / Escalations | Response
Quarterly | Executive Review | Strategic direction
8. STAKEHOLDER COMMUNICATION MATRIX
AUDIENCE | MESSAGE TYPE | CHANNEL | FREQUENCY
Steering Committee | Decisions & escalations | Dashboard + Meeting | Weekly
CFO | Financial & value metrics | Reports | Monthly
CIO / CTO | Operational & risk metrics | Dashboard | Weekly
Business Sponsor | Value realization & adoption | Executive summary | Monthly
Technical Teams | Tasks & dependencies | Slack / Standup | Daily
End Users | Change & training | Campaigns | Lifecycle
9. COMMUNICATION EFFECTIVENESS KPIs
Decision turnaround time
Escalation resolution SLA
Stakeholder awareness (%)
Adoption communication reach (%)
Report completeness rate (%)
Town hall engagement / participation (%)
Sponsor visibility cadence adherence (%)
10. INTEGRATION WITH YOUR 5-ARTIFACT FRAMEWORK
1. PRE-MORTEM FRAMEWORK
Surfaces risks, resistance, and stakeholder concerns early.
Feeds communication inputs early.
2. GOVERNANCE CONTROL SYSTEM
Uses communication to drive decision-making.
RAID updates flow through reporting.
3. STABILIZATION CONTROL MODEL
Incident communication during Hypercare.
Stability signals communicated to leadership.
4. ADKAR ADOPTION MATURITY SCALE
Drives stakeholder communication through Awareness → Reinforcement.
5. EXECUTIVE METRIC FRAMEWORK
Reporting feeds executive dashboards.
Metrics drive decisions.
COMMUNICATION IS NOT BROADCASTING — IT IS CONTROL IN MOTION
INFORMATION → ALIGNMENT → DECISION → EXECUTION
MISCOMMUNICATION → DELAY → RISK → FAILURE

Each layer of this model represents a control point—ensuring that information is not only shared, but translated into aligned decisions and controlled execution.

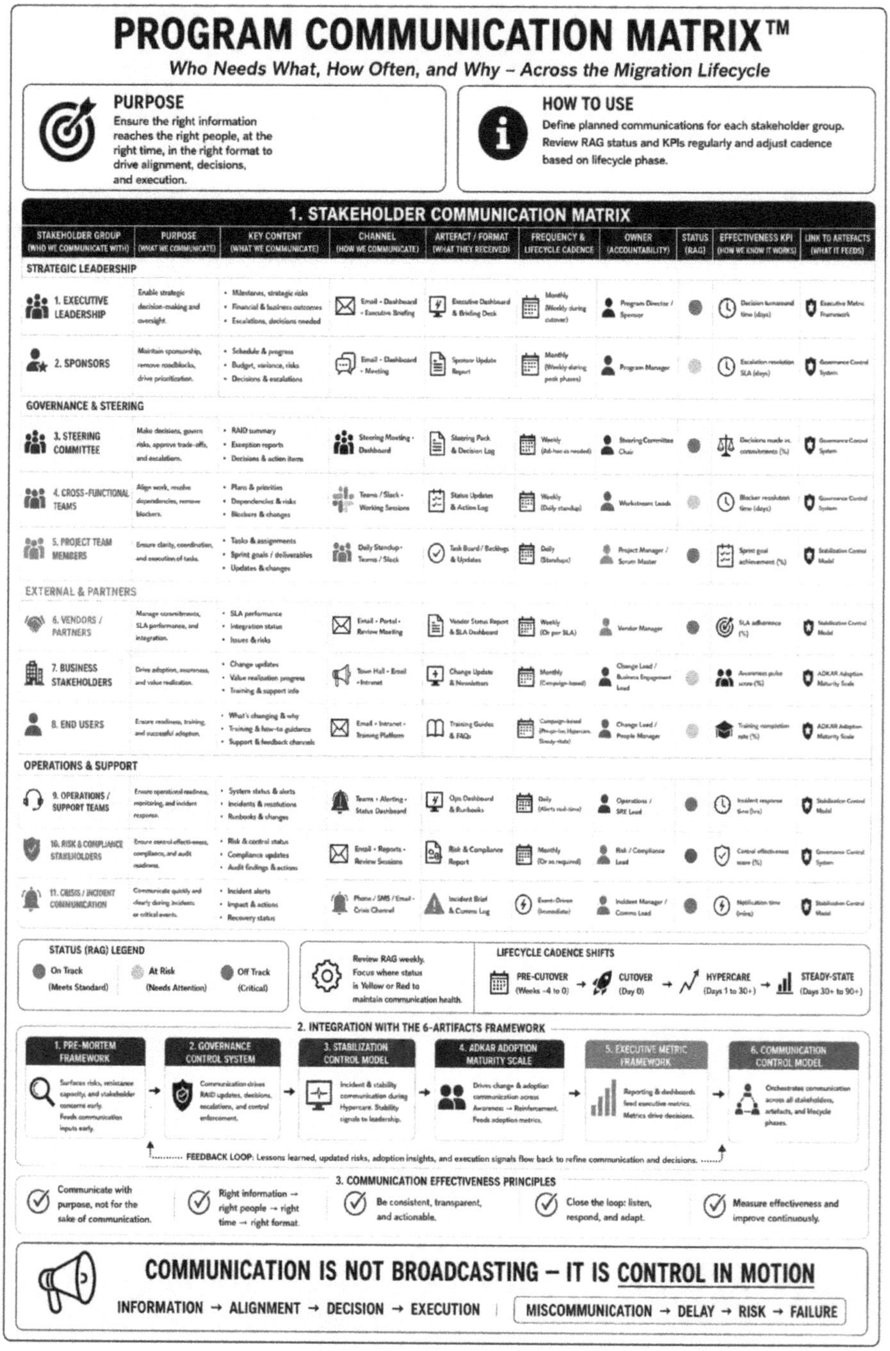

Cross-Functional Migration Governance

Migration programs fail when teams operate in isolation.

They succeed when execution is aligned across all domains.

Cross-functional governance ensures that:

Decisions are not fragmented

Risks are not hidden within silos

Dependencies are surfaced early

Accountability is clearly defined

Effective governance operates across layered responsibility:

Executives provide sponsorship and resolve major escalations

Sponsors and program boards manage priorities, funding, and risk posture

Architects validate technical direction and design integrity

Delivery teams execute the migration plan

Operations teams sustain the environment post-migration

This structure ensures that governance is not centralized—it is coordinated.

Breaking Silos Through Communication

Communication is the bridge between domains.

Without it:

infrastructure operates independently of applications

security operates independently of delivery

business stakeholders remain disconnected from execution

With structured communication:

infrastructure, network, security, identity, application, and data teams operate as one system

dependencies are understood before they become blockers

issues are surfaced before they become incidents

accountability becomes visible and enforceable

This is where communication becomes more than coordination.

It becomes control.

Control Principle — Communication Drives Execution

Execution does not fail because teams lack capability.

It fails because teams lack alignment.

And alignment is created through communication.

Communication ensures that:

decisions are informed

risks are visible

progress is understood

ownership is enforced

Without communication, execution becomes reactive.

With communication, execution becomes controlled.

Communication is not support—

it is the control system that holds execution together.

It is:

The system that synchronizes decisions
The mechanism that exposes risk
The structure that enforces ownership
The channel that maintains shared reality

The mechanism through which chaos is resolved—
and control is sustained.

PART VIII

Common Migration Failures

The recurring patterns behind enterprise migration failures — and the lessons they leave behind.

CHAPTER 13

The Seven Mistakes That Quietly Kill Migration Programs

Why Most Failures Are Operational Long Before They Are Technical

Migration programs rarely fail
because organizations lack technology.

They fail because execution loses structure.

Because assumptions replace validation.

Because movement begins
before control exists.

The failures below appear across cloud migrations, infrastructure transformations, platform consolidations, and enterprise modernization programs alike.

Different industries.

Different vendors.

Different platforms.

Yet the same breakdowns continue to emerge—

because the underlying failures are almost always operational—

not technical.

What follows is not merely a checklist.

It is the recurring pattern of how migration programs fail—

quietly at first—

long before instability becomes visible at the surface.

1. Beginning Execution Before Discovery Is Complete

Many organizations begin moving systems
while critical dependencies remain unknown.

Applications are migrated
before integrations are mapped.

Servers are moved
before upstream and downstream consumers are validated.

Network paths remain undocumented.

Authentication flows remain assumed—

rather than traced.

Discovery is not documentation.

It is control established
before execution begins.

When discovery is incomplete—

migration becomes reactive.

And reactive execution
introduces instability at scale.

One missed dependency
can destabilize an entire migration wave.

Not because the primary system failed—

but because something invisible behind it did.

2. Treating Migration as Infrastructure Movement Rather Than Business Change

Migration is often reduced
to servers, workloads, and target environments.

Migration changes more—
than where systems operate.

It changes how the business operates around them.

Support models shift.

Security postures change.

Operational workflows evolve.

Runbooks become obsolete.

End-user behavior changes—

or fails to.

Technical success alone
does not guarantee operational success.

A migrated system
the business cannot properly support—

is not a successful migration.

It is relocated instability
with a new ticket queue.

3. Letting Timelines Override Readiness

Many migration programs become driven
by executive commitments,
contract deadlines,
financial pressure,
or vendor end-of-support dates.

Over time—

the timeline begins to dictate execution.

This is where governance quietly begins to fail.

Execution must never begin
because the calendar demands it.

Execution begins
when readiness conditions are validated.

Dependencies confirmed.

Rollback rehearsed.

Runbooks approved.

Coverage staffed.

Risk understood.

When readiness gates are skipped
to protect a date—

the outcome becomes predictable:

compressed testing,
partial validation,
weak rollback preparation,
and elevated operational exposure.

Speed without control
is not acceleration—

it is exposure
with a deadline.

4. Treating Rollback as a Concept Instead of a Rehearsed Procedure

Almost every migration plan
claims to have rollback.

Far fewer possess rollback
that has actually been operationalized.

Defined trigger conditions.

Explicit authority.

Recovery thresholds.

Validated restoration timing.

Tested recovery paths.

Without these—

rollback becomes a word in a document,

not a capability the organization truly possesses.

And this reality usually appears
during live instability—

when the cost of uncertainty becomes operational.

Rollback strategy must be tested
before execution begins—

not invented during failure conditions.

A rollback
that has never been rehearsed—

is not a safety net.

It is a hypothesis.

5. Underestimating Identity as the Real Control Plane

Identity sits at the center
of modern enterprise architecture.

And authentication failures
can halt an otherwise healthy migration within minutes.

IAM platforms.

Federation services.

MFA enforcement.

Certificates.

Conditional access policies.

Directory synchronization.

Privileged access controls.

All of these introduce execution dependencies—

many of which organizations discover too late.

Identity is often treated
as a parallel workstream.

In reality—

identity frequently becomes
the operational control plane
of the migration itself.

Because when identity fails—

everything behind it fails with it.

And the symptoms rarely point
to the actual cause.

6. Treating Testing as a Phase Rather Than a Continuous Discipline

Testing is frequently compressed
into a single pre-cutover window.

This creates a dangerous illusion:

that validation occurs once—

and remains permanently true afterward.

But migration environments
do not remain static.

Configurations drift.

Policies evolve.

Dependencies change.

Performance behavior shifts under real production load.

Validation must therefore remain continuous—

before execution,
during execution,
and after execution.

Testing is not a checkpoint.

It is an operational discipline
sustained across the entire migration lifecycle.

The organizations that execute this well
treat validation as permanent infrastructure—

not temporary project activity.

7. Confusing Cutover With Completion

Organizations often celebrate successful cutover prematurely.

Because cutover is visible.

The war room.

The dashboards.

The completion emails.

The executive announcements.

But migration success—
is not proven during movement.

It is proven during stabilization.

This is where the quieter failures emerge:

performance degradation,
monitoring blind spots,
certificate expirations,
policy conflicts,
support escalation overload,
capacity exhaustion,
and operational drift.

This is why hypercare exists.

Migration does not end at cutover.

Cutover merely transitions execution
into stabilization.

And there is one final trap—
one that quietly affects many programs:

Confusing activity with control.

Meetings increase.

Dashboards multiply.

Tickets accelerate.

War rooms expand.

Executive briefings intensify.

Yet beneath all of that activity—

execution quality may still be deteriorating.

Real progress is not measured
by motion.

It is measured by:

validated readiness,
controlled execution,
stable operations,
risk reduction,
and demonstrated recovery capability.

Because migration success
is not defined by how much movement occurred—

but by how much instability was prevented.

Lessons from Enterprise Migration Failures

Enterprise migration failures consistently share common patterns:

discovery was incomplete, readiness was overstated, support was underprepared, or leadership visibility was weak.

A critical lesson is that migration success cannot be scheduled into existence.

It must be engineered and governed.

Validation must reflect real operating conditions—

and communication itself must be treated as a control.

The patterns behind these failures are not abstract—they are consistently observed across real-world migrations.

The following matrix captures the most common failure points, why they occur, and the structural controls required to prevent them.

COMMON MIGRATION FAILURES & CONTROL RESPONSE MATRIX

Identifying Failure Patterns and Applying Structural Controls

#	MISTAKE	WHY IT CAUSES FAILURE	CONTROL RESPONSE	VALIDATION SIGNAL
1	Treating migration as only a technical task	Ignores business readiness, communication, and user impact.	Integrate business validation, stakeholder alignment, and OCM from the start.	Business sign-off obtained; OCM plan approved; stakeholder engagement active.
2	Ignoring system dependencies	Hidden APIs, data flows, and identity paths break post-cutover.	Perform deep dependency mapping during Discovery Phase.	Dependency map signed off by system owners and architects.
3	No rollback plan	No safe recovery path during failure.	Establish tested rollback and contingency plans before cutover.	Rollback dry-run executed successfully and documented.
4	Declaring success too early	Cutover ≠ operational stability.	Define success through validation, monitoring, and stabilization.	Stability criteria met; SLA/SLO met for 7 consecutive days.
5	Ignoring post-migration monitoring	Issues surface only under real-world load.	Implement monitoring, hypercare, and incident response tracking.	Monitoring dashboards active; MTTD & MTTR within targets; incident closure rate ≥ 95%.
6	Poor stakeholder communication	Misalignment delays decisions and escalations.	Use structured communication cadence (Program Communication Matrix).	Communication matrix current; cadence met; stakeholder feedback tracked.
7	Weak change management	User adoption fails without readiness support.	Apply ADKAR / Prosci for adoption and readiness.	Adoption ≥ target by defined milestone; readiness assessments complete; satisfaction score ≥ 80%.
8	No wave planning	Large-scale single moves concentrate operational risk.	Execute migration in controlled waves with sequencing.	Wave plan approved; waves executed as planned; dependencies respected.
9	Lack of governance discipline	Decisions drift without oversight cadence.	Maintain governance cadence, steering committee reviews, and executive oversight.	Governance cadence met; decisions reviewed by steering committee; decision log current.
10	Unmanaged risks and assumptions	Risks and assumptions go untracked until they surface as incidents.	Active RAID management with assumption-validation checkpoints.	RAID log current; risks owned; assumptions validated and reviewed.

WITH STRUCTURE (Positive Path): **FAILURE** (Problems occur) → **PATTERN** (Patterns emerge) → **CONTROL** (Controls applied) → **STABILITY** (Stable outcomes)

WITHOUT STRUCTURE (Negative Path): **ASSUMPTION** (Assumptions made) → **EXPOSURE** (Gaps exposed) → **DISRUPTION** (Incidents and disruption)

STRUCTURE IS WHAT PREVENTS FAILURE BEFORE IT OCCURS.
Perceived readiness is not enough. Validated readiness delivers stability.

These patterns are not isolated incidents.

They represent systemic behaviors that repeat across organizations—regardless of size, industry, or technical maturity.

Why These Failures Persist Across Organizations

These mistakes are not isolated.

They repeat across industries, environments, and levels of technical maturity.

Not because organizations lack capability—

but because they underestimate complexity.

In most cases, failure does not originate from technical limitations.

It originates from:

Assumptions replacing validation

Urgency overriding structure

Communication treated as coordination rather than control

Planning disconnected from operational reality

Migration failures persist because organizations move forward with perceived readiness rather than validated readiness.

What appears to be progress is often unchallenged assumptions moving into execution.

And once execution begins, those assumptions become exposure.

The Role of Communication in Preventing Failure

Many of these failures are not technical breakdowns.

They are communication breakdowns.

When communication is weak:

Dependencies remain undiscovered
Risks are not escalated
Stakeholders operate with different expectations
Decision-making becomes delayed or misaligned

As established, communication is not support—

it is the control system that holds execution together.

It ensures that:

What is known is shared
What is unknown is surfaced
What is assumed is challenged

Without structured communication, even well-designed

migrations fail—not

because they were wrong,

but because they were not aligned.

How These Failures Are Prevented

Avoiding these mistakes is not about working harder.

It is about working with structure and discipline.

These failures are prevented when:

Discovery is treated as mandatory—not optional

Planning is validated before execution begins

Migration is executed in controlled waves—not large-scale events

Communication is continuous, structured, and enforced

Governance mechanisms actively track risks, assumptions, and dependencies

Success is defined by validation—not by cutover

Prevention is not reactive.

It is designed into the migration from the very beginning.

From Failure Patterns To Operational Discipline

These mistakes highlight a deeper truth:

Migration failure is rarely accidental.

It is usually predictable.

And if it is predictable—it is preventable.

The difference between failure and success is not effort.
It is operational discipline.
Discipline begins where understanding ends.

Avoiding failure requires structure
that can be:
repeated,
measured,
and scaled.

This is where migration moves—
Beyond principles
and into execution discipline.

The next chapter introduces the
Operational Playbook—
where execution becomes
repeatable,
measurable,
and scalable.

PART IX

Operational Playbook

Where execution becomes repeatable, measurable, and scalable — the operating model that makes controlled migration permanent.

CHAPTER 14

Operational Playbook

Where Execution Becomes Repeatable, Measurable, and Scalable

This section does not introduce new concepts.

It brings together what has already been established—
and shows how controlled migration operates in practice.

At this stage, the question is no longer:

"What should be done?"

But:
"How does it come together in a real environment?"

1. Operating Model — Defining Control, Ownership, and Flow

At execution level, the operating model is no longer theoretical.

It defines how migration actually runs:

Who owns decisions
How work flows across teams
How escalation is handled in real time

When ownership is unclear, accountability disappears.

When flow is undefined, execution slows.

In controlled migrations, the operating model is visible, enforced, and understood by all participants.

2. Runbooks — Executing Under Pressure

Runbooks translate planning into action.

They define exactly how tasks are executed under real conditions—especially when pressure is highest.

During migration, there is no time for interpretation.

Execution must be:

Clear
Sequenced
Repeatable

A well-defined runbook removes ambiguity and ensures that teams act with precision when it matters most.

3. Governance Cadence — Establishing Operational Discipline

Governance is not a concept.

It is a rhythm.

Daily checkpoints.

Weekly reviews.

Cutover war rooms.

Cadence ensures that decisions are made on time, risks are surfaced early, and alignment is maintained across teams.

Without cadence, governance weakens.

With cadence, execution remains controlled.

4. KPIs & Metrics — Visibility Into Performance and Stability

Metrics provide visibility into reality.

They answer a simple question:

Is the system performing as expected?

At execution level, metrics must be:

Relevant
Timely
Actionable

Without visibility, issues remain hidden.

With visibility, teams can respond before impact escalates.

5. Incident & Problem Management — Responding, Recovering, Learning

Incidents are not exceptions.

They are part of execution.

What matters is not whether issues occur—
but how they are handled.

Controlled environments:

Respond quickly
Restore service efficiently
Capture lessons systematically

Recovery is immediate.

Learning is continuous.

6. Change Management — Introducing Change Without Chaos

Every migration introduces change.

Technical change.

Operational change.

Behavioral change.

Without structure, change creates disruption.

With discipline, change becomes adoption.

Successful environments ensure that users, support teams, and leadership are prepared—not surprised.

7. Communication Framework — Alignment in Critical Moments

Communication is not information.

It is alignment.

During migration, clarity must exist across:

Technical teams
Business stakeholders
Leadership

Messages must be:

Timely
Relevant
Decision-focused

Because in critical moments, miscommunication is not a delay—

it is a risk.

8. Tooling & Automation — Bridging Process and Execution

Tools do not define execution.

They enable it.

Automation reduces manual effort, enforces consistency, and accelerates response.

But without structure, tools amplify chaos.

In controlled environments, tooling supports the process—

not replaces it.

9. Knowledge Management — Institutionalizing What Is Learned

Every migration generates insight.

What worked.

What failed.

What must improve.

If that knowledge is not captured—

it is lost.

Mature organizations institutionalize learning so that each migration becomes more efficient, more predictable, and more controlled than the last.

10. Continuous Improvement — From Lessons to Evolution

Migration is not a one-time event.

It is a capability.

Each execution cycle reveals opportunities to improve:

Process
Tools
Governance
Decision-making

Continuous improvement ensures that the organization evolves—

not repeats.

From Execution to Capability

Execution is where the operating model is tested.

Not in planning.

Not in strategy.

But in the behavior of systems, teams, and decisions under pressure.

Everything in this book leads to this point.

From understanding complexity—
to defining control.

From shaping mindset—
to establishing execution discipline.

From principles—
to operational reality.

Execution discipline requires:

The operating model defines control

Runbooks guide execution

Governance enforces discipline

Metrics provide visibility

Incident response restores stability

Change management enables adoption

Communication maintains alignment

Tooling supports consistency

Knowledge preserves learning

Continuous improvement drives evolution

Individually, these elements are important.

Together, they form a system.

Because migration success is not determined by effort.

It is determined by how well the system holds—

when it is under pressure.

In controlled environments, execution is not reactive.

It is structured.
Not improvised—
but designed.

This is the difference between organizations that complete migrations—

and those that master them.

Migration is not about moving systems.

It is about controlling change.

And when structure, discipline, and leadership align—
migration is no longer a risk.

It becomes a capability.

PART X

Execution Command Center™

Applying the Migration System in real-world conditions — where structure is tested, decisions are pressured, and execution must hold.

CHAPTER 15

Applying the Migration System in Real-World Conditions

This Section Is Not Meant to Be Read—It Is Meant to Be Used

This section is not a continuation of theory.

It is the application of control under real conditions—
where structure is tested, decisions are pressured, and execution must hold.

Everything introduced in this book—
from discovery and validation to governance, rollback, and stabilization—

comes together here.

Because migration success is not defined by design.

It is defined by execution under pressure.

Execution Does Not Break Under Normal Conditions

Execution does not fail when everything is clear.

It fails when:

Time is constrained

Information is incomplete

Dependencies surface late

Teams are misaligned

Decisions must be made quickly

Under these conditions, even well-designed plans begin to drift.

This is where most migrations lose control.

Not because the framework was wrong—

but because it was not operationalized.

The Execution Command Center exists to ensure that:

Structure holds under pressure

Decisions remain controlled

Execution remains aligned

The Execution Command Model

Execution in migration is not a linear activity.

This integrated control model can be visualized as a continuous execution system, where risk, rollback, stabilization, and execution operate together in real time.

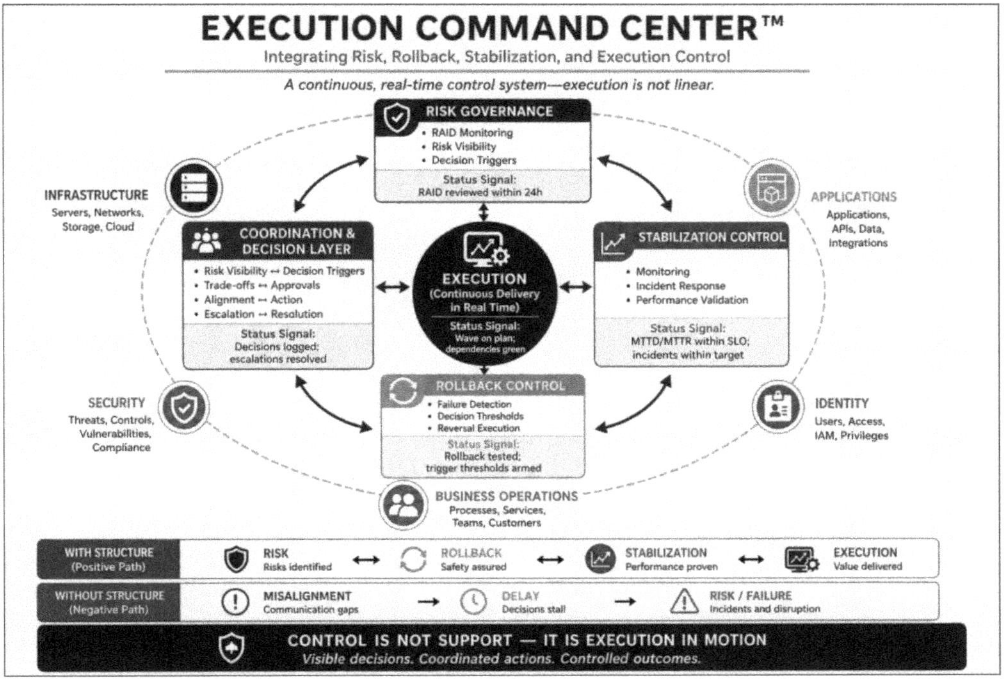

Each layer represents a control point—ensuring that execution remains visible, decisions remain structured, and outcomes remain controlled under pressure.

It is a coordinated system operating in real time across:

Infrastructure

Applications

Security

Identity

Business operations

To manage this complexity, execution must be centralized into a controlled environment:

The Command Center.

This is not a physical room.

It is an operational model where:

Visibility is unified

Decisions are coordinated

Accountability is immediate

Communication is controlled

The War Room Model — Coordinated Execution Under Pressure

During critical phases—especially cutover and early stabilization—execution shifts into a war room model.

This is where control becomes visible.

At this stage:

Technical leads operate in real time

Program leadership monitors execution flow

Decisions are made without delay

Escalations are resolved immediately

Roles are clearly defined:

Program Lead — Maintains overall control and decision authority

Technical Leads — Execute domain-specific actions (Infra, App, Security, Identity)

Operations / Support — Monitor system behavior and surface incidents

Business Representatives — Validate impact and usability

This structure eliminates ambiguity.

There is no uncertainty about:

Who owns the issue

Who makes the decision

Who communicates the outcome

Without this model, execution fragments.

With it, execution becomes controlled.

How the Governance System Operates During Execution

The governance system introduced earlier does not change during execution—

It becomes active.

During live migration:

Risks are continuously reviewed and updated

Dependencies are surfaced in real time

Execution sequencing is actively adjusted

Leadership visibility is maintained through structured reporting

Governance is no longer periodic.

It becomes continuous.

This is the difference between:

Managing a plan

And controlling execution

Execution Flow — From Cutover to Stabilization

Execution follows a controlled progression:

1. Pre-Cutover Readiness Confirmation

Validation gates are confirmed

Rollback readiness is verified

Decision authority is aligned

2. Cutover Execution

Systems transition according to defined sequencing

Dependencies are monitored in real time

Decision checkpoints are enforced

3. Failure Handling (If Triggered)

Execution pauses

Rollback decisions are evaluated

Controlled reversal is initiated if required

4. Controlled Resumption

Root cause is identified

Execution path is adjusted

Migration resumes under controlled conditions

5. Stabilization Entry

Monitoring intensifies

Incident response accelerates

System behavior is validated under real use

Execution is not a straight line,

It is a controlled progression through uncertainty.

Decision-Making Under Uncertainty

In real migrations, decisions are rarely made with complete information.

Leaders must act when:

Data is incomplete

Signals are conflicting

Risk is emerging but not fully defined

This is where structure becomes critical.

Controlled decision-making requires:

Defined escalation paths

Clear ownership

Known decision thresholds

Alignment between technical and business impact

Without structure, decisions become reactive.

With structure, decisions remain controlled—even under uncertainty.

Incident Handling in Live Migration

Incidents are not exceptions.

They are expected.

What defines success is not the absence of incidents—

It is the ability to control them.

During execution:

Detection

Issues are identified through monitoring, alerts, or user feedback

Triage

Severity is assessed based on impact and urgency

Containment

Immediate actions are taken to limit exposure

Resolution

Root cause is addressed through controlled intervention

Communication

Stakeholders are informed with clarity and alignment

Incident handling must be:

Fast

Structured

Controlled

Without this, minor issues become major failures.

Execution Reality — What Actually Happens

No migration unfolds exactly as planned.

In real environments:

Dependencies appear late

Configurations behave differently

Performance shifts under load

Communication gaps emerge

This is not failure.

This is reality.

The purpose of the migration system is not to eliminate these conditions—

It is to absorb them without losing control.

Controlled environments do not avoid disruption.

They manage it.

Continuous Alignment Across Teams

Execution fails when teams operate in isolation.

It succeeds when all domains operate as one system.

This requires:

Continuous communication

Shared visibility

Clear ownership

Coordinated decision-making

Infrastructure, security, applications, identity, and business teams must not operate independently.

They must operate as a unified execution system.

This alignment is not optional.

It is enforced.

From Execution to Capability

Execution is not the end of migration.

It is the proving ground.

Every migration produces:

Insights

Patterns

Lessons

If these are not captured, they are lost.

If they are structured, they become capability.

Mature organizations do not repeat migrations.

They evolve them.

Continuous Improvement — From Lessons to Evolution

Each execution cycle strengthens the system.

Improvements occur across:

Process

Governance

Tooling

Decision-making

This ensures that:

Execution becomes more predictable

Risk becomes more manageable

Outcomes become more consistent

Migration becomes not a one-time effort—

But an organizational capability.

Execution Discipline — Enforcing Control at the Operational Level

Execution is not maintained through awareness.

It is maintained through discipline.

In controlled environments, discipline is not assumed—

it is enforced through structured validation at every stage of execution.

During execution, these checklists function as enforcement mechanisms—ensuring that readiness is continuously validated and that execution does not drift under pressure.

They ensure that:

Readiness is verified

Dependencies are validated

Risk conditions are understood

Execution remains predictable

Without this layer, even well-structured execution models begin to drift.

With it, execution remains grounded in reality.

Execution discipline must be applied across every domain involved in migration.

Each layer of the environment—Infrastructure, Application, and Cloud Platform—requires its own validation controls to ensure that execution remains consistent, visible, and controlled.

Execution begins at the foundation. Infrastructure must be stable before anything else can hold.

During live execution, control is enforced through domain-level validation checkpoints.

Execution is not performed as a checklist.

It is executed as a controlled sequence across time, ownership, and decision points.

This sequence can be visualized as a controlled execution model across time—where readiness, decision-making, and stabilization are actively enforced rather than assumed.

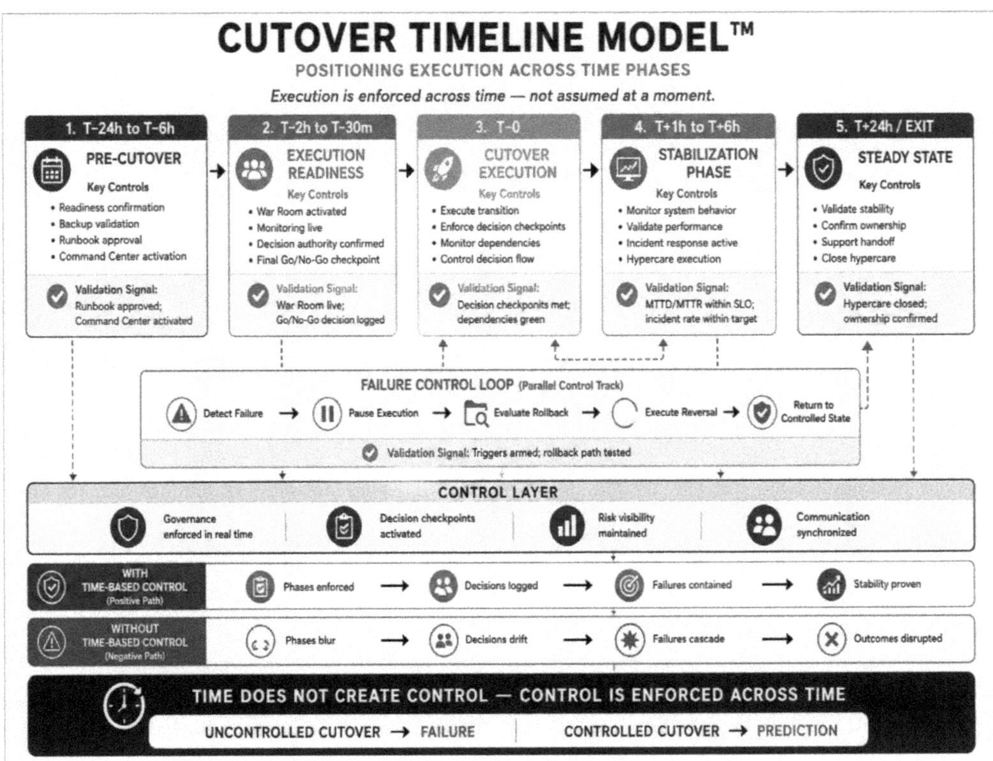

At this level, execution is no longer theoretical.

It becomes operational—where each phase is enforced through structured runbooks, decision checkpoints, and real-time control.

This operational alignment can be visualized as an integrated execution system—where timeline control, runbook discipline, and decision enforcement work together to make execution predictable.

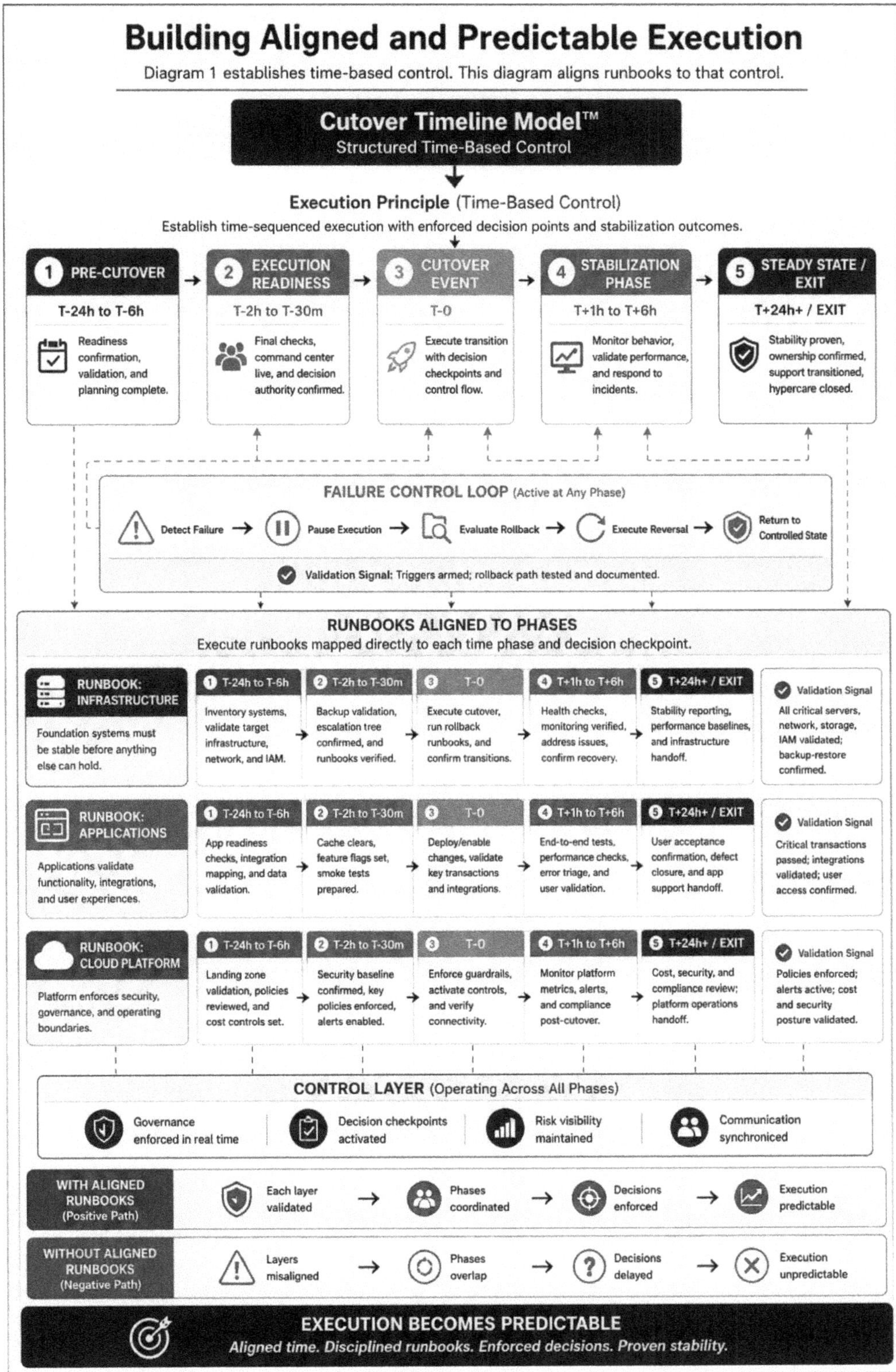

Building Aligned and Predictable Execution
Diagram 1 establishes time-based control. This diagram aligns runbooks to that control.
Cutover Timeline Model™
Structured Time-Based Control
Execution Principle (Time-Based Control)
Establish time-sequenced execution with enforced decision points and stabilization outcomes.
1 PRE-CUTOVER
T-24h to T-6h
Readiness confirmation, validation, and planning complete.
2 EXECUTION READINESS
T-2h to T-30m
Final checks, command center live, and decision authority confirmed.
3 CUTOVER EVENT
T-0
Execute transition with decision checkpoints and control flow.
4 STABILIZATION PHASE
T+1h to T+6h
Monitor behavior, validate performance, and respond to incidents.
5 STEADY STATE / EXIT
T+24h+ / EXIT
Stability proven, ownership confirmed, support transitioned, hypercare closed.
FAILURE CONTROL LOOP (Active at Any Phase)
Detect Failure
Pause Execution
Evaluate Rollback
Execute Reversal
Return to Controlled State
Validation Signal: Triggers armed; rollback path tested and documented.
RUNBOOKS ALIGNED TO PHASES
Execute runbooks mapped directly to each time phase and decision checkpoint.
RUNBOOK: INFRASTRUCTURE
Foundation systems must be stable before anything else can hold.
1 T-24h to T-6h
Inventory systems, validate target infrastructure, network, and IAM.
2 T-2h to T-30m
Backup validation, escalation tree confirmed, and runbooks verified.
3 T-0
Execute cutover, run rollback runbooks, and confirm transitions.
4 T+1h to T+6h
Health checks, monitoring verified, address issues, confirm recovery.
5 T+24h+ / EXIT
Stability reporting, performance baselines, and infrastructure handoff.
Validation Signal
All critical servers, network, storage, IAM validated; backup-restore confirmed.
RUNBOOK: APPLICATIONS
Applications validate functionality, integrations, and user experiences.
1 T-24h to T-6h
App readiness checks, integration mapping, and data validation.
2 T-2h to T-30m
Cache clears, feature flags set, smoke tests prepared.
3 T-0
Deploy/enable changes, validate key transactions and integrations.
4 T+1h to T+6h
End-to-end tests, performance checks, error triage, and user validation.
5 T+24h+ / EXIT
User acceptance confirmation, defect closure, and app support handoff.
Validation Signal
Critical transactions passed; integrations validated; user access confirmed.
RUNBOOK: CLOUD PLATFORM
Platform enforces security, governance, and operating boundaries.
1 T-24h to T-6h
Landing zone validation, policies reviewed, and cost controls set.
2 T-2h to T-30m
Security baseline confirmed, key policies enforced, alerts enabled.
3 T-0
Enforce guardrails, activate controls, and verify connectivity.
4 T+1h to T+6h
Monitor platform metrics, alerts, and compliance post-cutover.
5 T+24h+ / EXIT
Cost, security, and compliance review; platform operations handoff.
Validation Signal
Policies enforced; alerts active; cost and security posture validated.
CONTROL LAYER (Operating Across All Phases)
Governance enforced in real time
Decision checkpoints activated
Risk visibility maintained
Communication synchronized
WITH ALIGNED RUNBOOKS (Positive Path)
Each layer validated
Phases coordinated
Decisions enforced
Execution predictable
WITHOUT ALIGNED RUNBOOKS (Negative Path)
Layers misaligned
Phases overlap
Decisions delayed
Execution unpredictable
EXECUTION BECOMES PREDICTABLE
Aligned time. Disciplined runbooks. Enforced decisions. Proven stability.

At this point, execution is no longer driven by isolated tasks.

It is driven by phased control—

Where each runbook action aligns to a time-based checkpoint, a decision boundary, and a stabilization outcome.

Infrastructure Execution Runbook — Time-Sequenced Control

Infrastructure Layer — Command-Driven Sequence:

Confirm current-state inventory of servers, storage, network paths, IAM, and monitoring.

Validate target compute, storage, network, and security configuration.

Confirm backup and restore capability before cutover.

Approve change window and escalation tree.

Complete cutover runbook and rollback runbook.

Verify monitoring, logging, and alert routing.

Run post-migration infrastructure health checks.

Conduct stabilization reporting and support handoff.

Applications validation confirms whether the environment functions as intended under real operating conditions

Application Execution Runbook — Controlled Validation Sequence

Application Layer — Behavior Validation Flow:

Validate application architecture and dependency map.
Confirm configuration values, certificates, secrets, and environment variables.
Test application startup, APIs, queues, schedulers, and integration points.
Run database connectivity and transaction validation.
Confirm user access, role mapping, and critical workflow testing.
Review defect thresholds and rollback triggers.
Obtain technical and business sign-off.

The cloud environment enforces the boundaries of scalability, security, and operational control.

Cloud Platform Runbook — Execution and Governance Control

Platform & Governance Layer — Control Enforcement:

Confirm selected 6R strategy for each in-scope workload.
Validate landing zone, IAM boundaries, network segmentation, and tagging standards.
Confirm cloud monitoring, cost visibility, and logging.
Verify autoscaling, backup, DR, and resilience configurations.
Review cloud-specific security controls and compliance requirements.
Track stabilization metrics and cost behavior after go-live.

Cloud governance sustains operational consistency, financial visibility, and control integrity after migration.

Role and Domain Foundations

Role of the Infrastructure Technical Project Manager

The Infrastructure Technical Project Manager does not manage tasks.

They manage control.

In infrastructure, cloud, and platform transformation programs, complexity does not come from individual systems—

It comes from how those systems interact under pressure.

Compute, network, identity, security, and applications do not fail independently.

They fail at their intersections.

This is where the role of the Infrastructure Technical Project Manager becomes critical.

They operate as the integrator across domains—

Ensuring that engineering execution, security enforcement, operational readiness, and business expectations remain aligned throughout the migration lifecycle.

This role extends far beyond coordination.

It requires technical fluency—not to configure systems, but to understand how systems behave, where dependencies exist, and how risk propagates across the environment.

An effective Infrastructure PM must be able to:

Understand infrastructure dependencies across compute, network, identity, storage, and security

Anticipate cutover risks and validate rollback feasibility

Assess operational readiness beyond stated completion

Recognize how architectural decisions impact execution outcomes

Identify where assumptions replace validation

This level of awareness is not about becoming an engineer.

It is about developing execution awareness.

This relationship between leadership, control, and execution can be visualized as structured control model:

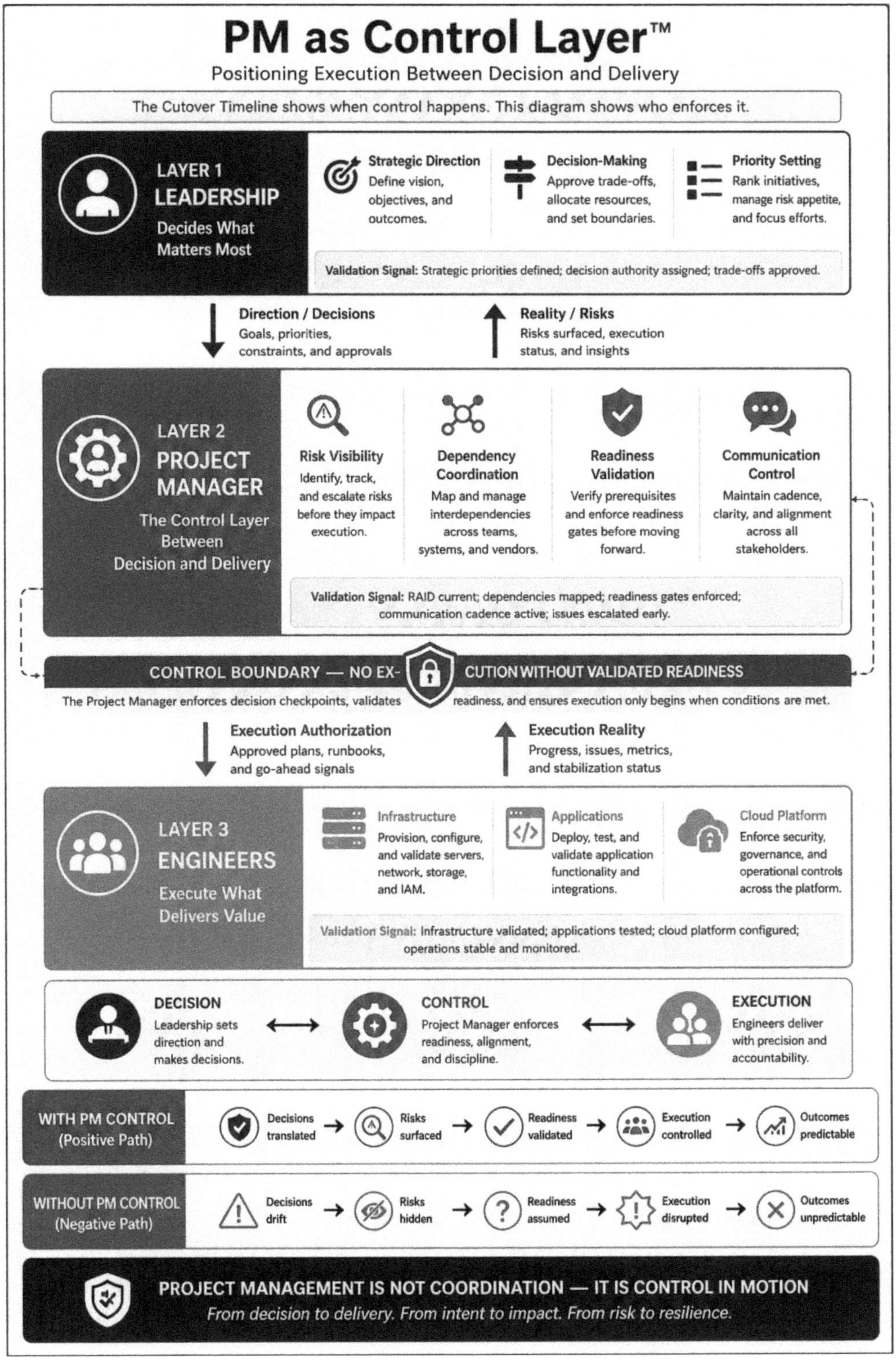

PM as Control Layer™
Positioning Execution Between Decision and Delivery
The Cutover Timeline shows when control happens. This diagram shows who enforces it.
LAYER 1
LEADERSHIP
Decides What Matters Most
Strategic Direction
Define vision, objectives, and outcomes.
Decision-Making
Approve trade-offs, allocate resources, and set boundaries.
Priority Setting
Rank initiatives, manage risk appetite, and focus efforts.
Validation Signal: Strategic priorities defined; decision authority assigned; trade-offs approved.
Direction / Decisions
Goals, priorities, constraints, and approvals
Reality / Risks
Risks surfaced, execution status, and insights
LAYER 2
PROJECT MANAGER
The Control Layer Between Decision and Delivery
Risk Visibility
Identify, track, and escalate risks before they impact execution.
Dependency Coordination
Map and manage interdependencies across teams, systems, and vendors.
Readiness Validation
Verify prerequisites and enforce readiness gates before moving forward.
Communication Control
Maintain cadence, clarity, and alignment across all stakeholders.
Validation Signal: RAID current; dependencies mapped; readiness gates enforced; communication cadence active; issues escalated early.
CONTROL BOUNDARY — NO EX- CUTION WITHOUT VALIDATED READINESS
The Project Manager enforces decision checkpoints, validates readiness, and ensures execution only begins when conditions are met.
Execution Authorization
Approved plans, runbooks, and go-ahead signals
Execution Reality
Progress, issues, metrics, and stabilization status
LAYER 3
ENGINEERS
Execute What Delivers Value
Infrastructure
Provision, configure, and validate servers, network, storage, and IAM.
Applications
Deploy, test, and validate application functionality and integrations.
Cloud Platform
Enforce security, governance, and operational controls across the platform.
Validation Signal: Infrastructure validated; applications tested; cloud platform configured; operations stable and monitored.
DECISION
Leadership sets direction and makes decisions.
CONTROL
Project Manager enforces readiness, alignment, and discipline.
EXECUTION
Engineers deliver with precision and accountability.
WITH PM CONTROL (Positive Path)
Decisions translated → Risks surfaced → Readiness validated → Execution controlled → Outcomes predictable
WITHOUT PM CONTROL (Negative Path)
Decisions drift → Risks hidden → Readiness assumed → Execution disrupted → Outcomes unpredictable
PROJECT MANAGEMENT IS NOT COORDINATION — IT IS CONTROL IN MOTION
From decision to delivery. From intent to impact. From risk to resilience.

This model makes one thing clear: engineers execute, leadership decides but the project manager ensures that execution remains controlled between the two.

Because in real migrations, failure rarely comes from what is visible.

It comes from what was not understood.

Beyond Technical Knowledge — The Discipline of Control

There is a common misconception in organizations:

That Infrastructure Technical Project Managers must reach the level of engineering depth to be effective.

This is not only unrealistic—it is misdirected.

The value of the Infrastructure PM is not in configuring systems.

It is in ensuring that systems can be delivered, validated, and sustained under real conditions.

What matters is not how deeply the PM can engineer—

but how effectively they can:

Drive clarity across technical teams

Surface hidden dependencies

Challenge incomplete readiness

Align stakeholders under pressure

Enable decisions when information is incomplete

Technical knowledge supports the role.

But leadership, structure, and communication define it.

The PM as the Control Layer

In a controlled migration environment:

Engineers execute.

Systems operate.

But the Project Manager ensures that:

Execution remains aligned

Decisions remain structured

Communication remains clear

Risk remains visible

Without this layer, even strong engineering teams drift into:

Misalignment

Delayed decisions

Hidden dependencies

Uncontrolled risk

With it, execution becomes:

Coordinated

Predictable

Governed

Communication as a Control Mechanism

Infrastructure migrations are not stabilized through technical execution alone.

They are stabilized through communication.

Because:

Dependencies must be understood across teams

Risks must be surfaced before they escalate

Decisions must be made with shared visibility

Business impact must be aligned with technical action

This is why communication is not support.

It is control in motion.

The Infrastructure Technical Project Manager ensures that:

Technical information is translated into decision-ready insight

Leadership receives clarity—not noise

Teams operate with shared understanding

Execution remains synchronized across domains

The Infrastructure Technical Project Manager does not replace engineering depth.

They make it effective.

They do not need to know everything.

But they must ensure that everything that matters is:

Understood

Validated

Aligned

Controlled

Because in infrastructure migration:

Success is not determined by how well systems are designed.

It is determined by how well execution is controlled—

when complexity, pressure, and uncertainty converge.

Core Infrastructure Domains Every PM Should Understand

Infrastructure migration does not fail within individual domains.

It fails at the intersections between them.

A strong Infrastructure Technical Project Manager does not need to configure systems—but must understand how compute, network, identity, storage, and security interact under real conditions.

Because in execution, no domain operates alone.

Each introduces dependencies.

Each introduces risk.

And each influences whether a migration holds—or collapses.

Compute Infrastructure:

Physical servers, virtual machines, containers, and cloud compute platforms.

This domain defines how workloads run.

Migration considerations include sizing, availability, autoscaling behavior, and runtime stability under load.

Network Infrastructure:

Routers, switches, load balancers, firewalls, VPNs, SD-WAN, and routing paths.

This domain defines how systems connect.

Migration considerations include connectivity, latency, segmentation, DNS resolution, and traffic redirection during cutover.

Storage Infrastructure:

SAN, NAS, object storage, block storage, backup systems, and replication platforms.

This domain defines how data is stored and protected.

Migration considerations include capacity, backup integrity, throughput, latency, and IOPS under real usage.

Identity and Access Infrastructure:

Active Directory, Entra ID, Okta, SSO, MFA, RBAC, service accounts, and privileged access systems.

This domain defines who can access what—and how.

Migration considerations include authentication continuity, access mapping, federation integrity, and privilege enforcement.

Cloud Infrastructure:

AWS, Azure, GCP, landing zones, VPCs/VNets, cloud-native security controls, and cost governance.

This domain defines the operating environment.
Migration considerations include environment readiness, policy alignment, scalability, and cost visibility under load.

End-User Computing (EUC):

Laptops, mobile devices, virtual desktops, endpoint management, and workspace delivery platforms.

This domain defines the user experience.

Migration considerations include device readiness, profile performance, access consistency, and support preparedness.

Security Infrastructure:

SIEM, endpoint protection, SASE, logging controls, segmentation policies, certificate and secrets management, and Zero Trust enforcement.

This domain defines how the environment is protected and observed.

Migration considerations include enforcement continuity, audit visibility, detection capability, and incident response readiness.

The Reality of Cross-Domain Execution:

This interaction can be understood as a control system — where dependencies converge, risks propagate, and control is either maintained or lost.

This model defines how execution is structured across time.

But structure alone does not ensure control.

Execution must be aligned to it in real time.

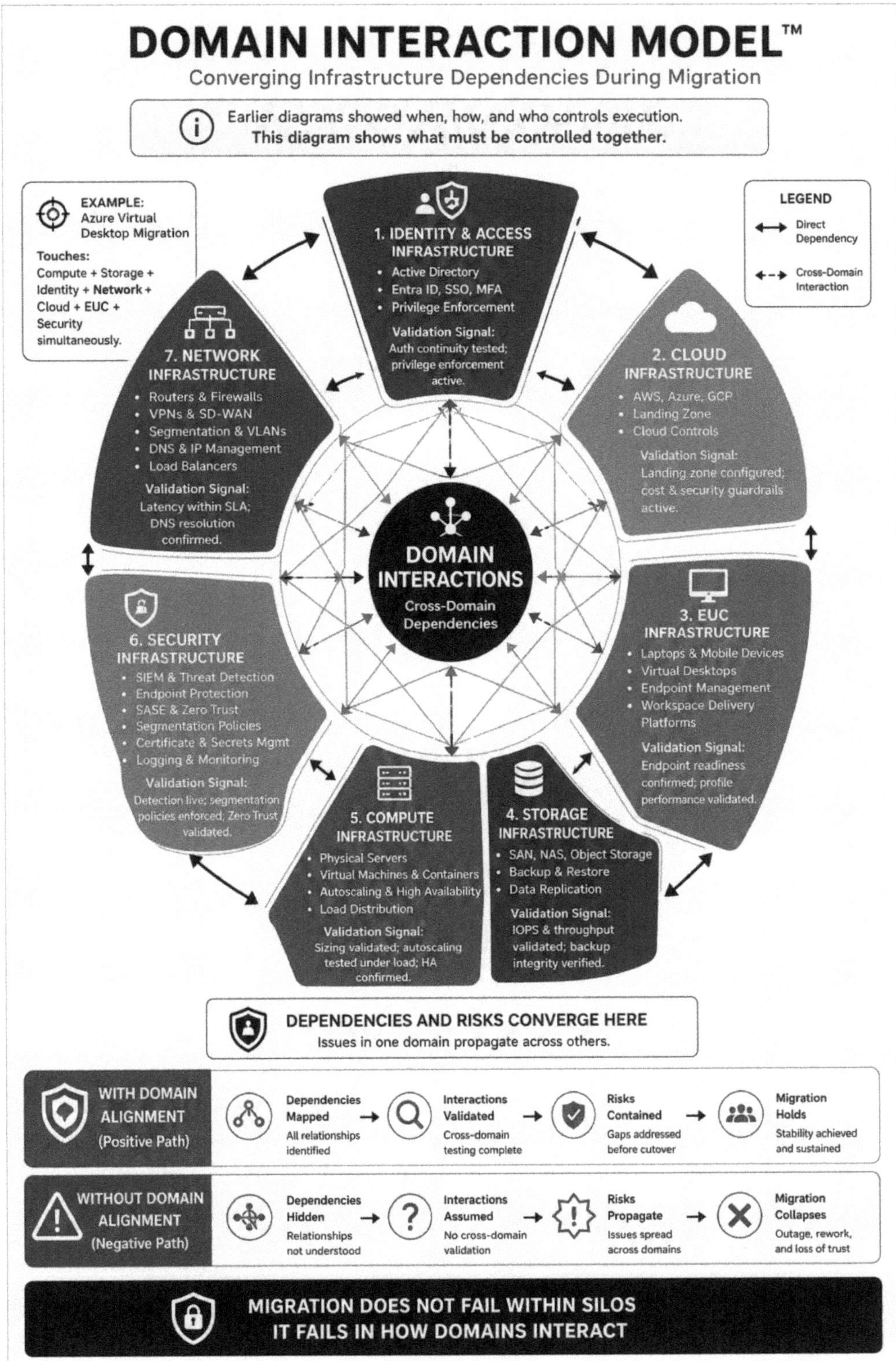
DOMAIN INTERACTION MODEL™
Converging Infrastructure Dependencies During Migration
Earlier diagrams showed when, how, and who controls execution.
This diagram shows what must be controlled together.
EXAMPLE: Azure Virtual Desktop Migration
Touches: Compute + Storage + Identity + Network + Cloud + EUC + Security simultaneously.
LEGEND
Direct Dependency
Cross-Domain Interaction
1. IDENTITY & ACCESS INFRASTRUCTURE
Active Directory
Entra ID, SSO, MFA
Privilege Enforcement
Validation Signal: Auth continuity tested; privilege enforcement active.
2. CLOUD INFRASTRUCTURE
AWS, Azure, GCP
Landing Zone
Cloud Controls
Validation Signal: Landing zone configured; cost & security guardrails active.
3. EUC INFRASTRUCTURE
Laptops & Mobile Devices
Virtual Desktops
Endpoint Management
Workspace Delivery Platforms
Validation Signal: Endpoint readiness confirmed; profile performance validated.
4. STORAGE INFRASTRUCTURE
SAN, NAS, Object Storage
Backup & Restore
Data Replication
Validation Signal: IOPS & throughput validated; backup integrity verified.
5. COMPUTE INFRASTRUCTURE
Physical Servers
Virtual Machines & Containers
Autoscaling & High Availability
Load Distribution
Validation Signal: Sizing validated; autoscaling tested under load; HA confirmed.
6. SECURITY INFRASTRUCTURE
SIEM & Threat Detection
Endpoint Protection
SASE & Zero Trust
Segmentation Policies
Certificate & Secrets Mgmt
Logging & Monitoring
Validation Signal: Detection live; segmentation policies enforced; Zero Trust validated.
7. NETWORK INFRASTRUCTURE
Routers & Firewalls
VPNs & SD-WAN
Segmentation & VLANs
DNS & IP Management
Load Balancers
Validation Signal: Latency within SLA; DNS resolution confirmed.
DOMAIN INTERACTIONS
Cross-Domain Dependencies
DEPENDENCIES AND RISKS CONVERGE HERE
Issues in one domain propagate across others.
WITH DOMAIN ALIGNMENT (Positive Path)
Dependencies Mapped
All relationships identified
Interactions Validated
Cross-domain testing complete
Risks Contained
Gaps addressed before cutover
Migration Holds
Stability achieved and sustained
WITHOUT DOMAIN ALIGNMENT (Negative Path)
Dependencies Hidden
Relationships not understood
Interactions Assumed
No cross-domain validation
Risks Propagate
Issues spread across domains
Migration Collapses
Outage, rework, and loss of trust
MIGRATION DOES NOT FAIL WITHIN SILOS
IT FAILS IN HOW DOMAINS INTERACT

These domains do not operate in isolation.

A single migration—such as Azure Virtual Desktop or a Zero Trust implementation—simultaneously touches compute, storage, identity, network, cloud, EUC, and security.

This is where most organizations lose control.

Not because individual domains are misunderstood—

but because their interactions are not validated as a system.

Execution Principle

Migration leadership is not about managing domains.

It is about managing their convergence.

Because success is not determined by whether each domain works—

but whether they work together

under real conditions,

at the same time.

Execution Control and Delivery Artifacts

Production Cutover Deliverables

Production cutover is not an event.

It is a controlled transition.

And control is not achieved through execution alone—but through the artifacts that define, validate, and govern that execution.

Before any migration enters production, a mature program produces a structured set of deliverables that ensure readiness is not assumed—but proven.

These artifacts are not created for documentation.

They are created to establish control before execution begins.

Core Cutover Deliverables

At a minimum, the following deliverables must be defined prior to production transition:

Production Readiness Checklist

Confirms that infrastructure, access controls, monitoring, security policies, backups, and capacity are fully prepared and validated.

Infrastructure Validation and Test Results

Provide evidence that authentication, connectivity, policy enforcement, application behavior, and integrations function as expected.

Cutover Plan

Defines execution sequencing, ownership, timing, dependencies, communication flows, and go/no-go decision points.

Rollback / Backout Plan

Establishes reversal logic—trigger thresholds, recovery sequencing, restoration timing, and decision ownership under failure conditions.

Operations Runbook

Prepares support teams for monitoring, troubleshooting, escalation, and incident response after go-live.

Go-Live Authorization

Captures formal approval across technical, operational, security, and business stakeholders.

Hypercare Support Plan

Defines stabilization structure—monitoring cadence, reporting visibility, incident triage, and exit criteria into steady-state operations.

Lifecycle Alignment — From Planning to Readiness

These deliverables are not created at the end.

They are built progressively across the migration lifecycle:

Initiation and Planning establish governance foundations—charter, scope, WBS, schedule, communication plan, and risk structures.

Design and Build produce architecture, integration models, provisioning logic, and configuration baselines.

Testing and Validation generate execution evidence—test results, defect tracking, and formal readiness validation.

Deployment Readiness consolidates all artifacts into a controlled cutover package.

Critical Distinction — Definition vs Execution

Defining these deliverables does not ensure control.

Using them correctly does.

This section establishes what must exist.

The next phase of the framework—Execution Command Center™—defines how these artifacts are applied under real-world conditions to maintain control during execution.

Execution Principle

Cutover success is not determined at the moment of execution.

It is determined by the quality of preparation that precedes it.

Because in production:

There is no time to discover.

Only time to execute.

Interview and Leadership Readiness

Migration Interview Questions and Model Answers

How do you validate that a migration was successful?

A migration is considered successful only when the target environment proves stable under real operating conditions.

Validation should include infrastructure health checks, application performance verification, authentication and access testing, database connectivity, integration validation, and user acceptance for critical workflows.

Monitoring dashboards should also be reviewed to confirm there are no anomalies in latency, error rates, or service behavior.

How do you handle rollback during a migration?

Every migration wave should include a rollback plan before execution starts.

The rollback strategy may include DNS failback, infrastructure snapshot restoration, traffic reversal, database restore, or reactivation of the prior environment.

From a PM perspective, rollback must be documented, rehearsed when feasible, time-boxed, and clearly understood by engineering and leadership.

How do you prioritize systems for migration?

Systems should be prioritized based on business criticality, technical complexity, dependency exposure, support readiness, and operational risk.

Most programs begin with lower-risk systems, move to moderate integrations, and then migrate mission-critical platforms after the model has been proven.

How do you identify dependencies before migration?

Dependency discovery should be performed through workshops involving application owners, infrastructure teams, network engineers, DBAs, support teams, and business stakeholders.

The output should capture APIs, databases, identity providers, routing paths, firewall rules, scheduled jobs, vendor connections, and upstream and downstream business dependencies.

How do you minimize downtime during migration?

Downtime is minimized through maintenance-window control, rehearsal migrations, target-environment validation, phased traffic redirection, operational staffing, and active monitoring during cutover.

The PM ensures stakeholder communication, support coverage, and governance are aligned with the execution plan.

How do you handle scope creep in complex IT programs?

Scope creep should be treated as a formal change decision rather than an informal expansion of delivery.

The PM compares the request against the approved scope baseline, documents the impact to cost, schedule, resources, and risk, and routes it through change control so leadership can make an informed decision.

The following 55 questions provide a practical readiness lens for discovery, planning, cutover, and stabilization

The 55 Questions Every Migration PM Must Ask Before Migration Begins

Successful migrations begin with disciplined questioning.

Before a migration wave proceeds, the PM should confirm not only technical readiness, but also business alignment, operational preparedness, governance controls, rollback viability, and post-go-live sustainability.

What systems are being migrated?
Why is the migration necessary?
What business outcomes justify the migration?
What migration strategy (6R) applies?
What dependencies exist?
What APIs or integrations exist?
What identity providers are used?
What databases support the application?
What infrastructure components must migrate?
Is the target environment provisioned?
Are network routes configured?
Are firewall rules validated?
Are monitoring tools configured?
Are IAM roles configured?
Are certificates valid?
Are secrets managed securely?
Are support teams trained?
Are operational runbooks documented?
Are monitoring dashboards ready?
Are incident procedures defined?
Is a migration war room established?
Are stakeholders aligned?
Are governance boards established?
Are change control procedures defined?
Is executive reporting scheduled?
Are migration waves defined?
Are maintenance windows approved?
Have rehearsal migrations been conducted?
Are rollback procedures tested?

Are validation checklists prepared?
Is a hypercare period defined?
Are performance baselines established?
Are system metrics monitored?
Are integration tests complete?
Are user acceptance tests complete?
Has operational ownership transferred?
Have risks been mitigated?
Have lessons learned been documented?
Has executive sign-off been obtained?
Did migration deliver business value?
Are users satisfied?
Did system reliability improve?
Did operational costs decrease?
Did teams gain knowledge?
Is the architecture scalable?
Is disaster recovery operational?
Is the environment secure?
Is monitoring effective?
Is the organization ready for future migrations?
What improvements should be made next time?
How do you validate that a migration was successful?
What rollback strategy is in place if the migration fails?
How do you identify hidden system dependencies?
How do you prioritize migration waves?
What metrics should be monitored during post-migration stabilization?

Author Signature and Intellectual Foundations

Philosophical Signature of the Author

This work is not written in a conventional technical voice.

Its structure, cadence, and rhythm are intentional.

It is designed not only to inform—

but to control how information is processed.

Why the Writing Feels Cinematic

The writing in this book follows a deliberate progression:

A statement is introduced.

It is interrupted.

Then it is resolved.

This is not stylistic preference—it is structural design.

The influence of Georg Wilhelm Friedrich Hegel is present in this pattern:

thesis → tension → synthesis.

Each idea is not simply delivered.
It is developed, challenged, and then clarified.

This creates movement—

and that movement is what gives the writing its cinematic quality.

Why Sentences Break Rhythm

The pauses.

The separations.

The abrupt lines.

They are intentional.

Influenced by René Descartes, thought in this work is constructed deliberately—

one unit at a time.

At the same time, the layering of ideas reflects the influence of Immanuel Kant—

where understanding is built through structured reasoning, not passive reading.

The interruptions in rhythm serve a purpose:

They slow the reader down.

They force attention.

They prevent assumptions from passing as understanding.

This is not writing for speed.

It is writing for clarity.

Underlying Tension and Human Interpretation

Not all meaning is stated directly.

Some is implied.

Some is felt.

This reflects the influence of Sigmund Freud—

where underlying tension and subtext shape interpretation as much as explicit content.

What is not said is often as important as what is said.

Stimulus, Response, and Structured Reinforcement

The flow of ideas also follows a behavioral pattern.

A concept is introduced.

A response is triggered.

A reinforcement follows.

This reflects the work of B. F. Skinner—

Building on the behavioral tradition of Ivan Petrovich Pavlov—

where understanding is strengthened through repetition and structured reinforcement of the desired response.

The goal is not exposure to ideas—

but retention and application.

From Philosophy to Structure

At its core, this writing is governed by a single principle:

Structure defines understanding.

This is where philosophy transitions into execution.

The influence of Villard Denis (Davertige) is foundational here.

Through his guidance, I learned to treat every line of thought with the discipline of chemistry—

where nothing is lost, only transformed.

An idea is never discarded.

It is refined.

Repositioned.

Integrated into a larger structure.

From Thought to Execution

This philosophical foundation does not exist in isolation.

It connects directly to the discipline of project management.

Hegel defines movement of thought

Kant defines structure of understanding

Descartes defines precision of reasoning

B.F. Skinner defines behavioral reinforcement

Davertige defines preservation and transformation of ideas

Together, they form a system.

That system is applied here:

Structure → Control → Execution

This is why the writing behaves the way it does.

It is not meant to be consumed passively.

It is meant to be processed, retained, and applied.

This book is not written to be read once.

It is written to be revisited—

each time revealing more structure than before.

Because understanding is not delivered in a single pass.

It is built.

Personal Intellectual Influence

I acknowledge my mentor, Villard Denis (Davertige) (1940–2004)—

a poet of rare depth, once described by Alain Bosquet as "a genius in a wild state."

His work did not merely influence how I write—

it shaped how I think.

Through him, I learned to treat every line of thought with the discipline of chemistry—

where nothing is lost, only transformed.

Every idea, once formed, must be preserved, refined, and structured into meaning.

That principle lives within this book.

References

Enterprise Frameworks & Methodologies

Amazon Web Services. (2023). AWS well-architected framework. Amazon Web Services. https://aws.amazon.com/architecture/well-architected/

AXELOS. (2019). ITIL® foundation: ITIL 4 edition. The Stationery Office.

ISACA. (2019). COBIT® 2019 framework: Governance and management objectives. ISACA.

National Institute of Standards and Technology. (2020). Security and privacy controls for information systems and organizations (SP 800-53 Rev. 5). U.S. Department of Commerce. https://doi.org/10.6028/NIST.SP.800-53r5

Project Management Institute. (2021). The standard for project management and a guide to the project management body of knowledge (PMBOK® guide) (7th ed.). Project Management Institute.

Leadership & People

Chamorro-Premuzic, T. (2014, August). Curiosity is as important as intelligence. Harvard Business Review. https://hbr.org/2014/08/curiosity-is-as-important-as-intelligence

Goleman, D. (1995). Emotional intelligence: Why it can matter more than IQ. Bantam Books.

Goulston, M. (2010). Just listen: Discover the secret to getting through to absolutely anyone. AMACOM.

Hiatt, J. M. (2006). ADKAR: A model for change in business, government and our community. Prosci Learning Center Publications.

Maxwell, J. C. (2007). The 21 irrefutable laws of leadership: Follow them and people will follow you (10th anniversary ed.). Thomas Nelson.

Peshawaria, R. (2011). Too many bosses, too few leaders: The three essential principles you need to become an extraordinary leader. Simon & Schuster.

Useem, M. (2001). Leading up: How to lead your boss so you both win. Crown Business.

Decision Science & Risk Thinking

Klein, G. (2007, September). Performing a project premortem. Harvard Business Review, 85(9), 18–19.

Behavioral Science

Maslow, A. H. (1943). A theory of human motivation. Psychological Review, 50(4), 370–396. https://doi.org/10.1037/h0054346

Skinner, B. F. (1953). Science and human behavior. Macmillan.

Public Policy & Government

Kamarck, E. (2026, February 23). How many people can the federal government lose before it crashes? Brookings Institution. https://www.brookings.edu/articles/how-many-people-can-the-federal-government-lose-before-it-crashes/

Lucas, R. (2025, February 4). What is the Department of Government Efficiency, or DOGE? NPR. https://www.npr.org/2025/02/04/nx-s1-5286314/department-of-government-efficiency-doge-explainer-elon-musk

Wallace, G. (2025, September 24). Trump administration rehires hundreds of federal employees laid off by DOGE. CNN. https://www.cnn.com/2025/09/24/politics/doge-federal-workers

Enterprise Migration & Cloud Strategy

Goldratt, E. M. (1984). The goal: A process of ongoing improvement. North River Press.

Orban, S. (2016). 6 strategies for migrating applications to the cloud. Amazon Web Services Cloud Enterprise Strategy Blog.

Philosophical Foundations

Aristotle. (2009). Nicomachean ethics (W. D. Ross, Trans.). Oxford University Press.

Dalí, S. (1948). 50 secrets of magic craftsmanship. Dial Press.

Descartes, R. (1996). Discourse on method and meditations on first philosophy (D. A. Cress, Trans.). Hackett Publishing. (Original work published 1637)

Freud, S. (1961). The ego and the id (J. Strachey, Trans.). W. W. Norton & Company. (Original work published 1923)

Hegel, G. W. F. (1977). Phenomenology of spirit (A. V. Miller, Trans.). Oxford University Press. (Original work published 1807)

Kant, I. (1998). Critique of pure reason (P. Guyer & A. W. Wood, Trans.). Cambridge University Press. (Original work published 1781)

Rousseau, J.-J. (2002). *The social contract and the first and second discourses* (S. Dunn, Ed. & Trans.). Yale University Press. (Original work published 1762).

Shaw, G. B. (1903). Man and superman. Archibald Constable & Co.

Reference and Visualization Library

Migration Diagram Catalog

Migration execution is not only driven through plans and runbooks—it is reinforced through visualization.

In complex environments, clarity is not achieved by more documentation.

It is achieved by seeing how systems, dependencies, and decisions connect in motion.

The Migration Diagram Catalog serves as a structured visual library designed to support execution at every level of the migration lifecycle.

It translates abstract concepts into operational understanding—enabling stakeholders, engineers, and leadership to align quickly, communicate effectively, and act with confidence under pressure.

These diagrams are not decorative.

They are execution tools.

They are used to:

Clarify system relationships and dependencies

Support decision-making during design and execution

Align cross-functional teams around a shared understanding

Communicate complex architecture in a simplified, actionable format

Reinforce governance, control points, and execution flow

The companion diagram deck is designed to be actively used—not referenced passively.

Each visual can be inserted into:

Executive briefings

Migration planning sessions

Architecture and design reviews

War room execution environments

Operational runbooks and playbooks

The catalog below reflects the structured inventory of diagrams available within the companion slide deck, organized to support both strategic communication and real-time execution.

Migration Validation — Proving Operational Readiness Through Control

Validation is not a checklist.

It is the control mechanism that confirms whether execution is holding under real conditions.

In migration programs, systems do not fail because validation is missing.

They fail because validation is treated as a formality—rather than an enforcement of operational truth.

A system is not validated because it is deployed.

It is validated only when it continues to perform correctly:

Across dependencies

Under load

Over time

Validation as an Execution Control Layer

Validation operates within execution—not after it.

It ensures that each phase of the migration:

Produces expected outcomes

Maintains system integrity

Does not introduce unmanaged risk

This is where execution is either confirmed—or exposed.

Because migration does not test systems in isolation.

It exposes them in motion.

This operational reality can be visualized as a validation control system—where system integrity is enforced across domains in real time.

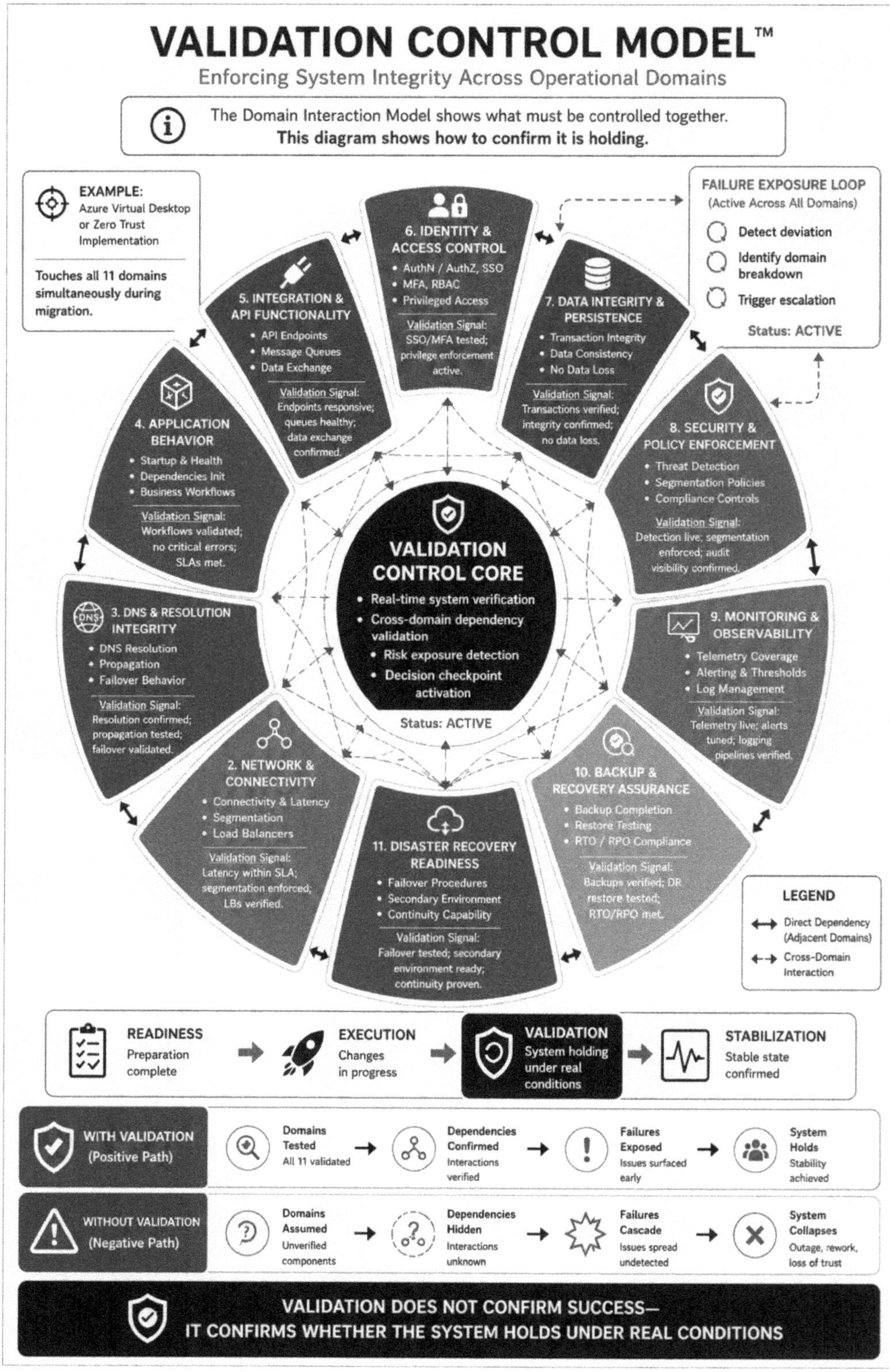
VALIDATION CONTROL MODEL™
Enforcing System Integrity Across Operational Domains
The Domain Interaction Model shows what must be controlled together.
This diagram shows how to confirm it is holding.
EXAMPLE:
Azure Virtual Desktop or Zero Trust Implementation
Touches all 11 domains simultaneously during migration.
FAILURE EXPOSURE LOOP
(Active Across All Domains)
Detect deviation
Identify domain breakdown
Trigger escalation
Status: ACTIVE
6. IDENTITY & ACCESS CONTROL
• AuthN / AuthZ, SSO
• MFA, RBAC
• Privileged Access
Validation Signal: SSO/MFA tested; privilege enforcement active.
5. INTEGRATION & API FUNCTIONALITY
• API Endpoints
• Message Queues
• Data Exchange
Validation Signal: Endpoints responsive; queues healthy; data exchange confirmed.
7. DATA INTEGRITY & PERSISTENCE
• Transaction Integrity
• Data Consistency
• No Data Loss
Validation Signal: Transactions verified; integrity confirmed; no data loss.
4. APPLICATION BEHAVIOR
• Startup & Health
• Dependencies Init
• Business Workflows
Validation Signal: Workflows validated; no critical errors; SLAs met.
8. SECURITY & POLICY ENFORCEMENT
• Threat Detection
• Segmentation Policies
• Compliance Controls
Validation Signal: Detection live; segmentation enforced; audit visibility confirmed.
VALIDATION CONTROL CORE
• Real-time system verification
• Cross-domain dependency validation
• Risk exposure detection
• Decision checkpoint activation
Status: ACTIVE
3. DNS & RESOLUTION INTEGRITY
• DNS Resolution
• Propagation
• Failover Behavior
Validation Signal: Resolution confirmed; propagation tested; failover validated.
9. MONITORING & OBSERVABILITY
• Telemetry Coverage
• Alerting & Thresholds
• Log Management
Validation Signal: Telemetry live; alerts tuned; logging pipelines verified.
2. NETWORK & CONNECTIVITY
• Connectivity & Latency
• Segmentation
• Load Balancers
Validation Signal: Latency within SLA; segmentation enforced; LBs verified.
10. BACKUP & RECOVERY ASSURANCE
• Backup Completion
• Restore Testing
• RTO / RPO Compliance
Validation Signal: Backups verified; DR restore tested; RTO/RPO met.
11. DISASTER RECOVERY READINESS
• Failover Procedures
• Secondary Environment
• Continuity Capability
Validation Signal: Failover tested; secondary environment ready; continuity proven.
LEGEND
Direct Dependency (Adjacent Domains)
Cross-Domain Interaction
READINESS
Preparation complete
EXECUTION
Changes in progress
VALIDATION
System holding under real conditions
STABILIZATION
Stable state confirmed
WITH VALIDATION (Positive Path)
Domains Tested
All 11 validated
Dependencies Confirmed
Interactions verified
Failures Exposed
Issues surfaced early
System Holds
Stability achieved
WITHOUT VALIDATION (Negative Path)
Domains Assumed
Unverified components
Dependencies Hidden
Interactions unknown
Failures Cascade
Issues spread undetected
System Collapses
Outage, rework, loss of trust
VALIDATION DOES NOT CONFIRM SUCCESS—
IT CONFIRMS WHETHER THE SYSTEM HOLDS UNDER REAL CONDITIONS

At this level, validation is no longer observational—it becomes an active control layer that continuously verifies whether execution is holding under real conditions.

Validation Control Domains

Validation must be executed across the following domains to confirm full system integrity:

Infrastructure Stability

Verify compute performance (CPU, memory, storage utilization)

Confirm resource allocation and system availability

Validate performance under expected and peak load conditions

Network and Connectivity

Confirm end-to-end connectivity across all network paths

Validate latency, routing behavior, and segmentation controls

Ensure load balancers, firewalls, and VPN access operate correctly

DNS and Resolution Integrity

Validate DNS resolution across internal and external systems

Confirm propagation behavior and failover handling

Ensure resolution aligns with cutover expectations

Application Behavior

Validate application startup and runtime stability

Confirm service dependencies initialize correctly

Ensure workflows execute as expected under real usage conditions

Integration and API Functionality

Validate API endpoints, queues, and integration services

Confirm upstream and downstream system communication

Ensure data exchange occurs without latency or failure

Identity and Access Control

Validate authentication mechanisms (SSO, MFA, federation)

Confirm authorization and role-based access enforcement

Ensure privileged access controls function as defined

Data Integrity and Persistence

Validate database connectivity and transaction processing

Confirm data integrity following migration or replication

Ensure no data loss, corruption, or inconsistency

Security and Policy Enforcement

Validate security controls, policies, and segmentation rules

Confirm threat detection, logging, and enforcement mechanisms

Ensure compliance visibility and audit readiness

Monitoring and Observability

Confirm monitoring systems are active and collecting signals

Validate logging pipelines and alerting mechanisms

Ensure visibility across infrastructure, application, and security layers

Backup and Recovery Assurance

Validate backup completion and accessibility

Perform restore testing where required

Confirm recovery objectives (RTO/RPO) are achievable

Disaster Recovery Readiness

Validate failover procedures and recovery workflows

Confirm secondary environment readiness

Ensure continuity capability is operational—not theoretical

Validation Within the Control Loop

Validation is not separate from execution.

It is part of the same control system:

Readiness → Establishes authority

Execution → Moves the system

Validation → Confirms system integrity

Stabilization → Proves sustainability

Validation ensures that execution does not drift into failure.

Control Principle — Validation Under Real Conditions

A system is not validated because it appears functional.

It is validated only when it continues to operate correctly under real conditions—

without degradation, inconsistency, or hidden failure across domains.

Migration Readiness Scorecard (CIO Tool)

Migration readiness is not determined by activity.

It is determined by measurable conditions that confirm the organization is prepared to execute without uncontrolled risk.

The Migration Readiness Scorecard is an executive-level control instrument designed to translate technical readiness into decision clarity.

It provides leadership with a structured method to assess whether a migration should:

Proceed

Pause

Or be re-evaluated

This is not a reporting tool.

It is a decision framework—where readiness is measured across domains, and execution is authorized only when control conditions are met.

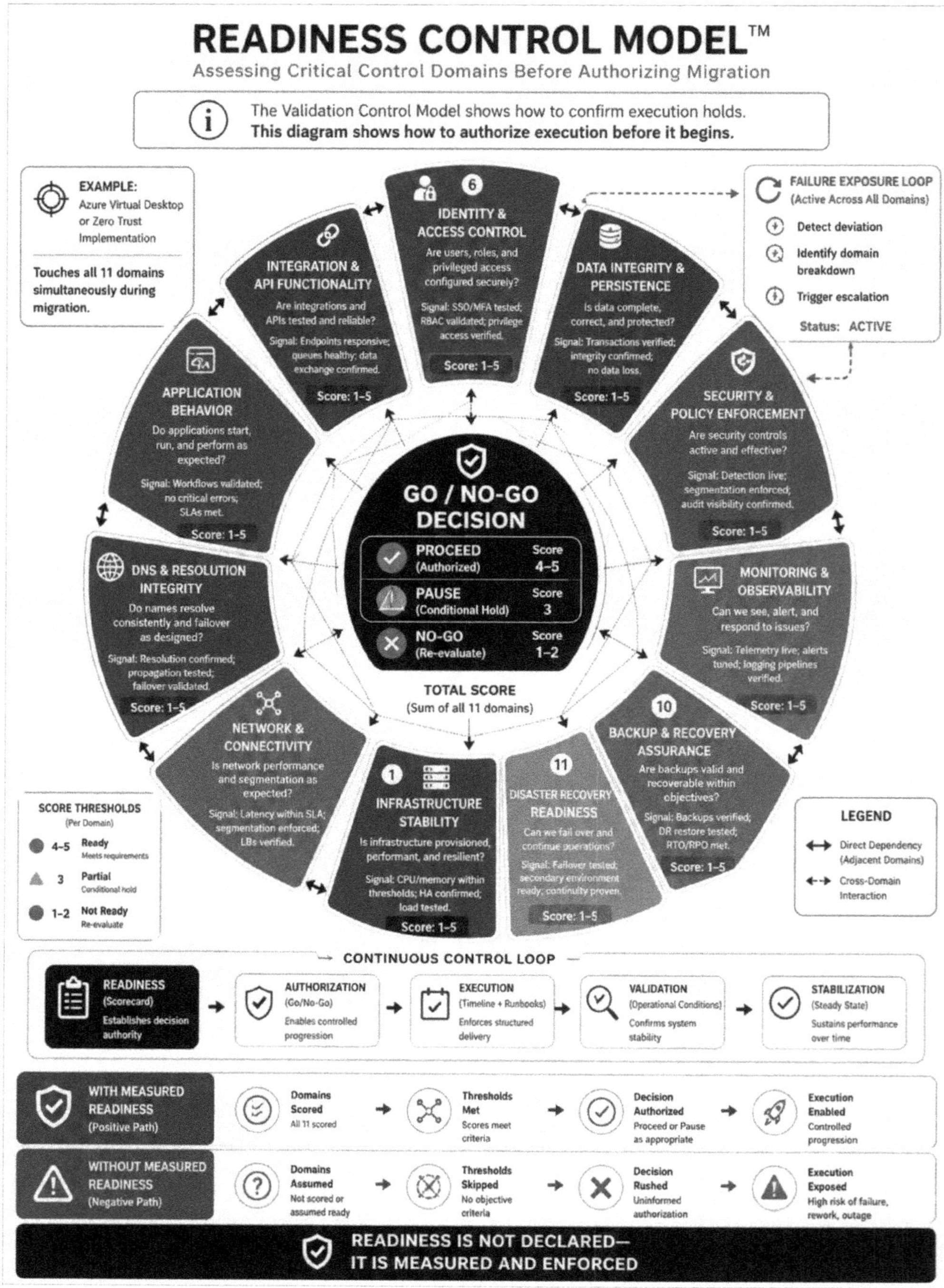
READINESS CONTROL MODEL™
Assessing Critical Control Domains Before Authorizing Migration
The Validation Control Model shows how to confirm execution holds.
This diagram shows how to authorize execution before it begins.
EXAMPLE:
Azure Virtual Desktop or Zero Trust Implementation
Touches all 11 domains simultaneously during migration.
FAILURE EXPOSURE LOOP
(Active Across All Domains)
Detect deviation
Identify domain breakdown
Trigger escalation
Status: ACTIVE
6
IDENTITY & ACCESS CONTROL
Are users, roles, and privileged access configured securely?
Signal: SSO/MFA tested; RBAC validated; privilege access verified.
Score: 1-5
INTEGRATION & API FUNCTIONALITY
Are integrations and APIs tested and reliable?
Signal: Endpoints responsive; queues healthy; data exchange confirmed.
Score: 1-5
DATA INTEGRITY & PERSISTENCE
Is data complete, correct, and protected?
Signal: Transactions verified; integrity confirmed; no data loss.
Score: 1-5
APPLICATION BEHAVIOR
Do applications start, run, and perform as expected?
Signal: Workflows validated; no critical errors; SLAs met.
Score: 1-5
SECURITY & POLICY ENFORCEMENT
Are security controls active and effective?
Signal: Detection live; segmentation enforced; audit visibility confirmed.
Score: 1-5
GO / NO-GO DECISION
PROCEED (Authorized) Score 4-5
PAUSE (Conditional Hold) Score 3
NO-GO (Re-evaluate) Score 1-2
DNS & RESOLUTION INTEGRITY
Do names resolve consistently and failover as designed?
Signal: Resolution confirmed; propagation tested; failover validated.
Score: 1-5
MONITORING & OBSERVABILITY
Can we see, alert, and respond to issues?
Signal: Telemetry live; alerts tuned; logging pipelines verified.
Score: 1-5
TOTAL SCORE
(Sum of all 11 domains)
NETWORK & CONNECTIVITY
Is network performance and segmentation as expected?
Signal: Latency within SLA; segmentation enforced; LBs verified.
1
INFRASTRUCTURE STABILITY
Is infrastructure provisioned, performant, and resilient?
Signal: CPU/memory within thresholds; HA confirmed; load tested.
Score: 1-5
11
DISASTER RECOVERY READINESS
Can we fail over and continue operations?
Signal: Failover tested; secondary environment ready; continuity proven.
Score: 1-5
10
BACKUP & RECOVERY ASSURANCE
Are backups valid and recoverable within objectives?
Signal: Backups verified; DR restore tested; RTO/RPO met.
Score: 1-5
SCORE THRESHOLDS
(Per Domain)
4-5 Ready Meets requirements
3 Partial Conditional hold
1-2 Not Ready Re-evaluate
LEGEND
Direct Dependency (Adjacent Domains)
Cross-Domain Interaction
CONTINUOUS CONTROL LOOP
READINESS (Scorecard) Establishes decision authority
AUTHORIZATION (Go/No-Go) Enables controlled progression
EXECUTION (Timeline + Runbooks) Enforces structured delivery
VALIDATION (Operational Conditions) Confirms system stability
STABILIZATION (Steady State) Sustains performance over time
WITH MEASURED READINESS (Positive Path)
Domains Scored All 11 scored
Thresholds Met Scores meet criteria
Decision Authorized Proceed or Pause as appropriate
Execution Enabled Controlled progression
WITHOUT MEASURED READINESS (Negative Path)
Domains Assumed Not scored or assumed ready
Thresholds Skipped No objective criteria
Decision Rushed Uninformed authorization
Execution Exposed High risk of failure, rework, outage
READINESS IS NOT DECLARED—
IT IS MEASURED AND ENFORCED

From Readiness to Execution Control

Readiness alone does not deliver outcomes.

It authorizes execution.

Once readiness has been validated and a go decision is made, control shifts from assessment to time-sequenced execution.

This is where the migration transitions from:

Readiness → Authorization

Authorization → Execution

Execution → Validation under real conditions

Execution Alignment Across Models

The Migration Readiness Scorecard does not operate in isolation.

It directly feeds the execution system:

Cutover Timeline Model™ — Defines when execution occurs.

Execution Runbooks — Define how execution is performed.

Validation Controls — Confirm whether execution holds under real conditions.

Together, they form a continuous control loop:

Readiness authorizes execution.

Execution follows structured timelines.

Runbooks enforce control at each phase.

Validation confirms system integrity under real conditions.

End-to-End Control Flow

Migration execution is not a single event.

It is a controlled system:

Readiness (Scorecard) → Establishes decision authority.

Authorization (Go/No-Go) → Enables controlled progression.

Execution (Timeline + Runbooks) → Enforces structured delivery.

Validation (Operational Conditions) → Confirms system stability.

Control Principle — Execution Under Authority

Execution must never begin without validated readiness.

Once execution begins, it must be governed through:

Time-based checkpoints

Domain-level validation

Continuous monitoring

Controlled decision flow

Because without this alignment—

Execution becomes movement without control.

Execution must be driven by validated readiness conditions—not timelines.

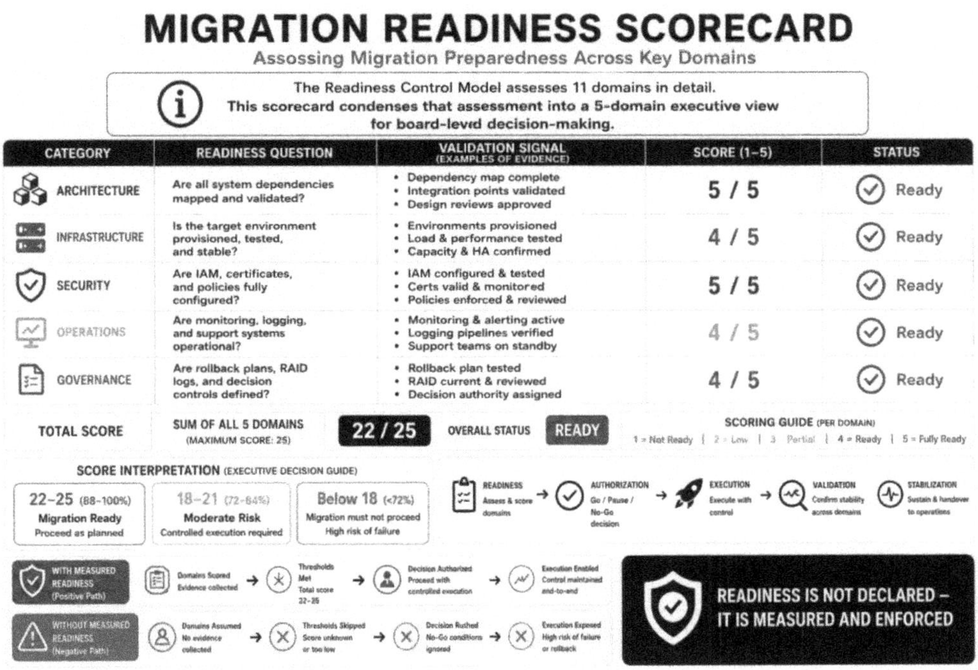

Score Interpretation

22–25 → Migration Ready

18–21 → Moderate Risk — Controlled execution required

Below 18 → Migration must not proceed

Principle of Control — Systems Must Hold Under Real Conditions

A system is not ready because it appears complete.

It is ready only when each domain has been validated, aligned, and proven to operate under real conditions—

without introducing unmanaged risk into execution.

Migration War Room Model

Migration execution does not operate in isolation.

It operates under coordination.

The Migration War Room is not a physical space.

It is a centralized control environment where leadership, engineering, and operations converge to enforce execution, resolve uncertainty, and maintain system integrity under real conditions.

This is not a battlefield.

It is a decision environment—where alignment is achieved through structured dialogue, real-time validation, and controlled escalation.

The objective is not debate.

The objective is clarity.

Because during migration, misalignment is risk.

And unresolved risk becomes failure.

Purpose — Why This Exists

The War Room exists to establish a single point of control during execution.

It ensures that:

Decisions are made in real time

Dependencies are validated across domains

Risks are identified before they escalate

Execution remains aligned with defined control conditions

Without a War Room, execution fragments.

With it, execution becomes coordinated, visible, and controlled.

Operational Function — Control in Motion

The War Room functions as the execution nerve center.

It is where:

System behavior is continuously monitored

Cross-domain dependencies are validated

Issues are surfaced and resolved immediately

Decisions are made with full visibility

This is where execution is actively governed—not observed.

Because migration does not fail in isolation.

It fails in the gaps between teams.

The War Room eliminates those gaps.

This operational model can be visualized as a centralized execution control system—where cross-domain coordination, decision flow, and escalation are enforced in real time.

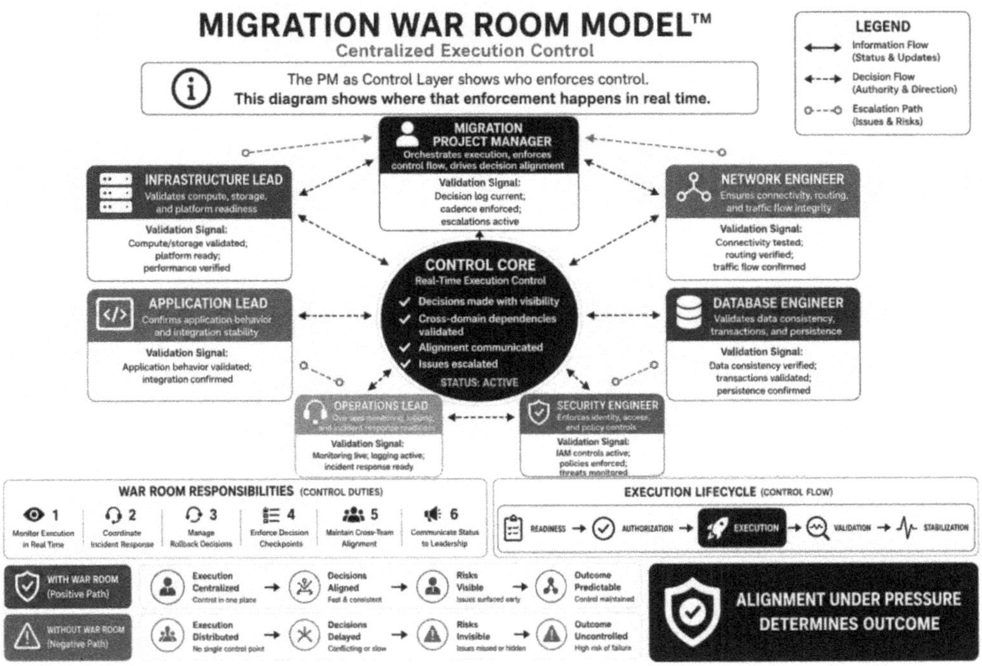

At this level, the War Room is no longer a coordination point—it becomes a control layer that actively governs execution, aligns decisions, and prevents drift across domains.

Core Participants — Cross-Domain Control Structure

Execution requires representation across all critical domains.

The War Room must include:

Migration Project Manager — Orchestrates execution, enforces control flow, and drives decision alignment

Infrastructure Lead — Validates compute, storage, and platform readiness

Application Lead — Confirms application behavior and integration stability

Network Engineer — Ensures connectivity, routing, and traffic flow integrity

Database Engineer — Validates data consistency, transactions, and persistence

Security Engineer — Enforces identity, access, and policy controls

Operations Lead — Oversees monitoring, logging, and incident response readiness

Each role is not advisory.

Each role is accountable for domain-level validation during execution.

War Room Responsibilities — Execution Enforcement

The War Room operates through active control responsibilities:

Monitor Execution in Real Time

Track system behavior across infrastructure, application, network, and security layers

Coordinate Incident Response

Detect, escalate, and resolve issues before they propagate across domains

Manage Rollback Decisions

Evaluate failure thresholds and execute reversal when control conditions are violated

Enforce Decision Checkpoints

Ensure execution does not proceed without validated readiness at each phase

Maintain Cross-Team Alignment

Synchronize communication, ownership, and execution across all participants

Communicate Status to Leadership

Provide clear, accurate, and decision-ready updates under pressure

War Room as a Control Layer

The War Room is not separate from execution.

It is part of the control system:

Readiness → Establishes conditions

Execution → Moves the system

War Room → Enforces control in real time

Validation → Confirms system integrity

Stabilization → Proves sustainability

Without this layer:

Execution becomes distributed.

Decisions become delayed.

Risk becomes invisible.

Control Principle — Alignment Under Pressure

Execution under pressure does not create alignment.

It exposes whether alignment exists.

The War Room ensures that:

Decisions are made with full visibility

Dependencies are validated across domains

Risks are addressed before they escalate

Because in migration:

Failure is not caused by lack of effort.

It is caused by lack of coordinated control.

Architecture Diagram Reference Index — Structural Models for Execution

Architecture is not documentation.

It is the visual expression of how systems are designed to operate under real conditions.

In migration programs, diagrams are often treated as static artifacts—created once, reviewed briefly, and then set aside.

But execution does not follow documentation.

It follows structure.

The Architecture Diagram Reference Index exists to provide a curated set of visual models that support understanding, alignment, and decision-making across the migration lifecycle.

Each diagram represents a system view—not in isolation—but as part of a broader execution environment where dependencies, control points, and operational behavior must be understood before execution begins.

This is not a library of images.

It is a reference system for how architecture supports execution.

Purpose — Why This Matters

Migration complexity does not come from individual components.

It comes from how those components interact.

Architecture diagrams provide:

Visibility into system dependencies

Clarity across infrastructure, application, and data layers

Alignment between technical design and execution strategy

A shared language across engineering, operations, and leadership

Without architectural clarity, execution becomes assumption-driven.

With it, execution becomes structured and predictable.

How to Use This Index

The diagrams in this index are not intended to be reviewed passively.

They are designed to be used actively throughout the migration lifecycle:

During Discovery — to map dependencies and understand system interactions

During Planning — to align architecture with migration strategy (6R model, wave planning)

During Execution — to validate that system behavior aligns with design expectations

During Validation and Stabilization — to confirm that architecture holds under real conditions

Each diagram should be referenced as a control artifact—supporting decision-making, validation, and execution alignment.

Architecture Diagram Reference Index

Core Architecture Models

Traditional Data Center Architecture

Represents on-premises infrastructure design, including compute, storage, network segmentation, and operational dependencies.

Hybrid Cloud Architecture

Illustrates integration between on-premises environments and cloud platforms, including identity federation, connectivity, and workload distribution.

Zero Trust Access Architecture

Defines identity-centric security models, emphasizing least privilege, continuous verification, and policy enforcement across access layers.

Migration Strategy & Execution Models

Migration Wave Model

Visualizes phased migration sequencing, workload grouping, and risk-controlled execution across defined waves.

Blue-Green Deployment Model

Represents parallel environment deployment to enable controlled cutover, rollback capability, and minimal service disruption.

Data & Platform Architecture

Database Replication Architecture

Illustrates data synchronization, replication strategies, failover design, and consistency controls across environments.

Cloud Monitoring Architecture

Defines observability layers, including logging, metrics, alerting, and telemetry across infrastructure and applications.

Governance & Control Models

Migration Governance Model

Represents decision structures, control checkpoints, RAID management, and execution oversight across the migration lifecycle.

Architecture Within the Control System

Architecture does not operate independently.

It is part of the execution system:

Readiness → Architecture defines what must be validated

Execution → Architecture guides how systems are transitioned

Validation → Architecture confirms whether systems behave as designed

Stabilization → Architecture ensures long-term operational integrity

Without architectural alignment, execution drifts.

Without validation against architecture, stability is assumed—not proven.

Control Principle — Structure Defines Behavior

Systems do not behave as intended because they are documented.

They behave as designed—only when that design is understood, validated, and enforced during execution.

Architecture is not a representation of the system.

It is the foundation upon which controlled execution depends.

Execution does not happen in isolation.

It is not meetings.

It is not updates.

It is not coordination disguised as progress.

Execution is command.

It is the ability to:
See clearly under pressure
Decide without hesitation
Act without fragmentation

And most importantly—

Maintain control
when everything else begins to move.

Because in the end—

The system does not fail in planning.

It fails in execution.

And execution—

is where truth begins to surface.

Execution reveals what planning conceals.

What holds—
and what collapses.

What was real—
and what was assumed.

Everything converges here.

Synthesis — Execution Under Control

Everything you have just seen—

was never theoretical.

Execution is where truth is revealed.

Not in planning.
Not in intention.
Not in the language of strategy—

But in what holds under pressure.

Across this book, frameworks were introduced.

Phases were defined.

Models were structured.

But none of them exist for theory.

They exist for control.

Because migration is not about movement.

It is about maintaining integrity while

systems,

people,

and environments change simultaneously.

Execution under control is not a concept—
It is a discipline.

A discipline that requires:

Clarity before action
Validation before commitment
Structure before scale

And when those conditions are met—

Execution stops being reactive.

It becomes intentional.

What this book has shown—

through structure,

through failure,

through lived experience—

is this:

Control is not something you apply at the end.

It is something you build from the beginning.

Because when execution begins without it—

Failure is already in motion.

And when execution is controlled—

Even failure becomes data.

Even setbacks become direction.

Even pressure becomes clarity.

This is the synthesis:

Execution does not define effort.

Execution defines truth.

Final Word — The Journey and What Remains

This was never just a book about migration.

It was a confrontation—

With complexity.

With failure.

With systems that resist structure
and environments that test discipline.

And through all of it—

One truth remained constant.

Control is not given.

It is built.

Over time.
Under pressure.

Through decisions that are not always seen—
but are always felt in the outcome.

This work did not come from theory.

It came from experience.

From environments that supported execution—
and from those that quietly collapsed beneath it.

From moments where structure held—

And moments where its absence
revealed everything.

Because in the end—

You do not rise to the level of your plans.

You fall to the level of your control.

And that is where execution lives.

Not in perfection—

But in discipline.

Not in certainty—

But in clarity.

Not in speed—

But in stability under pressure.

What you carry forward from this book
should not be the framework alone.

Frameworks evolve.

Tools change.

Technologies will continue to advance.

But the ability to:

See clearly
Act deliberately
Maintain control under pressure

That remains.

That is the work.

And if there is anything to take from this—

It is this:

Migration is not about moving systems.

It is about controlling change.

And those who learn to do that—

do not just deliver projects.

They shape outcomes.

They stabilize environments.

They lead transformation—

intentionally.

This is not the end of the journey.

It is the point where execution becomes yours.

What begins as structure—

Is only proven when it is tested.

Appendices

Cloud Migration PM Bible™

"Definitions are not decoration. They are the structure beneath understanding."

The appendices that follow are not a glossary in the traditional sense. They are a working reference — a control layer designed to support how this book is read, returned to, and applied. Every term included here appears in the manuscript with intention. None is decorative. Each one supports a decision, a discipline, or a distinction that matters in execution.

Appendix A defines the conceptual and technical vocabulary of controlled migration — frameworks, models, and disciplines referenced throughout. Appendix B provides the structured list of acronyms and abbreviations encountered across the work, with their full expansions.

Together, they reflect the principle that has guided this entire framework — that clarity is not optional, and that language, when used with discipline, becomes a form of control.

APPENDIX A

Migration Glossary

This glossary defines the principal terms, frameworks, and concepts referenced throughout Cloud Migration PM Bible™. Entries are arranged alphabetically. Terms marked with the trademark symbol (™) are proprietary models introduced by the author and developed in detail within the manuscript. References to the 6R framework, ADKAR, Prosci, COBIT, NIST, ITIL, and PMI represent established industry models cited in the appropriate contexts. Where definitions intersect — for example, between Rehost and Lift-and-Shift, or between RPO and Disaster Recovery — cross-references are provided to preserve continuity of meaning across the work.

A

6R Framework — A widely used migration strategy model — Rehost, Replatform, Refactor, Repurchase, Retain, Retire — that defines what is done to each workload when transitioning to a new environment. The 6R model originated within the AWS migration practice and has since become an industry standard across infrastructure, application, and cloud migrations.

7R Framework — An expansion of the 6R model that adds Relocate, addressing hypervisor-level moves — most commonly VMware Cloud on AWS scenarios in which a virtualization platform is moved without re-architecting workloads.

Active Directory (AD) — Microsoft's on-premises directory service used to manage users, groups, computers, and access policies. Often a foundational dependency in identity migrations and federations with cloud identity providers.

ADKAR — A change adoption framework developed by Prosci, standing for Awareness, Desire, Knowledge, Ability, and Reinforcement. It helps migration leaders assess whether impacted users and support teams are ready to adopt the new environment.

AIOps — Artificial Intelligence for IT Operations. The application of machine learning and analytics to operational data — logs, metrics, events — to detect anomalies, correlate incidents, and accelerate response.

Architecture Assessment — A structured review performed before execution that evaluates whether a system's design can operate correctly in the target environment. It does not test systems — it predicts their behavior under cloud, identity, latency, and dependency conditions.

Autoscaling — The capability of a cloud platform to automatically increase or decrease compute resources in response to load. A common validation point post-migration, particularly for high-traffic and latency-sensitive workloads.

Availability Zone (AZ) — A physically separate data center location within a cloud region, used to improve resilience and high availability.

B

Big Bang Migration — An execution approach in which a system — or multiple systems — is moved in a single cutover event, with no coexistence between the source and target environments. Effective only when readiness, rollback, and coordination are fully established.

Blue-Green Deployment — A release method in which production traffic is switched from the current environment to an identical new environment, allowing rapid rollback if issues occur.

Business Continuity (BCP) — The discipline of preserving critical business operations during disruption. In migration, BCP defines acceptable downtime, recovery sequencing, and operational fallback paths.

C

Canary Deployment — A release strategy in which a small subset of users or traffic is routed to the new environment first, before full rollout. Used to limit exposure and validate behavior under controlled conditions.

Change Freeze — A defined period during which no non-essential changes may be introduced into the production environment. Typically enforced before, during, and shortly after cutover.

CMDB (Configuration Management Database) — A repository used to track IT assets, configurations, and relationships. Helpful for migration planning, but should not be treated as complete without validation workshops.

Controlled Migration Execution™ — A discipline introduced in this work — anchored on three foundations (Mindset, Structure, and Validation) and four operational pillars (Validation, Risk Management, Rollback Strategy, and Monitoring & Stabilization) — through which migration is delivered as a coordinated system rather than a sequence of tasks.

Cutover — The planned transition point at which service, traffic, users, or workloads move from the source environment to the target environment.

Cutover Plan — A structured execution document defining sequencing, ownership, timing, dependencies, communication flows, and go/no-go decision points across the cutover window.

D

Decision Validation & Readiness Gate — The control point between planning and execution at which decisions are examined, challenged, and confirmed. Migration must not proceed until validated readiness is established, not assumed.

Dependency Mapping — The structured identification of how systems, applications, identities, and data interact across the operational ecosystem. In migration, dependencies determine sequencing, rollback boundaries, and integration risk.

Discovery — The first phase of the Dual-Phase Migration Model — where the environment is examined, dependencies are identified, and risks are evaluated before any movement occurs. Discovery is not a formality; it is a control mechanism.

Disaster Recovery (DR) — The structured capability to restore service after a significant disruption. Validated through failover procedures, secondary environment readiness, and recovery objectives (RTO/RPO).

Dual-Phase Migration Model — A simplifying lens introduced in this work that separates Discovery from Implementation, ensuring that understanding precedes execution in every migration program.

E

End-User Computing (EUC) — The infrastructure domain covering laptops, mobile devices, virtual desktops, endpoint management, and workspace delivery platforms — defining the user experience after migration.

Entra ID — Microsoft's cloud-based identity and access management service (formerly Azure Active Directory), commonly used in modern migrations for SSO, MFA, and conditional access.

Equipollent Leadership Model™ — A leadership construct introduced in this work — based on the principle that respect must be offered equally regardless of status. Defines four archetypes: Relational Contributor, Equipollent Leader, Passive Participant, and Transactional Authority.

Execution Command Center™ — An operational model — not a physical room — in which visibility, decision-making, and accountability converge during migration execution, particularly during cutover and stabilization.

F

Federation — The trust relationship between identity providers that allows users to authenticate once and access resources across boundaries — for example, between Active Directory and Entra ID, or between Okta and Entra ID in hybrid environments.

G

Gantt Chart — A visual representation of a schedule over time. A Gantt chart can illustrate an Integrated Master Schedule (IMS) but is not the IMS itself.

Go/No-Go — The formal decision point at which leadership authorizes — or halts — execution based on validated readiness criteria.

Governance Cadence — The disciplined rhythm of reviews — daily during cutover and hypercare, weekly during standard delivery — that ensures risks are surfaced, decisions are made on time, and execution remains aligned.

H

Hypercare — A short-term post-go-live support period with elevated monitoring, faster response times, daily reporting, and close coordination across support teams. Hypercare is not extended support — it is a controlled operational state.

Hypervisor — A platform layer that creates and manages virtual machines (VMs). Relevant in Relocate strategies, where workloads are moved at the hypervisor level rather than re-architected.

I

IAM (Identity and Access Management) — The controls, systems, and policies used to manage authentication, authorization, and access governance.

Infrastructure as Code (IaC) — The practice of provisioning and managing infrastructure through machine-readable definition files rather than manual configuration. Common in cloud landing zones and repeatable migration deployments.

Integrated Master Schedule (IMS) — A comprehensive, logically linked schedule that integrates all project activities, dependencies, and timelines across programs. The IMS is the structured schedule itself; a Gantt chart is one way to visualize it.

IOPS (Input/Output Operations Per Second) — A storage performance metric measuring how many read and write operations a storage system can process per second. In migration programs, IOPS is critical when validating storage health after cutover, since an application may appear operational while still suffering from degraded disk performance. High-transaction systems, databases, VDI platforms, and latency-sensitive applications are especially affected. PMs do not need to engineer storage tuning themselves, but must confirm that storage performance baselines, expected throughput, and post-migration test results meet business and technical requirements.

L

Landing Zone — A preconfigured cloud environment that includes networking, IAM, logging, policy controls, and governance standards to support secure workload onboarding.

Latency — The amount of time it takes for data to travel from one point to another. In migrations, latency often affects application responsiveness, database transactions, and user experience.

Lift-and-Shift — The colloquial term for the Rehost strategy — moving an application largely as-is, often from on-premises virtual machines to cloud-based virtual machines, without architectural redesign.

M

MFA (Multi-Factor Authentication) — An authentication method requiring two or more verification factors before granting access. A foundational control in identity migration and Zero Trust enforcement.

Migration Wave — A grouped set of systems, applications, or services migrated together based on risk, complexity, and dependency logic. Waves reduce disruption and create incremental learning cycles.

Migration Wave Tracker — A governance artifact that provides visibility into wave sequencing, risk distribution, dependencies, and execution progress across the program.

Monitoring and Observability — The combined discipline of collecting logs, metrics, traces, and alerts to verify system behavior — and to understand why systems behave as they do, particularly under real-world load.

MTTR (Mean Time to Recover / Resolve) — A measure of how quickly teams restore service after an incident.

N

Network Operations Center (NOC) — The operational team responsible for monitoring and managing network and infrastructure environments, particularly post-cutover. In some organizations, the NOC is replaced or supplemented by an SRE/DevOps function or managed service provider.

O

Okta — A cloud-based identity provider commonly used for SSO, MFA, and lifecycle management — frequently encountered in migrations involving federated identity architectures.

Operational Playbook — The structured set of operating model definitions, runbooks, governance cadences, KPIs, and continuous improvement disciplines through which controlled migration becomes repeatable, measurable, and scalable.

P

Parallel (Dual-Run) Migration — An execution approach in which both old and new environments operate simultaneously for a defined period — enabling comparison, validation, and fallback before full cutover. Common in regulated and mission-critical environments.

Phased (Wave-Based) Migration — An execution approach in which systems are moved gradually, in controlled groups (waves), with each wave validated before the next begins. The most common — and most controlled — approach in enterprise environments.

Pilot Migration — A small-scale, controlled migration executed to validate the model — including infrastructure readiness, runbooks, and rollback — before larger waves proceed.

P.R.E.M.O.T. Model™ — The operational engine of the PRE-MORTEM Risk Discovery Framework™ — a six-step sequence (Project Failure Simulation, Risk Brain Dump, Expose & Share, Map & Cluster, Order & Prioritize, Treat & Track) that converts failure-first thinking into governance-ready risk artifacts.

PRE-MORTEM Risk Discovery Framework™ — A proactive risk management model introduced in this work that simulates project failure in advance to systematically uncover hidden risks, challenge assumptions, and embed mitigation strategies into execution plans before work begins. Builds upon the original pre-mortem concept introduced by Gary Klein, formalizing it as a structured, governance-integrated methodology.

Production Readiness Checklist — A control artifact confirming that infrastructure, access, monitoring, security policies, backups, and capacity have been fully prepared and validated prior to production transition.

Prosci Change Management Framework — A widely used organizational change management model — Prepare, Manage, Reinforce — that defines how organizations structure, communicate, and sustain change at scale. Complements ADKAR, which addresses change at the individual level.

R

RAID Log / RAID Register — A live governance artifact used to track Risks, Assumptions, Issues, and Dependencies — assigning ownership, mitigation, escalation thresholds, and timelines. The RAID Log is not a document; it is a control mechanism.

RAG Status — A red-amber-green reporting model used to communicate delivery health to leadership.

Readiness Gate — A formal checkpoint in the migration lifecycle at which planned work is examined and challenged before execution begins. Execution does not proceed until readiness is validated.

RED Lens (RED-P Model) — An organizational diagnostic and execution model adapted in this work from Rajeev Peshawaria's original RED concept — Role, Environment, Development — extended with Priority to convert diagnosis into action.

Refactor (Re-Architect) — A 6R strategy in which the application is redesigned to take advantage of cloud-native capabilities — microservices, containers, serverless compute, or managed integration patterns. The most transformative — and most demanding — strategy.

Rehost — A 6R strategy in which the application is moved largely as-is, typically from on-premises VMs to cloud-based VMs. Also called lift-and-shift.

Replatform — A 6R strategy that introduces limited optimization without redesigning the application — for example, moving a self-managed database to a managed service.

Repurchase — A 6R strategy in which a legacy or custom system is replaced with a SaaS or packaged solution, shifting complexity from technology to organizational transformation.

Retain — A 6R strategy reflecting a deliberate decision to keep a workload in its current environment — often due to regulatory, latency, or hardware constraints. Retain must be controlled, documented, and revisited.

Retire — A 6R strategy in which an application is decommissioned because it provides little or no value, has been replaced, or whose maintenance cost exceeds its benefit. One of the most overlooked — and most valuable — strategies.

Rollback — A controlled return to the prior stable environment when the target state fails validation or creates unacceptable business risk.

RPO (Recovery Point Objective) — The maximum acceptable amount of data loss measured in time — defining how recent a recovery point must be after a disruption.

RTO (Recovery Time Objective) — The maximum acceptable duration of service unavailability after a disruption — defining how quickly the system must be restored.

Runbook — A structured execution document defining exactly how a task or sequence of tasks is performed under real conditions. In migration, runbooks remove ambiguity from cutover, rollback, and stabilization.

S

SASE (Secure Access Service Edge) — A cloud-delivered security architecture that combines networking and security capabilities — often relevant in modern migration and remote access models.

Service Account — A non-human account used by applications, services, or scheduled jobs to authenticate against systems. Often a hidden dependency in migration; service account access frequently breaks during identity transitions if not mapped in advance.

SIEM (Security Information and Event Management) — A security platform that aggregates and analyzes log data, events, and alerts across the environment for detection and response.

Single Sign-On (SSO) — An authentication mechanism that allows a user to access multiple applications with one set of credentials, typically backed by SAML or OIDC federation.

Subnet — A logical subdivision of an IP network. In cloud migrations, subnet design — combined with routing and firewall rules — defines connectivity and segmentation behavior.

T

Technical Proof of Concept (TPOC) — A controlled validation activity confirming that an architecture behaves as predicted under real conditions — including identity, performance, integration reliability, and operational readiness. TPOC is not where architecture is discovered; it is where architecture is validated.

Telemetry — Quantitative data — metrics, traces, and logs — emitted by systems, used to verify behavior, detect anomalies, and inform decisions during execution and stabilization.

V

Validation — The discipline that separates assumed readiness from proven readiness. Validation must occur across infrastructure, applications, identity, data, and operations — and must be designed before execution, not improvised after cutover.

Virtual Desktop Infrastructure (VDI) — A platform that delivers desktop environments from centrally hosted infrastructure to end-user devices. Frequently encountered in EUC migrations and Azure Virtual Desktop deployments.

Virtual Private Cloud (VPC) / Virtual Network (VNet) — An isolated network environment within a cloud provider — VPC in AWS and GCP, VNet in Azure — through which subnets, routing, and security boundaries are defined.

W

War Room (Migration War Room Model) — A centralized control environment — physical or virtual — in which leadership, engineering, and operations converge to enforce execution, resolve uncertainty, and maintain system integrity in real time during cutover and stabilization.

Wave — See Migration Wave.

Z

Zero Trust — A security model in which no user or device is trusted by default. Access is continuously verified through identity, context, and policy.

Zero Trust Network Architecture (ZTNA) — An identity-centric security architecture that enforces least privilege, continuous verification, and policy-based access across users, devices, and applications — replacing traditional network-perimeter trust models.

Zscaler Client Connector (ZCC) — An endpoint agent used by the Zscaler security platform to enforce policy and route traffic. Frequently encountered in modern security migrations and Zero Trust transitions.

APPENDIX B

Acronyms and Abbreviations

The acronyms and abbreviations below appear throughout the manuscript. Each entry expands to its full form. Where additional context is required to distinguish between common usages — for example, between AWS, Azure, and GCP cloud-network nomenclature — that context is provided through Appendix A. Acronyms specific to the author's proprietary models are not included here; their full names appear in Appendix A and within the body of the work.

A

AD — Active Directory

ADKAR — Awareness, Desire, Knowledge, Ability, Reinforcement

AIOps — Artificial Intelligence for IT Operations

API — Application Programming Interface

AVD — Azure Virtual Desktop

AWS — Amazon Web Services

AZ — Availability Zone

B

BCP — Business Continuity Plan

C

CIO — Chief Information Officer

CMDB — Configuration Management Database

COBIT — Control Objectives for Information and Related Technologies

CPI — Cost Performance Index

CPU — Central Processing Unit

CQ — Curiosity Quotient

CRM — Customer Relationship Management

CTO — Chief Technology Officer

D

DBA — Database Administrator

DCIO — Deputy Chief Information Officer

DNS — Domain Name System

DR — Disaster Recovery

E

E2E — End-to-End (Testing)

EQ — Emotional Intelligence Quotient

ERP — Enterprise Resource Planning

ETL — Extract, Transform, Load

EUC — End-User Computing

G

GCP — Google Cloud Platform

H

HR — Human Resources

I

IaC — Infrastructure as Code

IAM — Identity and Access Management

IMS — Integrated Master Schedule

IOPS — Input/Output Operations Per Second

IQ — Intelligence Quotient

IT — Information Technology

ITIL — Information Technology Infrastructure Library

K

KPI — Key Performance Indicator

M

MFA — Multi-Factor Authentication

MTTR — Mean Time to Recover (or Resolve)

N

NAS — Network-Attached Storage

NIST — National Institute of Standards and Technology

NOC — Network Operations Center

O

OCM — Organizational Change Management

OIDC — OpenID Connect

P

PMBOK — Project Management Body of Knowledge

PMI — Project Management Institute

PMO — Project Management Office

PMP — Project Management Professional

POA&M — Plan of Action and Milestones

POC — Proof of Concept

R

RAG — Red, Amber, Green (status reporting)

RAID — Risks, Assumptions, Issues, Dependencies

RBAC — Role-Based Access Control

RPO — Recovery Point Objective

RTO — Recovery Time Objective

S

SaaS — Software as a Service

SAML — Security Assertion Markup Language

SAN — Storage Area Network

SASE — Secure Access Service Edge

SD-WAN — Software-Defined Wide Area Network

SID — Security Identifier

SIEM — Security Information and Event Management

SLA — Service Level Agreement

SME — Subject Matter Expert

SMTP — Simple Mail Transfer Protocol

SOP — Standard Operating Procedure

SPI — Schedule Performance Index

SRE — Site Reliability Engineering

SSO — Single Sign-On

SV — Schedule Variance

T

TLS — Transport Layer Security

TPOC — Technical Proof of Concept

U

UAT — User Acceptance Testing

V

VDI — Virtual Desktop Infrastructure

VM — Virtual Machine

VNet — Virtual Network (Microsoft Azure)

VPC — Virtual Private Cloud (AWS / GCP)

VPN — Virtual Private Network

W

WBS — Work Breakdown Structure

Z

ZCC — Zscaler Client Connector

ZIA — Zscaler Internet Access

ZTNA — Zero Trust Network Architecture

"What is named with precision can be controlled with discipline."

CLOUDMIGRATIONPMBIBLE™

Gérald L'Ouverture Noël

Cloud Migration PM Bible™

Index

Cloud Migration PM Bible™

"What is named with precision can be retrieved with discipline."

This index covers principal terms, frameworks, models, methodologies, and concepts referenced throughout the work. Page numbers refer to the final manuscript pagination.

Entries are organized alphabetically by letter section. Italicized references such as "see" and "see also" direct the reader to the principal entry where a concept is fully developed. Page ranges (e.g., 173–187) indicate continuous coverage of a topic across multiple pages; comma-separated entries indicate distinct discussions of the term in different parts of the manuscript.

Proprietary frameworks introduced in this work — marked with the trademark symbol (™) — are indexed both by their full name and by the chapter or part in which they are formally established. Cross-references to authors, philosophers, and external frameworks are provided to support the reader's continued study beyond this volume.

A

B

C

D

E

F

G

H

I

J

K

L

M

N

O

P

R

S

T

V

W

Z